Transformative Practice: New Pathways to Leadership

Sue L.T. McGregor

Transformative Practice: New Pathways to Leadership

Published in the United States in 2006 by:

    Kappa Omicron Nu Honor Society

Copyright © 2006 Sue L.T. McGregor.

This publication is distributed by:

    Kappa Omicron Nu Honor Society
    4990 Northwind Drive, Suite 140
    East Lansing, MI 48823-5031

    (T): 517.351.8335 (F): 517.351.8336.

The opinions expressed by the author are her own and do not necessarily reflect the policies of Kappa Omicron Nu.

ISBN 1-929083-08-2

Cover and book design by Lisa Wootton Booth.

Printed in Lansing, Michigan by Spartan Printing.

Transformative Practice: *New Pathways to Leadership*

This book is dedicated to
my Grandmothers,
my Mom and Dad, and
my husband and best friend, Peter.

Transformative Practice: New Pathways to Leadership

Transformative Practice: New Pathways to Leadership

Table of Contents

Caveats vii
Preface ix
Chapter 1: Understanding Paradigm Shifts 1
Chapter 2: Understanding Postmodern
   Thinking 21
Chapter 3: Transdisciplinary Inquiry 55
Chapter 4: Sustaining the Life Energy of
   the Profession: Insights from the
   Holomovement Principle 83
Chapter 5: Transformative versus
   Transactional Leadership 97
Chapter 6: Reflective Human Action
   (RHA) Leadership Theory 109
Chapter 7: Leadership Responsibilities
   of Professionals 133
Chapter 8: Transformative Change
   Agents 163
Chapter 9: Typology of Styles 183
Chapter 10: Critical Science Approach
   to Practice 205
Chapter 11: Perspective Transformation
   and Reflective Inquiry 229
Chapter 12: Critical Discourse Analysis 245
Chapter 13: Authentic Educational
   Pedagogies 265
Chapter 14: Intellectual Curiosity and
   Skeptical Thinking 279

Transformative Practice: New Pathways to Leadership

Chapter 15: Philosophical Well-being 295
Chapter 16: Communities of Practice 309
Chapter 17: Knowledge Management: Turning Personal Knowledge into Professional Knowledge 331
Chapter 18: Globalization–Top-Down and Bottom-Up 351
Chapter 19: Re-conceptualizing Human and Social Development 371
Chapter 20: Transforming Consumption 389
Postscript from the Editor, Dorothy I. Mitstifer 415
Index 417

Transformative Practice: New Pathways to Leadership

Caveats

The premise of this book is that practice needs to be transformed in order to embark upon a new century of leadership and professional work. For clarification, the book will use the terms "the profession" or "a profession" and, when especially relevant, use home economics/family and consumer sciences as a working example. A recent personal experience led me to believe that this book has application to many professions.

Ideally, the material in this book would be available on the Internet in PDF files. But, I chose another approach. I want to acknowledge Dr. Dorothy Mitstifer, Executive Director of Kappa Omicron Nu. She has given me a voice for my ideas. She has been my staunch and undaunting mentor, pushing me in directions I did not even know I needed to go. This book is a result of her strong mentoring role in my professional life. Also, I wanted to give back to Kappa Omicron Nu in some way since it plays such a key leadership role. We are working out an arrangement wherein a percentage of the profits go directly to KON. I made this decision as a way to give back for all that I have gained from the organization, and from Dorothy, since I became a member.

Of special note is the recent article, co-written with global colleagues, that created a satire of home economics, claiming that we are addicted to technical practice (McGregor et al., 2004). Dorothy eagerly posted this at the innovative Human Sciences Working Papers Archives at www.kon.org for the entire world to read. Writing that paper prompted me to finish and publish this book.

Transformative Practice: New Pathways to Leadership

Preface

This book was intentionally written to speak to a broad international audience. The context for the evolution of the profession is different in each country, but the paradigm shift called for in the book applies around the world. Getting locked into a paradigm that is not working any more inhibits professional momentum, generates inertia, slows communication, interferes with innovation, and creates tunnel vision (lack of peripheral vision). Anything is better than this state of affairs. Although there are no guarantees, professional life on the other side of the current paradigm should be full of momentum, be dynamic and evolving, full of rich, reflective communication, and replete with innovative practice and a clear, far-reaching vision.

The book is organized into five sections, starting with *paradigm shifts*, followed by *postmodernism*, *transdisciplinary* (rather than interdisciplinary) *practice*, and a new idea from quantum physics—the *holomovement principle*. This principle offers a model for visualizing a profession that is very alive, dynamic, and holistic, rather than divided and fragmented.

The second section examines leadership and the assumption that too many professionals are overly comfortable with the transactional leadership approach. This type of leadership follows the top-down, boss/subordinate model and relies upon exchanges, rewards, and punishments. It only recognizes the power of individuals in particular positions. The chapters on transformative

Transformative Practice: New Pathways to Leadership

leadership and Reflective Human Action (RHA) theory provide alternative leadership paradigms based around truth, vision, authenticity, ethics, and spirituality. Dorothy Mitstifer's chapter on leadership responsibilities for professionals offers a new model that can help us to understand that anyone can be a leader. She provides a powerful discussion of the appropriateness of the RHA approach for developing leaders. The chapter on social change agents provides context for professional leadership. The final chapter in this section offers a taxonomy of styles and encourages an appreciation of the fact that not all members of a given profession self-identify in the same way. These different leadership styles profoundly impact the means by which leaders approach members of the profession to take on leadership roles.

Section three examines the current educational pedagogy and offers a glimpse into what it might look like if practice were transformed. The four chapters in this section focus on the critical science approach, transformative learning, critical discourse analysis, and authentic educational pedagogy. Although the critical science approach is not new, it is included in this book because there is too little evidence of its use in professional practice. There is a tendency to avoid a close examination of the power relationships that keep a few people in power while most remain oppressed. Critical discourse analysis is a powerful tool that can be used to dissect the lack of balance in these relationships. Transformative learning is a concept found in adult education. It encourages individuals to appreciate their inner power and holds that unexpected, disorienting

Transformative Practice: New Pathways to Leadership

events can force people to seek out and clarify that inner voice. Authentic education is based on the premise that professional learning should meet high standards for intellectual rigor and connectedness, all within a supportive environment that recognizes and values diversity. Dr. Janet Reynolds, of Queensland, Australia, prompted the inclusion of this pedagogical approach. It counters the common but flawed approach to teaching that operates within an expert, lecture-mode environment where students are perceived as disempowered, empty vessels.

The fourth section of the book deals with the philosophical growth of professionals. Members of today's evolving professions must become more *intellectually curious*. Professionals with this trait confidently resist ideas presented by others until they have first critically challenged and examined them using skeptical thinking. Questioning dogma and unspoken assumptions by expressing skeptical doubt is humbling and constructive. It facilitates rational thought and a full reexamination of options, and it opens unlimited mental vistas that lead to more professional rigor. A well-lived professional life is contingent upon philosophical well-being, and although technology, scientific knowledge, and aesthetics can make life easier and more pleasant, the art of philosophizing by engaging in skeptical, intellectual curiosity must come first. Philosophers have an extraordinarily rich repertoire of theoretical and paradigm perspectives at their disposal. Therefore, they are particularly adept at seeing the implications of the assumptions that undergird their practice and structure their life and work environments. To that end, chapters are included to cover

Transformative Practice: New Pathways to Leadership

intellectual curiosity, skeptical thinking, and philosophical well-being.

The next two chapters discuss approaches we can use to foster this intellectual and philosophical growth, specifically communities of practice and knowledge management. Professional practitioners must push the limits of their field of study; otherwise their body of knowledge becomes stagnant. This transcending work requires a special kind of practice, in a special kind of community. Communities of practice are social groups that share their expertise and passion about a topic and pursue ongoing interactions to further their learning in this domain. These groups are intended to steward a particular practice to nurture, enrich, spread, and entrench a valuable contribution to the profession. Knowledge management is related to this practice, because it is based on the principle that a profession's most valuable resource is the knowledge of its people. In other words, knowledge management holds that an organization's members embody its intellectual assets or intellectual capital. These intellectual assets, the proprietary knowledge of each individual, are critical to a profession's overall vision and strategic plan. A profession can gain the innovative ideas it requires to survive and thrive if it can manage this tacit knowledge by converting the ideas of its practitioners. To accomplish this, we must pursue the strategies, policies, and tools that are necessary for the profession to access, manage, nurture, and share in these intellectual assets.

The final section of the book deals with the juggernaut of globalization and the

Transformative Practice: New Pathways to Leadership

assumption that most people tend to see it as a good thing that is necessary for solid economic growth and prosperity. As we'll see in chapter two, this attitude represents a hangover from the age of modernism. The chapter on globalization provides a cursory overview that compares globalization from the corporate led, top-down approach to the counter movement or resistance that would structure civil society from the bottom-up. The following chapter goes hand-in-hand with this concept, as it discusses sustainable human and social development to augment and offset the negative impact of growth-led economic development. Professional practitioners need a balanced understanding of these major concepts to effectively support justice, peace, and security. Dr. Deirdre Shaw of Glasgow, Scotland, contributes the final chapter on ethical consumption. She offers a taxonomy of different types of concerned consumers, specifically those who follow the green, ethical, anti-consumer, and voluntary simplicity philosophies. I would like to thank Dr. Shaw for skillfully illuminating the systemic moral dilemma citizens face as they strive to transform their consumption behavior.

In conclusion, the title of the book is *Transformative Practice: New Pathways to Leadership*, because leadership represents the cornerstone of our professional future. This leadership must be transformative in nature and shaped by a profound paradigm shift that will affect professional practice on many levels. This new, transformative style of leadership will distinguish itself through a different pedagogy, and through new approaches to professional

development. We will see evidence of it in revised university and public school curricula, in refocused policy involvement, and in different approaches to private and public enterprise. It will also become apparent as we see more and different civil society involvement and as we pursue continuous personal growth and reflection.

Reference

McGregor, S. L. T., et al. (2004). *A Satire: Confessions of recovering home economists* at http://www.kon.org/hswp/archive/recovering.html

Transformative Practice: New Pathways to Leadership

Chapter 1: Understanding Paradigm Shifts

This entire book is predicated on the assumption that a profession has to be open to a paradigm shift. This chapter will address the issues of what is a paradigm, what is involved in shifting paradigms, why people resist these shifts, and what this book proposes for a paradigm shift within a profession.

The Process of Shifting Paradigms

The term paradigm has been around for a long time. It comes from the Greek word *paradeigma,* meaning "pattern." Today's usage refers to *thought patterns.* Lay people discuss such patterns using phrases like mind-set, worldview, and groupthink. These terms refer to a set of experiences, beliefs, values, and assumptions that profoundly affect the way a person perceives reality and responds to that perception. When this personal belief system changes, the person experiences a paradigm shift. Although it is often difficult to discern when the shift actually occurs, those who have experienced one often describe it as a *stepping away from,* a *transitioning to,* an *overthrowing,* or an *overturning.*

The replacement of one mind-set with another is a very complex social process, and it is possible for several paradigms to compete for attention within a single profession. An entire field can undergo a paradigm shift when, eventually, a state of crisis emerges because too many things happen that cannot be explained using the assumptions of the dominant paradigm (see sidebar). Under these circumstances, people become much more willing to explore ideas that were once unthinkable. Finally, a

Transformative Practice: New Pathways to Leadership

Paradigm Anomalies

It is common practice for international and private lending agencies to get Majority World countries to enter into structural adjustment programs (SAPs), which are now referred to as Poverty Reduction Strategy Papers (PRSPs). The intent is to use monetary and fiscal policies to adjust the economy in a country, assuming that a stronger economy will lead to less poverty. These initiatives have failed miserably. All of the 54 developing countries that implemented SAPs in the last decade ended up poorer than they were when they started. Advocates of SAPs cannot understand why their approach did not work. It must be the fault of the citizens of the country whom they are trying to help get out of debt. They believe that the assumptions behind SAPs are sound, that a free market approach leads to more justice and equality due to the trickle down effect.

Even though these atrocious anomalies have surfaced for the past three decades, SAPs are still being used. Lenders continue to adhere to the assumption that too much state involvement in the planned economy of developing and underdeveloped countries (versus private enterprise), coupled with uncontrolled Majority World state spending on the wrong things (health, social welfare, and education), leads to an indebted situation that can only be fixed if the government shifts from a planned to a market economy via SAP economic policies. The anomaly illustrates reality. When SAPs are introduced, expenditures on basic services (health, education, welfare, and social programs) are often severely curtailed while monies earned exporting goods and commodities to world markets are used to make payments on the huge loans, and to impact market activities, capital investment, and production activities rather than fund basic services. Poverty, injustice, inequality, and human rights infringements only get worse, despite the intended outcome (McGregor, 2005).

different mind-set emerges and gains its own followers. Adherents to the new philosophy then examine reality from a new set of beliefs, assumptions, and values. This new perspective then results in different interpretations, conclusions, and implementation of resultant decisions and insights (Wikipedia, 2005b, c).

Throughout this process, there are those who continue to cling to old or competing paradigms, leading to intense intellectual and philosophical "battles" as paradigm proponents try to advance their respective views of the world and their place in it (Wikipedia, 2005b). This resistance occurs because the mind-set is so deeply entrenched that people are often unaware of the habitual patterns in their

Transformative Practice: New Pathways to Leadership

thinking, while being utterly reliant upon them to help interpret reality. Being stuck in a particular mind-set without consciously critiquing it is known as mental inertia, and it is very difficult to escape. By definition, something that is inert will have a tendency to persist unchanged in the absence of external influences. When something, or someone, from outside challenges a well-entrenched mind-set, that challenge is met with a great deal of fear, anxiety, and resistance. That is why it takes so long for paradigm shifts to occur. When shifts finally do occur, however, people are able to see the world through a different set of lenses, and the ideas they consider accurate without proof or critique (assumptions) change along with what they believe to be true (belief system) and what is important to them (values). Indeed, the effort involved in implementing a different paradigm is small compared to that of finding and believing in the paradigm (Wikipedia, 2005a).

Paradigm shifts are a necessary part of professional growth and personal life stories. Things do change, and sometimes they *have to* change. Healthy, successful people then learn to adjust to these changes, but paradigm shifts can be hard to endure, nonetheless. We crave stability because we literally cannot function without a paradigm, because it is more comfortable to have a solid stance from which to view the world and take part in it. For these reasons, it makes perfect sense that a paradigm in flux can make life very difficult, but it can also be enlightening and empowering (McGregor, 2004).

Paradigm shifts often come from the young, primarily because older generations have more to

Transformative Practice: New Pathways to Leadership

conserve and cling to: youth, after all, have not had time to become so emotionally invested in the current world paradigm. Sometimes, however, elders do lead the charge. This may be because the wiser among them appreciate that any subjective truth in a society normally remains applicable for about 20 years, seldom longer. This phenomenon may help to explain why it takes about 20 years, or one generation, for a paradigm to shift (Healy, 1996).

Why People Resist Paradigm Shifts

Breton and Largent (2002) provided a very intriguing discussion of why it is so hard to get people to change paradigms. Their work described the mechanism for resistance to shifting paradigms within a professional field. To summarize, they suggested that citizens of the Western world are obsessed with *processes* in much the same way that addicts are drawn to drugs, alcohol, caffeine, food, tobacco, shopping, or gambling. They suggest that people can become addicted to work and high stress jobs, perfectionism, competition, unhealthy relationships, making money, spending money and slipping into debt, seeking fame, and even living out family dramas. To illustrate, they offered the metaphor of an iceberg: the symptoms of our addictions to these processes (gambling, debt, substance abuse) are visible above the water, while the deadly societal, economic, cultural, technological, and political processes that fuel them remain hidden and silent below the surface.

Breton and Largent (2002) also noted that because the symptoms are so familiar, they too become invisible. The result is a citizenry that is blind to the driving force behind cultural patterns. In this

way, the addictive processes continue to shape daily life while the populace remains incapable of critiquing the social, economic, and political agents that perpetuate their addictions. Science, industry, the media, government, and like-minded think tanks require a pliant, non-interfering social system to facilitate both ideology and agenda. They thrive on privatization, decentralization, deregulation, and globalization (McGregor, 2001). Characteristics of this process-driven, addictive social structure are now pervasive throughout our school systems, workplace labor procedures, corporate hierarchies, governmental policies, media messages, and even our religious and cultural belief systems. Each of these entrenched institutions clings to modes of operation that keep us blind and addicted, and the level of "thinking-distortion" that influences people within these systems is astonishing. Disagreement and resistance are seen as threats to the order of things, and that is why paradigm shifts are difficult. Growing beyond the old framework forces us to change our mental models to fix the distorted thinking that shapes everything we do, believe, and feel. Because these powerful mental models supply us with stability and certainty, we often struggle fiercely to keep them intact, even after they have outlived their usefulness and grown to cause more harm than good.

Paradigm Protective Cloaking Devices

One final comment before discussing the current and proposed paradigms in the profession: earlier, it was noted that people who hold a particular worldview have a vested interest in maintaining it because it defines who

Transformative Practice: New Pathways to Leadership

they are. The loss of the paradigm would mean a loss of the self. To offset this risk, paradigm defenders tend to develop a range of "cloaking devices" for self-protection. See if you recognize yourself in what follows. Such people (a) align themselves with peers who share the same mental models or worldview, (b) split themselves into compartments and then design filters for each "box" (specializations, areas of expertise, different subjects, different disciplines), and (c) avoid comparing these boxes in ways that might force them to question whether the values they use at work are the ones they want to use at home or in their community. By erecting walls between these filters, people actually end up not interacting with, or reflecting upon, various aspects of their lives. They keep each one separate until, one day, they "just do not like what they see in the mirror." This disconnect can result in a deep lack of consistency that leads to bewildering stress and angst. In addition, people who compartmentalize in this manner can more readily assert that "there is no one overall worldview," so the underlying, prevailing worldview can remain invisible and unexamined (Breton & Largent, 2002).

Breton and Largent (2002) pursued this idea further, noting that people who are using cloaking devices also (d) claim to be objective and free from value judgments, posing as unbiased observers. This practice is especially evident in the application of the scientific method of empirical research, and in acceptance of any knowledge stemming from this science. (e) People also make use of taboos to pretend that challenging aspects of their lives or practices do not exist. If they do not exist, they cannot be a problem so a profession does not have to deal with them. This phenomenon relates to the previous point about objectivity, because there are enduring professional taboos against reliance on any form of science that is not strictly empirical. If it cannot be measured, proven, and controlled, then the knowledge gained from the science is not valid. This taboo has led to deep divisions among practitioners of many professions in the past. It has also left no room for narrative, conscience, spirituality, or wisdom, either because there is no proof of their existence or the results cannot be generalized to the wider population. It is common for people who step on this particular taboo to be ridiculed, not promoted, even fired.

In the home economics/ family and consumer sciences profession, another taboo has involved settling on a final definition of "family." If we pretend that non-nuclear family forms do not exist or exist only as aberrations, we can pretend that we do not have to deal with that aspect of our practice. Until recently, the suggestion that consuming is a bad thing was also treated as taboo, but this perspective is now being challenged (McGregor, 2003a, b).

Finally, (f) people who try to protect themselves within a given paradigm create defensive routines to prevent embarrassment if someone comes too close to figuring out their mental models or worldviews. These defensive routines block communication with others and inhibit personal transformation because they deny access to the filters that have been established around the boxes. If one cannot access the filters, one stays locked within a given paradigm. This

allows the situation to worsen because mental breakthroughs are stifled (Breton & Largent, 2002). Yes, the person stays protected, but there is a price to be paid. Individuals who operate in this manner often shut out others and become alienated to the point of limiting relations to like-minded peers in order to feel any sense of belonging. In this scenario, the paradigm cycle perpetuates itself indefinitely.

Making the Current Paradigm Visible

Breton and Largent (2002) continued by asserting that the invisible paradigm is everywhere, touching every part of daily life. Because it is hidden, yet ubiquitous, people cannot see what is causing the system-wide unhappiness, and this renders them incapable of stopping it. Hawken (1994) wisely noted that if you ask any group of people, anywhere in the world, "*How many woke up this morning with the intention of destroying the world?*" no one would raise a hand. So, if people are destroying the world without intention, and yet they are doing it anyway, the action must be embedded in *how* they do things as opposed to being something that they consciously *want* to do. That insight told Hawken that the behavior could be reversed. Making the relevant paradigm(s) visible is the first step toward changing a harmful action.

Because a paradigm is the sum total of the belief-set, values, and practices prevalent in a given professional community at a given moment in its development (Kuhn, 1962), it is vitally important to reveal the nature of that prevailing paradigm. It is impossible to describe a proposed shift in the professional community's conception of its legitimate problems and standards if a

Transformative Practice: New Pathways to Leadership

benchmark is not provided. Recent work by McGregor (1997a, b, 1999) and McGregor et al. (2004) offered a deep analysis of existing professional paradigms within the field of family and consumer sciences and describes various ways in which the current mind-set is not adequate for the times. A summary of this discussion is shared here to illustrate the primary point by outlining weaknesses in the current worldview that is shaping most practice in home economics/family and consumer sciences.

First, the profession has been criticized for relying too heavily on the scientific or empirical paradigm during the last 100 years of practice, without questioning the relevance of the knowledge gained from this science in the context of contemporary individual and family life. Newer thinking has softened this critique somewhat, suggesting that what is lacking is a balance. Empirical science has its place, but so do critical, narrative, and other forms of the new sciences.

Second, this over-reliance on empirical science can result in an overuse of detached, coldly clinical thinking that leads to over-specialization and positions professionals as benevolent experts who are somehow "above it all." Families are called *clients*, implying an exchange relationship and dependency. Again, this critique has been moderated somewhat as professionals have begun to recognize that balance is needed. A responsive combination of technical, communicative, and empowerment approaches elicits more productive results when working with individuals and families. This approach has been labeled the "three systems of action" to signify that problems are

Transformative Practice: New Pathways to Leadership

mentally approached from three different directions. In effect, the three systems of action ask us to determine what combination of coping with, adapting to, and affecting social and political change is appropriate to any given situation.

Third, the profession went along with the reductionist, mechanistic mind-set of the Industrial Revolution to the detriment of individual and family well-being. It accepted the machine metaphor without question, leading us to perceive a false fragmentation of living systems that made each component appear disconnected and isolated. Different family forms were labeled, narrowly focused specializations were developed, professionals accepted the title of "expert," and university programs were created with no common philosophical orientation.

This fragmentation continues to engender professional ineffectiveness and divisiveness. One has to tick off which "division" one occupies when joining a professional association, as there is never a box labeled "Integrationist" or "Advocate for a common philosophy."

Fourth, a profession dedicated to human well-being did not take issue with capitalism as the pre-eminent market model. In some countries, the name of the profession was changed to include the word *consumer*. Since capitalism cannot work without consumers, and since we now live in a society that is deeply entrenched in consumer culture (necessitating a specific work ethic), the field of home economics/family and consumer sciences was complicit in creating the juggernaut of out-of-control consumerism. As such, the profession must bear some responsibility for the negative impact on those living elsewhere, on the future generation, on the environment, and on other species.

Fifth, professional rhetoric utilizes the term "interdisciplinary" when "multidisciplinary" would be more appropriate. Although this is not a bad thing in and of itself, it should be noted that an honest embrace of the interdisciplinary approach would involve preparing professionals to be synergistic thinkers. Instead, the profession continues to embrace programs of study that condone the expert mode and observe artificial boundaries between disciplines, such as food, clothing, family, housing, and resource management/consumption. Communication between specializations is severely inhibited, as well. Separate conferences are held for each discipline (save for the national association conferences), and separate professional associations exist to serve each narrow area of expertise. Divided we fall.

Sixth, there is an ongoing debate over the place of the human ecosystem perspective in the profession. This perspective was advanced as a means of moving beyond the systems model, itself a step forward from the microeconomic approach (Key & Firebaugh, 1989). To elaborate, the economic theory of the early 1900s depicted families as producers of household commodities and consumers of market goods and services. Social systems theory was then introduced in 1975, partly because of the *static* nature of economic theory. Social systems theory recognizes the family as a set of mutually dependent, *dynamically interacting* entities, and

acknowledges complex relationships between the family and its environments. The more contextual human ecosystem approach was advanced in the early 1980s as professionals began to combine separate paradigms by *integrating the social with the economic.* Some contend that internal and external systems of change must be addressed simultaneously. These professionals propose that the field delve further into complex reciprocal relationships between families and their micro, meso, and macro environments, the processes of change, equilibrium, and adaptation. Once accepted, the paradigm shift proposed in this approach will allow the profession to observe the *process* and the *context* of resource allocation within, and by, the family. It will also illuminate the *outcomes* of such allocations on others and on the environment.

Finally, because the field operates within the expert mode and relies on empirically-based science, research is performed "on" families instead of "with" families. Until recently, professionals did not recognize the merit of a dialectic, participatory, contextual approach. Instead, scholarly work took the form of controlled experiments that relied heavily on the laboratory, and professionals confined themselves to the role of the objective observer. This methodology offers no voice to those being studied and expresses no concern for the larger context within which they live their lives. Sophisticated statistical approaches allow researchers to hold things constant and pretend that change is not happening, demonstrating a lack of respect for any kind of science that is not grounded in purely empirical practices. If it cannot be counted, measured, validated, and

Transformative Practice: New Pathways to Leadership

replicated it is deemed unworthy of research, because any data gained through non-empirical methods of observation must be disregarded.

Conversely, dialectic theory encourages practitioners to (a) take everyday life into account, along with the common sense meanings in which the family is immersed, (b) respect the intrinsic value that family members place on things in the home, (c) conduct a critical analysis of social and cultural traditions to reveal the constraints they place on internal and external freedoms and on justice, and (d) view families within a totality of relationships that are enmeshed in conditions of power. Such relationships influence each member's self-interpretation of various situations and provide a sense of empowerment to improve their own lives.

Participatory research calls for the active involvement of, and often even control by, the objects or beneficiaries of the research. Participants' roles would include defining the questions, controlling the process, and interpreting the findings – ideally as originators, proponents, and executors of the research. A contextual approach necessitates that families take action when *they* are ready, not when the researchers are ready. A family's decision to act could take years, and the result of that action may take longer still to become evident. Researchers may, in fact, never know if their efforts have made an impact. Because society encourages us to rely on a quick fix that makes us feel needed, professionals tend to shy away from this long-term approach. Ironically, by maintaining complete control to achieve short-term gains, researchers who are attempting to improve the human condition often unwittingly

contribute to the disempowerment of individuals and families.

The insightful, forward thinking professionals who come together to identify ideological and paradigm trends in any profession often propose ideas for a new future. However, today's change agents are faced with a significant challenge as they work to achieve progress in the face of professional "push-back." Professions struggle to move forward by making progress on past recommendations while the world continues to evolve. With this evolution comes the pressing need to define and refine a paradigm appropriate to the field during changing times. The next section describes what that practice might look like if recent thinking about appropriate paradigms is augmented with new paths to leadership from a transformative perspective.

Proposed Paradigm Shift for the Profession

Practicing professionals do not lose faith in an established paradigm when nothing credible exists to take its place. Practitioners of a profession or discipline must judge how much the dominant paradigm fails to consider current reality. To that end, some professionals are bolder than most and are brave enough, and convinced enough, to declare the current paradigm and resultant practice in crisis, or at least in transition. These few people explore alternatives to the field's long held assumptions even though the majority of practitioners resist. Thank goodness a paradigm shift needs both protagonists and protestors, because they surely do exist in all professions (Wikipedia, 2005d). In the end, a profession's chances for survival and effectiveness depend upon members' willingness, readiness,

Transformative Practice: New Pathways to Leadership

and ability to change established ways of thinking—for the home economics/family and consumer sciences, it depends on an ability to develop alternatives to the scientific, mechanistic paradigm (Chorover, 1991).

Being locked into a paradigm that no longer works inhibits momentum, generates inertia, slows communication, interferes with innovation, and creates tunnel vision (Kirschner, 2002). When the state of affairs reaches this level, anything is better. Although there are no guarantees, professional life on the other side of an outdated paradigm is often full of momentum. The evolving profession becomes dynamic and full of rich, reflective communication replete with innovative practice and a clear, far-reaching vision. The new paradigm for the home economics/family and consumer sciences should mean porous, or better yet no boundaries between various disciplines within the profession. Practitioners would pose the right questions and seek better solutions by continually critiquing the human condition from a holistic, peace oriented, social justice perspective. Within this paradigm, everyone is recognized as a leader and effective leadership is based on personal transformation and reflection. In addition, members of the profession would become very receptive to the notion of Reflective Human Action theory (Andrews, Mitstifer, Rehm, & Vaughn, 1985) as a means for achieving an authentic, ethical, and spiritual practice. This new framework would also enable professionals to experience a growing respect for the various typologies people use to self-identify as members of a profession, and members would benefit

Transformative Practice: New Pathways to Leadership

greatly from the deep implications this self-identification has upon future professional development initiatives.

The evolving profession should be comprised of members who are ambassadors, with every person proudly representing the profession. Practitioners in all specializations could champion the cause of individuals and families while working collaboratively with them to pose and solve deep human problems, instead of posing as experts who simply address the symptoms. A holistic, empowerment approach would develop to embrace transformative learning, and practitioners could realize new opportunities for profession(al) growth by shifting from interdisciplinary to transdisciplinary practice (see Chapter 3). This shift would entail consideration of the merits of viewing professional practice through the lens of the new sciences (chaos theory, quantum physics, and living systems) with one possible model being the holomovement principle (see Chapter 4), or holism instead of fragmentation.

Philosophical well-being would serve as a beacon for a sustainable future and profession. This form of wellness would be augmented with an abiding intellectual curiosity and deep respect for skeptical thinking. The latter would involve taking up the habit of critical discourse analysis by engaging in practice from a critical science approach, always seeking insights into the power dynamics inherent in all aspects of human life. Revealing power relationships would involve deep respect for, and ongoing analysis of, the new faces of globalization (corporate-led, top down as well as civil society-led, bottom

Transformative Practice: New Pathways to Leadership

up) and the necessity of promoting and facilitating human, social, and economic development. A focus on inner and societal power would also imply a different pedagogical approach, namely *authentic pedagogy*, in the preparation of professional members. Learning in the profession would meet the standards of intellectual rigor and connectedness in a supportive environment that recognizes and values diversity. This mind-set would carry forward into professional practice.

In this new paradigm, we would see professionals committed to understanding what it means "to live in postmodern times." One deeply unsettling aspect of the postmodern era is the new face of consumerism. The new paradigm would explore the idea that the time has come for us to flesh out standards for ethical consumerism. As the field moves forward on each element of the new paradigm, members would create communities of practice as a way to manage and advance an evolving base of knowledge management. This approach would ensure that philosophies that worked in the past could be successfully married with the new principles that comprise the enhanced mind-set of the new paradigm.

Conclusion

Paradigm shift is a risky endeavor. This peril must be acknowledged, but we must also recognize that not shifting is even riskier when a good case can be made for the necessity of a paradigm shift. Because the changes proposed in this book are so big, we by no means have all of the answers. We do, however, want to start the philosophical discussion. This book is an attempt to

Transformative Practice: New Pathways to Leadership

expand ways for all of us to participate in a profession-wide dialogue about embracing and facilitating this paradigm shift.

Paradigms are typically overthrown only with great difficulty, because change requires that we take on new assumptions and expectations that will then transform our theories, methods, and analytical approaches. We must try not to fall into the trap of equating paradigm survival with personal survival. Instead, we must focus on the direction of the profession to determine what needs to be done to change, or reinforce, that course. Furthermore, collaborative efforts among like-minded people can enable paradigm developments to emerge that are greater and more significant than any one person could produce alone (Breton & Largent, 2002). The question now is whether professionals will individually and collectively take the lead to change paradigms so the profession can move forward into the new millennium. This book was written assuming the answer is a resounding, "YES."

References

Andrews, F. E., Mitstifer, D. I., Rehm, M., & Vaughn, G. G. (1995). *Leaders: Reflective human action – a professional development module*. East Lansing, MI: Kappa Omicron Nu.

Breton, D., & Largent, C. (2002). *On the reality of the 'Paradigm Conspiracy'*. Retrieved March 4, 2005 from http://www.trufax.org/paradigm/paradigm.html

Chorover, S. L. (1991). *Systems human ecology: Towards a new paradigm*. Retrieved March 4, 2005 from http://business.hol.gr/bio/HTML/PUBS/VOL3/lh_cho.htm

Hawken, P. (1994). *The ecology of commerce*. New York: Harper Business.

Healy, T. (1996). *Thomas Kuhn*. Retrieved March 2, 2005 from http://www.ee.scu.edu/eefac/healy/kuhn.html

Key, R., & Firebaugh, F. (1989). Family resource management: Preparing for the 21st century. *Journal of Home Economics*, 81(1), 13-17.

Kirschner, R. (2002). *Thrive in turbulent times... The paradigm shifts*. Retrieved February 3, 2003 from http://www.rickspeaks.com/Articles/TTT.html

Kuhn, T. (1962). *The structure of scientific revolutions*. Chicago: University of Chicago Press.

McGregor, S. L. T. (1997a). Envisioning our collective journey into the next millennium. *Journal of Home Economics Education*, 35(1), 26-38.

McGregor, S. L. T. (1997b). The impact of different paradigms on home economics practice. *Journal of the Home Economics Institute of Australia*, 4(3), 23-33.

McGregor, S. L. T. (1999). Reconnecting our professional community: A revitalization perspective. *Kappa Omicron Nu FORUM*, 10(2), 5-18. Online at http://www.kon.org/archives/forum/forum10_2.pdf

McGregor, S. L. T. (2001). Neoliberalism and health care. *International Journal of Consumer Studies*, 25(2), 82-89 (available at http://www.consultmcgregor.com).

McGregor, S. L. T. (2003a). Consumerism as structural violence. *Human Sciences Working Papers Archives*. Retrieved June 6, 2005 from http://www.kon.org/hswp/archive/consumerism.html

McGregor, S. L. T. (2003b). Consumer entitlement, narcissism and immoral consumption. *Human Sciences Working Papers Archives*. Retrieved June 6, 2005 from http://www.kon.org/hswp/archive/mcgregor_1.htm

McGregor, S. L. T. (2004). Transformative learning: We teach who we are. *Kappa Omicron Nu FORUM*, 14(2), retrieved June 6, 2005 from www.kon.org/archives/forum/14-2/forum14-2_article4.html

McGregor, S. L. T. (2005). Structural adjustment programmes and human well-being. *International Journal of Consumer Studies*, 29(3), 170-180.

McGregor, S. L. T., et al. (2004). A Satire: Confessions of recovering home economists. *Human Sciences Working Papers Archives*. Retrieved March 6, 2005 from http://www.kon.org/hswp/archive/recovering.html

Wikipedia. (2005a). *Mindset*. Retrieved March 2, 2005 from http://en.wikipedia.org/wiki/Mindset

Wikipedia. (2005b). *Paradigm*. Retrieved March 2, 2005 from http://en.wikipedia.org/wiki/paradigm

Wikipedia, (2005c). *Paradigm shifts*. Retrieved March 2, 2005 http://en.wikipedia.org/wiki/paradigm_shift

Wikipedia. (2005d). *The structure of scientific revolutions*. Retrieved March 4, 2005 from http://en.wikipedia.org/The_Structure_of_Scientific_Revolutions

Transformative Practice: New Pathways to Leadership

Chapter 2: Understanding Postmodern Thinking*

It is no longer uncommon to hear "We live in postmodern times," stated in a dramatic manner that assumes a profound ongoing societal impact. Professionals who wish to function effectively in postmodern times must first understand how scholars and others view this era and how it is different from other periods of human history. This chapter explores premodernism, modernism, and five different strands of postmodernism.[1] It concludes by detailing the consequences of adherence to any, some, or all of these five strands upon an individual's professional practice.

The Premodern Era (800s-late 1500s)

To obtain a clearer understanding of *postmodernism*, it is helpful to first define the modern and premodern eras. The premodern era is now considered the age of *faith and superstition*. Premodern, medieval cultures were based on a religious or sacred worldview where people lived at the mercy of their environs, spirits, religions, or gods (Scheurich, 2001). The Dark Ages and Middle Ages that comprise premodernism conjure images of King Arthur, Robin Hood, Joan of Arc, Thomas à Beckett, William the Conqueror, and rich feudal tales peopled by heralds, scribes, magicians, chivalric knights, pages, lords and ladies-in-waiting, and poverty-stricken peasants. A historic pre-cursor to the modern concept of human rights also arose during this period: the Magna

---

*Earlier version published in *Kappa Omicron Nu FORUM*, http://www.kon.org/archives/forum/13-2/mcgregor.html.

[1] This is a fundamental discussion that provides a brief historical overview to describe the events that have led us to this point. It does not provide a comprehensive analysis.

Transformative Practice: New Pathways to Leadership

Carta, signed in 1215, gave English nobility and other freeman rights to property and protection from arbitrary royal authority.

The premodern era was very religious, and dictates of the Church were accepted without question. There was little respect for human dignity and peasants typically held the legal and economic status of bonded servants, or serfs. They were not technically slaves because no one owned them and they did have some rights, such as the right to own property. Serfs were tenant farmers or craftsman who worked the Lord's land and paid a percentage of their crops in rent. They were obligated to work and to pay high fees to the landowner for nearly everything, including getting married. Serfs could not leave the land without the Lord's permission, and if they had a dispute with the Lord they could not seek an impartial hearing in the King's court, but had to make their case in the Lord's court.

Serfdom linked the farmer to the land and prevented social or geographical mobility. This arrangement was not invented in the Medieval period but it prevailed during this time. People believed in absolutes, and God was at the root of explanations for *everything*. That is why the role of the Church was so significant and why serfdom worked as a system. During Medieval times, it was accepted that only God (and by extension, the kings and lords who were *men* of the church) was capable of pure, incorruptible reason. Human judgment was suspect and assumed to be clouded by passions and materialism.

In 1347, everything changed when Europe was ravaged by the Black Death. Medieval medicine was incapable of combating the plague,

Transformative Practice: New Pathways to Leadership

reliant as it was on holy wells, pools, streams, and miraculous intervention. When the last of the dead were buried six years later, three profound changes had occurred. First, the Church began to lose power. Survivors could discover no Divine purpose in the pain they had suffered. If disaster of this magnitude was an act of God, then reliance on God's goodness was no longer absolute. Once people began to envision a change in the order of things, the age of unquestioned submission to Church, King, and Lord was over. Minds that were opened to admit these questions could never be closed again.

Second, the Medieval economy never recovered from the impact of the plague. So many people had died that there were serious labor shortages all over Europe. This led workers to demand higher wages, but landlords and Nobles refused those demands. By the end of the 1300s, peasant revolts broke out across Europe. At the same time, the word *peasant* began to be used in a derogatory manner that referred to a new lower class. Previously, a peasant was simply someone who comprised a part of the three orders in society: work, pray, and fight. Peasants were not the only segment of society in revolt. The phenomenon of popular uprisings was broader in scope and involved classes below the Nobles who desired to share in the wealth, status, and well-being of those more fortunate. There were five main reasons for these uprisings: (a) an increasing gap between the wealthy and poor, (b) declining incomes overall, (c) rising inflation and taxation, (d) the external crises of famine, plague, and war, and (e) religious backlashes.

Third, society began to move away from the idea of *miraculous* healing and toward the practice of

medical science. People lost faith in the myths that arose from ignorance of physical cause and effect and looked to modern science to explain the world. Eventually, people no longer accepted supernatural agencies, but instead relied only upon observation, experience, experiment, and thought (Dunnigan & Nofi, 1997). This was the beginning of the scientific paradigm that is so prevalent in post-modern times.

Transition to the Modern Era

Once the plague passed, society transitioned through several distinct eras along its path into the modern age. There is a drift of dates that occurs with all periods of history, so the years are intended only as a rough approximation.

Renaissance Era (1500-1700)

A brief Renaissance *Humanist* era preceded the Renaissance Era during the 1300-1400s, and ushered in a new focus on living well in the present (humanism) along with a renewed interest in the classics. The Renaissance Era itself began in earnest around 1500. Also sometimes referred to as Elizabethan Times, the Renaissance was peopled by such luminaries as Shakespeare, Leonardo da Vinci, and John Milton. It gave rise to the printing press, an emerging middle class, gunpowder, cannons, witch burnings, and the beginnings of democracy and civics. Florence was the world's preeminent city, and a compelling, still unparalleled blend of art and science existed during this period.

Again, during the Middle Ages people believed that only God was capable of reason, and men of the church were needed to convey the voice of God to the masses incapable of rational thought. The Renaissance era called

Transformative Practice: New Pathways to Leadership

this belief into question. People chose to arrive at meaningful conclusions *on their own*, rather than accept what was dictated by the church or by royalty. For the first time, philosophies arose to advance the notion that reason is possible for *everyone*, not just Priests, Kings, and Lords. Key proponents of this belief included Bacon (empiricism), Descartes (rationalism), Locke (natural, political rights), Adam Smith (capitalism), David Hume (naturalism), and Voltaire (separation of church and state). These philosophies spread quickly when, in 1454, Johannes Gutenburg perfected the portable printing press. This singular invention spurred an increased level of education and sparked a communication revolution on par with that advanced by the Internet today.

The Renaissance marks the transition from the Middle Ages to the Modern Age.

During this period, scientists developed the foundations of a thoroughly empirical worldview, and people began to reject the scholastic authority that had evolved in medieval universities. Where scholastics relied upon ancient authorities as sources of dogma and engaged in elaborate debates about how to *interpret* them properly, Renaissance scholars were very excited about the prospect of achieving new scientific knowledge. They studied the old texts to gain their *own* interpretation of them and they gladly embraced the new science. With the advent of the printing press, the knowledge they generated was spread far and wide. This era also saw a rise in commerce and exploration as well as an increasingly popular willingness to reject institutional authority (church, government, ruling class) in favor of greater individual freedom.

25

Transformative Practice: New Pathways to Leadership

There is general agreement that this era benefited only literate people of influence. Changes were largely intellectual and ideological, rather than substantive in nature. The plight of the masses remained largely unchanged from the Middle Ages, in spite of modest gains made in the peasant revolts. Still, while Renaissance innovations were elitist in the short-term, the long-term effects profoundly influenced all strata of society: new methods of learning, commerce, communication, and experimentation triggered eventual advancements in science, economics, medicine, education, technology, and politics that continue to benefit all socio-economic classes to this day.

Enlightenment Era (1700-1800s)

As Europe entered the 1700s, the Renaissance gave way to the Enlightenment period and modern science was born. The Enlightenment was an eighteenth-century intellectual movement that placed great emphasis on the use of *reason* in the development of philosophical, social, political, and scientific knowledge. During this era, people believed that human reason could combat ignorance, superstition, and tyranny to create a better world. The Enlightenment era was shaped by confidence in the power of human knowledge to overcome injustice and the social ills formerly attributed to supernatural forces. It also sought to replace impulsive political decisions made on a ruler's whim with sound governance based upon logic and reason (Brians, 2000).

Throughout this age, European intellectuals emphasized the need to base a "modern" society on a more secular worldview, one less

Transformative Practice: New Pathways to Leadership

grounded in religious doctrine. A secular view theorized and idealized the concepts of rationality and inevitable social progress; it held that this progress would advance through the emerging sciences and the scientific method. In concert with the development of natural science, the Enlightenment era brought the early rise of market capitalism, transnational banking, and the initial development of the nation-state. In earlier times, society was structured into hundreds of fiefdoms, each ruled by its own prince. Italy took that model further still, structuring itself in individual city-states.

Citizens of this age believed strongly in the value of the individual and had faith in the human capacity to think independently. It was no longer accepted that people had to rely upon an established authority to tell them what to think.

Enlightenment era thinkers also recognized the value of self-determination for the first time. A belief emerged that individuals were intelligent enough to make their own choices in life and did not need to have decisions made for them by others.

This period was also characterized by a manifest mastery over nature and the magnification of efficiency—everywhere. The great thinkers of the time developed natural laws using the scientific method and applied them universally. It was this age that gave rise to Newton's laws of physics, Darwin's theory of biological evolution, and the periodic table of elements. These new laws replaced medieval laws developed by the divine right of church officials and kings, but much of the dogma remained. Men were still making the laws, just using a different approach.

Transformative Practice: New Pathways to Leadership

Enlightenment describes an illumination in the darkness, or coming to the truth out of ignorance. The era was shaped by confidence in humanity to overcome social ills through logic and reason. This Age of Reason challenged many formerly incontrovertible assumptions by calling for

- secularism, which states that life can best be lived with no reference to God or the supernatural, religion is not in public sphere, and religion does not dictate politics;
- distrust of authority, particularly the Catholic Church. People rejected the overbearing, dogmatic authoritarianism of the Church and dispensed with absolute clerical rule;
- respect for human dignity;
- acceptance of the principle that reason would illuminate mankind and lead to perpetual social, political, economic, and scientific progress; and,
- cosmopolitanism, which held that people should not be subservient to authority but should be citizens of the world. This idea emerged in the context of rising capitalism, worldwide trade, expanding empires, world voyages and discoveries, and the emergence of the concept of human rights in 1789.

By the end of the Enlightenment era, humanity stood on the brink of the Modern age in a society that was

- based on a more secular worldview—less grounded in religious doctrine;
- founded on rationality through optimal decision-making based upon reason, logic, and scientific truth;
- built to facilitate the inevitable social progress that would stem from reason, education using the three R's, and absolute science;
- grounded in emerging sciences and the

scientific method, implementing a universal, *methodical* approach to the acquisition of knowledge. Natural laws took the place of medieval laws made by divine right;
♦ shaped by a deep respect for individuality with emphasis on the person. Self-interest became the focus over the state, the community, or "the other;"
♦ marked by faith in the human capacity for rational thought that does not require an established authority to tell people what to believe;
♦ committed to cumulative social progress through scientific endeavor. Enlightenment thinking held that society could follow the scientific method to advance naturally as mechanisms were analyzed using empirical evidence rather than faith;
♦ rooted in the value of self-determination to guide individuals in governing their own lives by making their own intelligent choices instead of relying on direction from others;
♦ characterized by a manifest mastery over nature as evidenced by colonialization and the use of slavery to extract natural resources; and,
♦ shaped by the magnification of efficiency throughout every aspect of life. Resources were scarce, waste was unthinkable.

The Modern Era (1800s-1950)

When we think of the modern era, many diverse images, inventions, and events spring to mind. This is the age of Art Deco and Art Nouveau, cubism, commercial advertising, moving pictures, vintage television, vaudeville, jazz, flappers, technological advances in machines, electronics, appliances and gadgets to simplify our lives, skyscrapers, transcontinental railways and highways, assembly lines, motels, a stock market

Transformative Practice: New Pathways to Leadership

crash, two world wars, the atom bomb, urban sub-divisions, and a focus on function over form (especially in architecture).

This is the age of reason, empiricism, and science. Modernism is a term that encompasses events and changes that occurred after the gains made in the Enlightenment Era. It refers to the rise of mass media, large-scale integration of isolated communities into societies, and departure from tradition and religion. The Modern period is also marked by a profound reliance on individualism, rational or scientific organization of society, and the advent of egalitarianism, which states that all persons are equal in fundamental worth or moral status. Humanity continues to cling to absolutes during the Modern era, but the absolute shifts from God to nature and finally to man himself. The self becomes the absolute that can be depended upon, not God or higher authorities. The human enterprise of Modern times was built upon an optimistic view of man, where reason finally pushes faith entirely out of the picture because it is no longer necessary.

In essence, modernism rejected the traditional, and long-established patterns were considered outdated or old-fashioned. Modernism approached problems with new ideas and techniques. It reexamined every aspect of existence to learn what was "holding back" progress. Stumbling blocks were replaced with new, therefore better, ways of advancing. This was especially true after the horrors of the First World War, when people became jaded and rejected the idea that mankind could make moral progress. Material progress would have to do.

Other defining events in the Modern Age included industrialization and the

Transformative Practice: New Pathways to Leadership

rise of representative democracy, urbanization, and mass literacy. Industrialization forced social and economic transformation through technological innovation, notably in automation, energy, engineering, telecommunications, and metallurgy. The later stages of modernity are characterized by several other defining features, including ubiquitous technology and science; mass production and industrial efficiency; the emergence of the middle class from among the aristocrats, underclasses, and the Church; centralized governmental power; and consumerism, defined as economics organized around consumption instead of production (Scheurich, 2001; Shepherd, 2000).

Governments evolved as centralized, hierarchal structures that seemed far removed from the citizens they were designed to benefit. People were no longer confined to a role dictated by the family or social class they were born into, but were able to move up, down, and around. This social mobility created a sense of liberty, but it also fostered competition, individualism, and the concepts of individual economic success and failure.

As the Modern age unfolded, Western European and North American societies gained unparalleled influence over other societies. This happened for two key reasons. First, these were the primary regions where rational thinking replaced reliance on religion, superstition, and convention. Second, the plunder of the developing world through colonization created exploitative relations with a majority of the world's population, relations that continue to this day. These factors allowed Western leaders to assume that, since the rational, scientific approach to problems

seems to give rise to the pursuit of economic wealth, such a system is reasonable for pursuing social development or "progress."

In the 1950s, people came to believe that they lived in a modern secular society that was better than earlier societies because of scientific advances. This modern society believed progress was built upon reason, the three R's of education, and absolute dedication to empirical science. Supernatural, outer space, and faith-based phenomena were considered myths to be explained away by science. The *modern* in this instance refers to a post-Enlightenment notion of the individual as a subject, free of state and church yet regulated and disciplined by increasingly powerful apparatuses of bureaucracy and surveillance. The modern age was marked by faith in progress and technology to improve the lot of the individual, even as these same individuals began to critique the impact of this progress and technology on their personal and public lives (Sturken & Cartwright, 2001). Key features of the Modern era are summarized in Table 1.

Finally, Modernism sought the singular, totalizing narrative: the grand unified theory through which all human activities may be anticipated, explained, and potentially influenced. Modernists believed that one overarching hypothesis could apply to all levels of society (Sturken & Cartwright, 2001). This grand narrative contains everything we have always been told and thus take for granted. It is a collection of modern ideas and knowledge that profoundly affects societal organization, the role of the individual within the society, and the power relationships that exist between society's institutions, such as government, labor

Transformative Practice: New Pathways to Leadership

Table 1.   Features of Modernity and the Late Modern Age
(Sturken & Cartwright, 2001)

- Rise of market capitalism via the mercantile system
- Development of transnational banking and worldwide trade
- Further development of the nation-state, with centralized power in the hands of a hierarchical government. Nation states mandated and controlled economic markets on behalf of citizens
- Formation of the middle class
- Rise of positivism as supernatural, faith-based beliefs lost credence to become mere myth to be explained away by science

Under the label *Late Modernity*, we see:

- Free market capitalism in the context of 21st century globalization
- Ubiquitous technology and science, or t*echnoscience*
- Mass production and industrial efficiency, in concert with the growth of the service and information society and related industries
- Economic policy organized around consumption, not production
- Rationalization taken to extremes of total efficiency, predictability, calculability, and control. This leads to dehumanization and devaluation of relationships
- Social Darwinism, and the notion of one truth as perpetuated by the Grand Narrative (success, competition, science, individualism) as the only way to interpret "how things work"
- Reductionism, or an obsession with ordering, classifying, and grouping things, which leads to unnatural fragmentation and compartmentalization of subjects and knowledge
- Continued patriarchy and social policies that devalue women, children, and the underpriviledged as illegitimate and unimportant
- Proof that we are biologically alike signifies that all are equal, but fails to end racism, discrimination, exclusion, marginalization, and war
- Earth dominated by man, with resources "there for the taking"
- Meaning and truth defined by individuals through personal life experiences
- Living things treated like machines within a *mastery over* system that is reflected in the management paradigm and the education system
- An assumption that everything is separate and disconnected. This dualism, binary, or cause and effect paradigm leads to irresponsible, distanced consumption
- A focus on the traditional nuclear family with clear division of gender roles. Different family *types* emerge, but the tendency toward reductionism ensures that they are assigned labels that indicate deviation from the norm
- Concern with conclusions and closures with proof, accompanied by no appreciation for process
- A belief that only matter has power, which leads to materialism and a desire to gain power over others by buying things

market, consumer market, economic system, education, health, transportation, religion, the media, and the family. This comprehensive narrative is perpetuated through patriarchically determined gender roles and divisions that support male domination, colonialism, subjectivity, empiricism, representation, technological and economic progress, and male-centric analysis in the form of <u>his</u>tory, rather than <u>a</u> story or <u>her</u>story.

Modernism meets Consumerism in the 1960s

Consumerism is a defining feature of the Modern era. It rose with industrialization, economic efficiency, and capitalism. It began in the mid 1600s and continues today, unabated. However, consumption in the 1600s did not look the way it does now. From 1600 through the 1800s (the late Renaissance and Enlightenment Ages), a culturally specific set of conditions gave rise to consumerism. People consumed to show that they were respectable. It was assumed that taste arose from good breeding, so the elite consumed the sugar, tea, coffee, and exotic imported fabrics gained through colonialism. The virtue of self-restraint allowed the elite to take a moral stance. If they consumed to take comfort in innocent pleasure, or if they consumed for convenience, they saw themselves as more efficient, constructive participants in the public sphere. Consuming coffee in coffeehouses was a way for men to transact business in a civil and respectable manner. Consuming tea at home was a way for women to be seen as civilizers, the moral hearth of the nation (Smith, 2002). For these reasons, and for the advancement of consumerism, most people accepted slave labor and colonization as leading-edge strategies

Transformative Practice: New Pathways to Leadership

for economic growth and imperialism.

This model changed in the Modern era of the late 1800s and early 1900s. Because producers needed people to buy their products, the advertising and marketing industries flourished. *Modern consumption* describes the gratification of individual material acquisitiveness. Products and services have little value as ends in themselves. Rather, they are social signals that allow people to identify with like-minded peers through the consumption and display of similar products or through the use of similar services.

In the 1960s, Modernism was determined to have lost its vitality because the avant-garde, the innovators, were engaged in activities that supported the emerging culture of consumerism. They became traditional. Some say this transition marked the beginning of the postmodern age.

It now appears that Modernism has gone wrong. The fundamental, original concept of rationality withered away when logic and reason were replaced with today's consumer-based rationality. The resultant consumer society is a vast floating complex of advertising images that produce an endless sign-play, destabilizing society's long-held symbolic meanings and sense of order in exact opposition to early Modernists goals. The long-term growth of the consumer culture has led people to believe that it is right to pursue new experiences and values via consumption rather than rely on familiar and traditional, albeit imposed, values and dogma. The global market is now characterized by the proliferation of identical goods and a growing consumer monoculture that makes it easier to sell things. As a result, consumerism has become the means by which

capitalism maintains control over the buying public.

Fallout from Modernism Leads to Postmodern Angst

As noted, modernism represented a new social order that believed in social progress and in the potential to advance human reason, scientific rationality, and technology in an economy driven by capitalism and consumption. Unfortunately, things did not go as planned. Progress manifested itself in material terms and celebrated the production of things, the exploitation of workers, and the destruction of the natural environment. Progress was also made manifest in the development of a massive amount of objective but value-free scientific knowledge, all while the masses remained ignorant and spiritually impoverished.

Community resilience declined, family strength and connectedness suffered, and individuals lost direction and began to define themselves by what they owned rather than by their own intrinsic value as global citizens (Baldwin, 2002). Anxiety, emotional disorders, and the breakdown of families and marriages were common results of this age. A new social formation emerged, generated by the random activities of lost individuals trying to make sense of the world and their place in it. For these individuals, "the social" was dissolving, and the bonds that once held them together could no longer be accepted without question. They tried to search out the ideal life but without success. This failure created fear, anger, frustration, greed, hatred, and the desire for revenge. Governmental attempts to erase the differences between people and impose national identities backfired, leaving a fragmented populous seeking leadership and

Transformative Practice: New Pathways to Leadership

focus. Political mentality was inspired by consumer choice, diverse life styles, and raw spectator curiosity in front of the television (Best, n.d.).

In the Modern Age, we became dependent upon technology and industry as we became addicted to consumerism. We regarded free market competition as a wholly good thing, and we highly valued our individualistic society (Notess, 2001). Not all technological developments led to human and social progress, however. Technological advancement, although always celebrated as a force for the good, occurs in the military as well as in medicine and agriculture. As a result, new weapons and new types of warfare, particularly chemical, germ, and biological warfare, are now available, as are space-based weapons. Developments in biotechnology and genetic engineering have created unknown risks for generations to come. Rational thinking, a cornerstone of Modernism, was used to justify actions of genocide and the extermination or exclusion of nonstandard human beings from concentration camps to insane asylums, and from penitentiaries to re-programming facilities for young homosexuals. This was not the progress Modernists intended. In fact, our enlightened society allowed capitalism to politically and militarily oppress others for the sole purpose of providing us with more products to buy and sell (Cronk, 1996) and more natural resources to consume.

The Postmodernism Era (1960-ongoing)

These unintended side-effects of modernization's partnership with growing consumerism have led to the emergence of post-modernistic thinking (Featherstone, 1995; Wikipedia, 2003a,b). To

Transformative Practice: New Pathways to Leadership

recap the historic flow and put the present into context, the premodern Dark and Medieval ages were eras of faith and superstition, followed by the modern age, which embraced reason, empiricism, and science. We currently live in the postmodern age of globalization and, more recently, the age of holism and interdependence. This is the newest form of postmodernism, which became an area of academic study in the mid eighties (Klages, 2003). It was named "postmodern" because those who first labeled it assumed that the modern age was over, although not everyone agrees that this is the case.

Kellner (2003) suggested that we are in an interregnum period, a time between eras when dominant or powerful trends are falling away but no new model has risen to replace them. Further, Kellner maintained that we are in a period of transition between an aging modern and an emerging postmodern era. This uncomfortable interlude occupies the borderland between two influential epochs, with each time period characterized by similar conditions. Others offered different explanations to describe the times we live in. Some asserted that what many referred to as postmodernism was actually the late stage of modernity (Eckersley, 1999; Griffin, 1993), while others claimed that postmodernism had already occurred. The latter group equated postmodernity with an earthquake, and suggested that we are now living through the aftershocks in a world that is forever changed (Trotter & Burke as cited in Wallace, 2003). Still others claimed that there is no such thing as postmodernism: that postmodernism is a set of ideas that has run its course and is morphing into the emerging project of globalization. Although

Transformative Practice: New Pathways to Leadership

postmodernism began as an economic construct, an examination of these disparate hypotheses makes it plain that the concept has grown to encompass an entirely new category of thinking (Richter, 2002). It also demonstrates that, regardless of what individual theorists believe regarding the nature of postmodernism itself, those investigating the issue are ultimately attempting to answer the same core questions: "If science and reason are not the answer, then what is? How do we get out of the box that modernism has put us in?" (Morley, 2002, p. 3).

Clarifying Some Terms - Ism, Ity, and Ern

> *Postmodernity* is the era in which postmodern ideas, attitudes, and values reign—when the mood of *postmodernism* is molding culture. This is the era of the *postmodern* society (emphasis added). (Grenz, 1996, pp. 12-13)

Before proceeding, it is important that we clarify the meanings of the various derivations of the word "postmodern:"

- ***Postmodernism*** refers to the intellectual mood and cultural expressions that are becoming dominant in contemporary society. These expressions call into question the ideals, principles, and values that lay at the heart of the modern mind-set.
- ***Postmodernity*** refers to the era in which we are living, the time when the postmodern outlook increasingly shapes our society.
- The adjective ***postmodern***, then, refers to the overall mind-set and its products.

In addition to the debate over whether or not we are actually living in a postmodern age, there is also wide disagreement over the working definition of "postmodern." Even those scholars who believe that we are, indeed, living in a postmodern age differ as

to what postmodernism is. Some say it is a historical and cultural condition (Lyotard, 1984). Others describe it is an artistic movement that corresponds culturally to a new configuration of politics and economics within the framework of late capitalism and globalization (Jameson, 1985). The latter group uses such terms as post-industrial, consumerism, and multi- or trans-national capitalism. They also explore the global village phenomena through the globalization of cultures, races, ideas, images, capital, and products in an information age. As you might expect, these proponents of the postmodernism-as-artistic-movement also explore the new models of artistic and stylistic eclecticism, including a mixing of different styles, cultures, and time periods to create a new form of art, fashion, architecture, and literature (Irvine, 1998).

Five different Strands of Postmodern Thinking

Individuals often speak of *the* postmodern way of looking at issues when, in fact, an assortment of postmodern agendas exists. Oord (2001) shared a very useful overview of the five prevailing approaches to understanding postmodernism, prefacing his discussion with the following:

> ". . . some notions flying under the postmodernism flag oppose or contradict other notions under the same banner . . . how does one decide which is authentic?. . . [This] proves to be difficult" (pp. 1-2).

Most authors gloss over these differences, and derive conclusions from the one-dimensional position that the postmodern movement simply represents a fundamental paradigmatic shift in our abiding worldview (e.g., Elkind, 1995). However, it is vitally important that we take time to identify

and analyze these diverse approaches, because each provides a different interpretation of the challenges we face in shaping professional practice for the future. The dominant features of Oord's (2001) five strands of postmodernism are summarized in Table 2 on the following page.

Popular Culture Postmodernism

Although there are many competing theories and approaches to the new study of popular culture (Storey, 2000), we will simplify the discussion by defining popular culture postmodernism as preoccupied with the idea of novelty. It is fascinated with the current, the latest, the most recent, and with contemporary innovations and with whatever happens to be in vogue (Oord, 2001). Ironically, the very concept of newness (novelty) has been commoditized by the postmodern consumer culture to such an extent that genuine innovation is increasingly difficult to imagine. In the face of a steady supply of new and improved cars, dish detergents, and widgets of every sort, newness itself has become a ruined nonsense word. It has been repeated so often that it has become little more than a self-parody, a repetition of the idea of newness in which nothing actually is novel (Berry & Siegel, 2001).

Popular culture is obsessed with technology, mass communication, mass marketing, the therapeutic orientation, and conspicuous consumption – all tools for the prolongation of newness, novelty, and consumerism (Horton, 2003). Since nothing save the relentless pace of change is constant, the result can best be summarized as a growing distrust of and disrespect for authority. This strand of postmodernism also leads to a disdain for rationality and a wide-

Table 2 - Five Different Strands of Post Modernism (Adapted from Oord, 2001)

Popular Culture	Deconstructive	Liberationist	Narrative	Constructive
Society is comprised of "early adopters"– preoccupation with the latest novelties, gadgets, innovations, and product improvements. *Everything is for sale*– consumerism gives life meaning and purpose through the acquisition of goods and services. *Commoditization abounds*– obsession with technology, mass communication, and marketing as methods for creating new commodities for sale. *Consumer entitlement is pervasive*– expectation of reward is widespread. Belief exists that rewards will be granted for behaving in a certain way.	*Everything is relative*–truth changes with circumstance and is different for everyone. There is no real knowledge, merely expressions of opinion. Nothing can be known with certainty. *Morality is not well defined*– right and wrong are a matter of personal taste or emotional preference. *There is no predictable order to things*–the focus is on differences, diversity, and free will. *Individuals lack a sense of commonality*–no over-arching narrative describes the world, so no common denominators bind diverse citizens together. *Economies are organized around consumption*– corporations gain power, States lose power, and citizens are reduced to consumers. *Nihilism and "whateverism" are pervasive*— youth are disillusioned. Life seems devoid of purpose. Individuals hold no loyalties and lack respect for social rules.	Liberationists can be divided into three distinct sub-groups: *Postmodern feminists*– desire liberation from the customs and terminology that perpetuate a position of female inferiority. *Ethnic postmodernists* –seek to overturn modern assumptions that confer equality based upon biological similarities. Focus on race and culture to promote the notion that the voices modern society has marginalized are legitimate and must be heard. *Ecological postmodernists* –seek freedom from modern assumption that the earth is subject to total human domination. Ecological postmodernists call for a responsible relationship between humanity and the environment.	*Intangibles are emphasized*– language and stories are valued over strictly empirical science. *There is strong interest in the illogical*– emotions, intuition, reflection, speculation, personal experience, customs, magic, myth, and the mystical are a legitimate focus of study. *Citizens rely on a community-based definition of truth*– knowledge, meaning, and truth are all constructed in individual communities, where the localized reality is then reflected in people's life-stories. Because these stories are created within a community and are experienced on a daily basis, they do not require scientific proof to confer legitimacy. *Culture-specific myths define reality*–what is right and true and full of meaning is determined by the local populace. There is no need for a grand narrative to describe the entire world.	*Judgment is reserved*–there is a possibility that humankind is standing on the threshold of *a new age*. A *holistic, interdisciplinary perspective is embraced*–new unity is encouraged between scientific, ethical, aesthetic, and religious institutions. *All relationships are seen as interwoven*– all organisms on earth are interrelated. Fundamental openness to other beings because all are linked in webs of interdependency. *Truth is a living, growing thing*– truth is neither singular nor static. *Internal states are recognized as co-equal*–Non-sensory experiences (dreams, memories, visions) are as valid as truths we gain from our five senses using the scientific method. *Goal-oriented philosophies are outmoded*–we must be more concerned with process and with growing beyond current limitations, or *becoming*.

Transformative Practice: New Pathways to Leadership

spread sense of consumer entitlement (Sacks, 1996). Indeed, popular culture postmodernism embraces consumerism so fully that it claims anyone who resists it is unable to come to grips with the paradigm shift we are experiencing (Burman, 1998).

Deconstructive Postmodernism

Deconstructive postmodernism, the most widely known form, does not promote replacing the old modern system with a better one as constructive postmodernism does. Instead, its proponents work to undermine or de-construct the modern era's knowledge, language centers, and worldview by overturning them. Proponents' primary goal is to bring about the downfall of modernism because they reject the era's main tenets. The doctrine of the supremacy of reason, the notion of one truth, and the belief that man and society can be perfected through continual progress are all utterly rejected by deconstructive postmodernists. Whereas modernism held that knowledge gained through logic, reason, and the scientific method was the only way of knowing that mattered, postmodernists posit that knowledge is open to interpretation, and that there is no one truth because a multiplicity of voices exist. Instead of knowing truth, we express opinions, indicate preferences, or simply go with our instincts (Berry & Siegel, 2001; Shepherd, 2000). Also, because postmodernists reject the grand narrative, they cannot acknowledge anything common to us all. This leads to a sense of separation and fragmentation.

Modernism was obsessed with classifications, groupings, and order. Deconstructive postmodernists believe that one thing leads to another, but insist that there is no neat

blueprint. They use the term rhizome, a mass of roots, to refer to this lack of pattern because a rhizome has no beginning or end. It is always in the middle, between things, with one point connecting to another via myriad lines with no predictable order (Berry & Siegel, 2001; Shepherd, 2000).

Throughout modernist culture, the State mandated and controlled the market on behalf of all citizens. The economy was organized around production, not consumption. Profit and competition were not suspect because the State provided counterbalance. In postmodern times, however, we have witnessed the advent of global telecommunications, mass media, information technology, and transportation. Corporations have gained power, States have lost power, citizens have become mere consumers, and economies have reorganized themselves around consumption (Kellner, 2003; Richter, 1996). These factors have led many to feel a sense of disillusionment, which in turn has led to a widespread undercurrent of nihilism and relativism within deconstructive postmodernism.

Nihilism is the belief that all values are baseless and that nothing can be known or communicated with certainty. Everything is illusion because there is no reality, so a true nihilist believes in nothing, has no loyalties, and has no purpose. Life itself is seen as meaningless. Relativism is closely linked to nihilism. It assumes that everything is relative to the particular vantage point it is viewed from, and it holds that no standpoint is uniquely privileged above the others. Relativist thought holds that all points of views are equally valid, all belief systems are equally true, and all moralities are equally good. Said another way, "The way I see things

Transformative Practice: New Pathways to Leadership

from my point of view is actually true – for me. If you see things differently, then that is true – for you." There is no separate or objective truth that does not rely upon each individual's perception. Everything is relative! Thus, we have nothing in common to ground us, and no basis for explaining the collective reality.

Liberationist Postmodernism

Liberationists seek emancipation from societal ills associated with modernism. Specifically, postmodern feminists focus on gender, because they wish to escape modern-era language that perpetuates ways of thinking that imply women are inferior. They encourage people to speak in ways that empower rather than oppress women. Ethnic postmodernists focus on racial and cultural liberation. They work to be free from the modernist assumption that equality is derived from biological similarities. They suggest instead that cultural uniqueness establishes one's value, and that this uniqueness is the basis for judging the legitimacy and validity of one's voice. Finally, ecological postmodernists focus on the environment and pursue freedom from the modernist assumption that the earth is in need of human domination. They call for humanity to responsibly nurture the earth and its resources.

Many liberationist postmodernists, regardless of their subgroup, reject deconstructive postmodernism because they feel nihilism and relativism are traits that subvert attempts to instigate deliverance from oppression (Oord, 2001). They particularly reject the deconstructive perspective that it is impossible to value liberation from oppression, along with deconstructionist notions that the voices of those struggling for liberation at the

45

margins of society do not have any legitimacy.

Narrative Postmodernism

Because the community one lives in profoundly shapes a person's point of view, life stories gleaned from individuals are actually variations of the community's overarching narrative. This basic tenet of narrative postmodernism attempts to overcome two traditions of modernism, specifically relativism (or individualism), and positivism. Narrative postmodernists do not accept the modern relativist assumption that meaning and truth are decided solely by the individual, nor do they believe in the positivist doctrine that denies the validity of knowledge gained through means other than the scientific method. Narrative postmodernists reject the modern assumption that there is one grand narrative that structures and informs all of our stories. They replace the concept of an overarching storyline with the notion that our culture-specific myths define what is right and true and full of meaning. From this standpoint, authority shifts from the individual to the community. Narrative postmodernists believe that knowledge, meaning, and truth are sociologically constructed within communities and are reflected in the stories of individual people. Empirical verification is not required nor desired, because the meaning of individual stories is independent of scientific inquiry when applied in the original context. This limitation is acceptable because the narrative arises from the community in which people live their daily lives.

Many are critical of narrative postmodernism because they feel that stifling communitarianism is even more devastating than the modernist era's uninhibited individualism.

Transformative Practice: New Pathways to Leadership

Critics also question whether this philosophy allows room for interfaith dialogue, since religious communities rely upon their own unique stories and find meaning exclusively in their own traditions. Finally, this viewpoint leaves many wondering if there is an overarching narrative large enough to encompass all of us when so many micro-narratives abound (Oord, 2001).

Constructive (Revisionary) Postmodernism

Constructive postmodernism, the most recent strand, attempts to overcome five undesirable features of modernity. First, it rejects the unnatural fragmentation of knowledge found in many school subject matters and in separate university disciplines. In its place, constructive postmodernists propose a holistic, interdisciplinary perspective that offers a new unity between scientific, ethical, aesthetic, and religious institutions. Second, constructive postmodernism conceives of societal structures as organic bodies that have a purpose. This is in stark contrast to the modern view, which holds that all living things are mechanized by nature. Modernists believed all creatures were mindless machines without purpose, and that humanity was simply the most advanced purposeless mechanism. Third, constructivists offer a worldview that is viable for our time specifically, instead of proposing a single interpretation to describe how things work within a grand narrative or theory. Fourth, constructive postmodernism recognizes non-sensory insights (memories, dreams, and visions) as valid forms of knowledge, instead of limiting knowledge to facts gained through the five senses. Finally, constructive postmodernism rejects the notion that individuals are isolated, along with modernity's pervasive dualisms. Instead, it follows systems and ecosystems theory and assumes that everything is interrelated, existing in relationship with all living organisms. The purpose of constructive postmodernism is to imagine a better, less destructive, more organic order beyond the modern world (Oord, 2001). It calls for a fundamental openness to other beings and holds that all entities are interwoven in webs of interdependency. In contrast, modernism enforced an otherness based on differences that led to alienation, apathy, hostility, arrogance, and dominance (Phipps, 2002).

Discussion

A profession that embraces deconstructivist postmodernism is setting itself up for despair, hopelessness, and cynicism. This strand of post-modernism is only useful in that it helps us to understand why people are doing what they are doing in terms of excessive consumerism, defeatism, violence, less than moral stances in society, and holding everything as value neutral and relative. However, by deconstructing existing society without applying the constructive insights, we do not serve professionals, individuals, families, or communities. To accept this interpretation of life after modernism would be to accept individualism, condone a lack of moral stance in society, and assume that we are all so different that we have nothing in common. It would also lead to the assumption that there are no patterns, nor is there any predictable order in life. This stance presents a very confining approach to practice. It restricts our efforts to simply helping people to get by, to cope with life as it is, rather than questioning our assumptions in order to address what life could and should be.

Transformative Practice: New Pathways to Leadership

Professionals who embrace the popular culture strand of postmodernism perpetuate a consumer-oriented society, along with all of the accompanying ills. Popular culture is obsessed with technology, mass communication, mass marketing, therapeutic orientation, and conspicuous consumption. These phenomena do nothing but prolong consumerist cravings for novelty. Accepting that consumerism is inevitable, that there is no alternative to the current global situation, that technology is only bad if you put it to harmful use, and that people are entitled to own unlimited amounts of everything paves the way for even more unsustainable consumption and production. It is not our place to be complicit in the destruction of our home, the earth, and its citizens.

If professionals embrace the other three strands of postmodernism, they will

- be open to a liberatory practice that has the potential to free people, other species, and the entire ecosystem from both self-imposed and systemic oppression (liberationist);
- respect the power of language and stories to balance the current focus on the scientific approach, and create an intellectual space for the unknown and unknowable (narrative); and
- value an ecosystem, holistic, global approach to practice (constructive).

This is the preferred approach for professionals in the new millennium. These three models enable us to understand the angst that people are feeling as we transition from the modern to the postmodern era. They also provide an ethical and moral stance from which to critique the world and make sustainable social change. Adherence to these philosophies makes room for peace and justice, human rights, human security, human responsibilities,

Transformative Practice: New Pathways to Leadership

and non-violence: concepts that are not found within the current mainstream of study.

Popular culture and deconstructive postmodern thinkers provide us with a framework for describing the state of the human condition in this era. They show us why our present state exists and shine light on the forces that perpetuate it. Conversely, liberationist, narrative, and constructive forms of postmodernism give us hope by pointing to solutions for professional practice that could truly better the human condition. They collectively call upon us to

- respect that we are on the threshold of a holistic, interconnected new age;
- facilitate unity between scientific, political, economic, ethical, aesthetic, and religious institutions;
- model and promote a responsible relationship with the earth that embraces stewardship instead of mastery;
- give voice to those marginalized by race, ethnicity, religion, and gender by creating a globalization from the bottom-up movement;
- use language that respects women and promotes gender-balanced power and influence;
- Factor language and stories into our analyses instead of relying solely upon scientific proof;
- achieve a balance between rational scientific knowledge and elements not governed by reason and logic, particularly "irrational" constructs like emotions, intuition, personal experience, dreams, and customs;
- appreciate that knowledge, meaning, and truth are constructed in local communities, not handed down within a grand narrative that preaches success, competition, profit, and individuality;
- open our minds to the idea that everything is

Transformative Practice: New Pathways to Leadership

connected within a complex web of relationships;
- respect the process of *becoming* instead of focusing on the end result;
- encourage fair trade and localization in mindful markets;
- pursue humane working conditions and an end to sweatshops and child labor; and,
- work toward indigenous respect and continuity.

Conclusion

In this postmodern era, we must be tolerant of uncertainty, comfortable with patterns and processes, attentive to empowerment and liberation, respectful of others and their diversity, and open to new perspectives and paradigms. Professionals will approach practice differently depending upon which view(s) of postmodernism they embrace, but it is imperative that we individually and collectively undertake a dialogue regarding the profession's understanding of the times we live in at the beginning of this new century. This understanding will help us to appreciate where others are coming from and where we want to go as a profession. Personal and professional practice cannot be transformed unless this understanding is examined, critiqued, and confirmed. We must be able to stand in certainty of our purpose and power if we want to evolve as a profession and assume transformative leadership roles.

References

Aglesworth, G. (2005). *Postmodernism.* Retrieved January 25, 2006 from http://plato.stanford.edu/entries/postmodernism/#2

Baldwin, E. E. (2002). Modernity, postmodernity, and family and consumer sciences. *Kappa Omicron Nu FORUM, 13*(2) at http://www.kon.org/archives/forum/Baldwin.html

Barker, C. (2000). *Cultural studies: Theory and practice.* London: Sage.

Berry, E., & Seigel, C. (2001). *Rhizomes, newness, and the condition of our postmodernity.* Accessed September 22,

51

Transformative Practice: New Pathways to Leadership

2003 at http://www.rhizomes.net/Issue1/rhizopods/newness1.html
Best, S. (n.d.). *The post-modern experience.* Accessed January 18, 2006 at http://www.sociology.org.uk/atssspl2.htm
Brainy Encyclopedia. (2004). *Cultural movement.* Retrieved January 25, 2006 from http://www.brainyencyclopedia.com/encyclopedia/c/cu/cultural_movement.html
Brians, P. (2000). *The enlightenment.* Retrieved November 12, 2004 from http://www.wsu.edu:8080/~brians/hum_303/enlightenment.html
Burman, R. (1998). *Popular culture and the logic of consumerism.* Accessed September 23, 2003 at http://www2.unl.ac.uk/~rpb001/global2.htm
Cronk, R. (1996). *Consumerism and the new capitalism.* Retrieved November 12, 2004 from http://www.westland.net/venice/art/cronk/consumer.htm
Davidson, A. (2002). *What is it to be modern.* Retrieved January 25, 2006 from http://www.freemasonry101.org/to_be_modern.htm
de Quincy, C. (2002). *Summary of paradigms.* Retrieved January 25, 2006 from http://www.deepspirit.com/sys-tmpl/contd5

Dunnigan, J., & Nofi, A. (1997). *Medieval life and the hundred years war.* Retrieved November 12, 2004 from http://www.hyw.com/books/history/1_Help_C.htm
Eckersley, R. (1999, January). Running on empty. *Australian Financial Review, 29,* 1-2,11.
Elkind, D. (1995). School and family in the postmodern world. *Phi Delta Kappan, 77*(1), 8-14.
Featherstone, M. (1995). *Undoing culture.* Thousand Oaks, CA: Sage.
Gay, P. (1996). *The enlightenment: An interpretation.* NY: N.W. Morton & Company.
Grenz, S. (1996). *A primer on postmodernism.* Grand Rapids, MI: Eerdmans.
Griffin, D., et al. (1993). *Founders of constructive postmodernism philosophy.* Albany, NY: SUNY.
Horton, M. (2003). Pop goes postmodernism. *Modern Reformation, 12* (4).
Irvine, M. (1998). *Approaches to po-mo.* Accessed July 31, 2003 at http://www.georgetown.edu/irvinemj/technoculture/pomo.html
Jameson, F. (1985). *Postmodern culture.* London: Pluto Press.
Jessup, M. (2001). Truth: The first causality of postmodernism consumerism [Electronic version]. *Christian Scholar's Review, 30*(3), 289-304.

Transformative Practice: New Pathways to Leadership

Kellner, D. (2003). *Globalization and the postmodern turn*. Accessed September 23, 2003 at http://www.gseis.ucla.edu/courses/ed253a/dk/GLOBPM.htm

Kemerling, G. (2001). *Renaissance thought*. Retrieved January 25, 2006 from http://www.philosophypages.com/hy/3t.htm

Klages, (2003). *Postmodernism* Accessed July 31, 2003 at http://www.colorado.edu/English/ENGL2012Klages/pomo.html.

Kjos, A. (2002). *Modern versus postmodern culture*. Retrieved January 25, 2006 from http://www.crossroad.to./charts/postmodernity-2.htm

Kleingeld, P., & Brown, E. (2002). *Cosmopolitanism*. Retrieved from http://plato.stanford.edu/entries/cosmopolitanism

Kupinse, B. (1998). *Modernism*. Retrieved January 25, 2006 from http://www.vanderbilt.edu/AnS/english/kupinse/modernism.html

Leffel, J., & McCallum, D. (2004, May 12). The postmodern challenge: Facing the spiritual age. *Christian Research Institute, (Statement DP-321)*. Retrieved January 25, 2006 from http://www.equip.org/free/DP321.htm

Livesey, C. (n.d.). *From here to post-modernity*. Retrieved January 25, 2006 from http://www.sociology.org.uk/p1line.htm

Lyotard, J. F. (1984). *The postmodern condition*. Minneapolis: University of Minnesota Press.

Mautz, N. B. (2003). *The development of Western Civilization: World history: Medieval world*. Retrieved September 9, 2003 from http://history.evansville.net/medieval.html

Morley, P. M. (2002). *Understanding the postmodern era*. Retrieved November 12, 2004 from http://www.maninthemirror.org/alm/alm39.htm

Notess, C. (2001). *Postmodernism, social change and polarization*. Accessed September 23, 2003 at http://www.greeleynet.com/~cnotess/forum/forum.htm

Oord, T. J. (2001). Postmodernism - What is it? *Diadache, 1*(2) Accessed September 23, 2003 at http://www.nazarene.org/iboe/riie/Didache/Didache_vol1_2/postmodernism.pdf

Phipps, R. (2002). *Beijing Whitehead conference report*. Accessed September 23, 2003 at http://www.alfred.north.whitehead.com/IPN/ipn_china.htm

Richter, R. (1996). *Corporate enterprise as postmodern practice*. Accessed September 22, 2003 at http://webpages.ursinus.edu/rrichter/essayfour.html

Richter, R. (2002). *Why study globalization?* Accessed September 17, 2003 at http://webpages.ursinus.edu/rrichter/friedman.htm#intro

Sacks, P. (1996). *Generation X goes to college.* Chicago: Open Court.

Scheurich, J. (2001). *Postmodernism.* Accessed July 31, 2003 at http://www.edb.utexas.edu/faculty/scheurich/proj6/pags/pm101_1.htm

Shepherd, V. (1999, June). *Postmodernism and the church.* Retrieved January 25, 2006 from http://www.victorshepherd.on.ca/Other%20Writings/postmode.htm

Shepherd, V. (2000, November). *Postmodernism.* Accessed September 23, 2003 at http://www.victorshepherd.on.ca/sermons/post-mod.htm

Smethurst, P. (1996). *Overview: Postmodernism and fiction (Liverpool John Moores University course).* Retrieved January 25, 2006 from http://www.hku.hk/english/courses2000/7006/overview.htm

Smith, W. D. (2002). *Consumption and the making of respectability.* New York: Routledge.

Stevens, C. (2002). *Postmodernism.* Retrieved January 25, 2006 from http://mingo.info-science.uiowa.edu/~stevens/critped/post.htm

Storey, J. (2000). *Cultural theory and popular culture.* Toronto: Pearson Education.

Sturken, M, & Cartwright, L. (2001). *Practices of looking: An introduction to visual culture.* New York: Oxford University Press.

Wallace, S. (2003). *About postmodernism.* Accessed September 23, 2003 at http://www.freewaybr.com/usfs.htm

Wikipedia. (2003a). *Modernism.* Accessed July 31, 2003 at http://www.wikipedia.org/wiki/modernism

Wikipedia. (2003b). *Postmodernism.* Accessed July 31, 2003 at http://www.wikipedia.org/wiki/Postmodernism

Wikipedia. (2006a, January 16). *Peasant.* Retrieved January 25, 2006 from http://en.wikipedia.org/wiki/peasant

Wikipedia. (2006b). *Secularism.* Retrieved January 25, 2006 from http://en.wikipedia.org/wiki/Secularism

Wikipedia. (2006c, January 24). *Serfdom.* Retrieved January 25, 2006 from http://en.wikipedia.org/wiki/Serf

Witecombe, C. L. (2000). *Modernism and postmodernism (part 4).* Retrieved January 25, 2006 from http://witcombe.sbc.edu/modernism/modpostmod.html

Wood, A. (2003). *Postmodernism and popular culture (chap. 7).* Retrieved January 25, 2006 from http://www2.sjsu.edu/faculty/wooda/171/171syllabus13chapter7.html

Transformative Practice: New Pathways to Leadership

Chapter 3: Transdisciplinary Inquiry*

Professionals across contemporary society are powering a growing trend as they forge bridges between disciplines in an attempt to resolve complex problems and situations. Although some fields are ahead of their time, having long advocated multidisciplinary (and rhetorically interdisciplinary) approaches to solving generational problems, there is a new approach emerging that merits our consideration as well. At the crux of this new trend toward transdisciplinary research and practice is the growing need for new kinds of knowledge: knowledge that is not generated within a single discipline but is instead gained through a temporary alliance between disciplines. It really is time to move beyond our penchant for forming specializations, because society's problems are far too complex to be explained from one point of view.

Mono, multi, and interdisciplinary approaches each generate new knowledge, and according to Nicolescu (1997), a Romanian quantum physicist, the latter two overflow the boundaries between distinct disciplines. The transdisciplinary approach, however, takes us *beyond* disciplines by weaving a new kind of

---

*Earlier version published in *Human Sciences Working Papers Archives*, http://www.kon.org/hswp/index.html.

As a quick side note, I attended a public symposium held by the Canadian Commission for UNESCO (May, 2004). The entire focus was on the transdisciplinary approach. Until attending this symposium, I was happy touting the merits of the interdisciplinary approach. The insights I took away from this day prompted me to write this chapter for other professionals.

55

knowledge. Because there is a need for all four types of disciplinary approaches, each will be discussed below but the primary focus will be on the transdisciplinary. For many readers, this chapter will represent a "close encounter of the third kind" with such new concepts at Copyleft, intellectual outer space, crossing through veils to different realities, isomorphies and patterns, metaphors, transversing disciplines, multiple realities, quantum complexities, honoring imaginations, zones of resistance, virtual creative commons, nuances of chaos theory, and living adaptive systems. Newcomers to these ideas are in for an exciting intellectual roller coaster ride.

Monodisciplinary

Because *Mono* means one, this approach to practice and research implies that only one discipline is brought to bear to solve a societal problem. Worse yet, a solution is sometimes drawn from a single branch of a given discipline if a field has become deeply fragmented into narrow specializations. This approach can foster a one-dimensional viewpoint among professionals within a given discipline, whether it is law, economics, sociology, or any other field of study. Colleagues naturally study the same research objects, share the same paradigm (worldview and set of assumptions about what is real), use common methodologies, and communicate using the same language and jargon (Regeer, 2002). Although single disciplinary work has valid applications, it is of limited use in solving intricate societal problems. A solitary lens is simply not adequate when the task requires a study of multi-faceted, dynamic issues.

Transformative Practice: New Pathways to Leadership

Multidisciplinary

Multidisciplinary research and practice take us beyond the involvement of just *one* discipline and into the realm of several disciplines working in tandem to solve a societal problem of common concern. A multidisciplinary approach would involve professionals within a root discipline, such as economics, turning to several other disciplines for help in solving a problem. Although many perspectives are shared in this model, the guiding intent is to serve the root discipline that initiated the collaboration. Once the work is done, all go back to their respective places (Nicolescu, 1997). In other words, a multidisciplinary event occurs when disciplines are simply mingled for the purpose of solving a problem while each discipline maintains its distinctiveness (Colins, 2002). Although the boundaries become porous to enable the flow of information between disciplines, the walls are restored when the group arrives at an answer that serves the needs of the root discipline.

Interdisciplinary

Whereas the multidisciplinary approach juxtaposes specialists by sitting them down beside each other at the table, the interdisciplinary approach coordinates their expertise (Lattanzi, 1998). *Inter* means between, so interdisciplinary work involves an interaction between two or more disciplines. Nicolescu (1997) clarified by stating that multidisciplinary work remains grounded in the framework of one discipline, but an interdisciplinary model involves the transfer of methods from one discipline to another to address (a) new applications, (b) new

57

analyses, or (c) the generation of an entirely new discipline. Within home economics/family and consumer sciences, Ellen Swallow Richards advocated an interdisciplinary approach to facilitate the new discipline's development over time. This model involved integrating several disciplines to generate a unified outcome or perspective that was sustained and substantial enough to create a completely new discipline (Colins, 2002). Although this effort was nominally successful in producing a single new field, McGregor et al. (2004) demonstrated that the profession has leaned more toward multidisciplinary, expert specializations than toward interdisciplinary problem solving over the past 100 years. Perhaps today's professionals can mend the breach by embracing a transdisciplinary approach.

When solving problems from the interdisciplinary approach, researchers analyze individual parts of the problem along parallel tracks. A new synergy emerges from the transfer of knowledge between disciplines. The intent is not to understand the world, but simply to solve a complex problem within it.

Conversely, transdisciplinary methods involve a dialogue in which approaches and assumptions are shared in order to weave together a new approach to complex social issues (Lattanzi, 1998). Transdisciplinary efforts move beyond sharing different analyses or creating new applications as they create a space for shared dialogue. That dialogue then leads to a joint analysis using new approaches that could not have existed without the crisscrossing of ideas to weave together a new web of knowledge.

Transformative Practice: New Pathways to Leadership

Society loses when we limit ourselves to the interdisciplinary approach, because it is not comprehensive enough to fully address the profound complexity of today's problems. The societal factors that give rise to poverty, unsustainability, exploitation, oppression, corporate-led globalization, capitalism, and free market ideology are simply too complex. We need a new approach that challenges us to push beyond the boundaries of contemporary thinking.

Transdisciplinary

Trans has several meanings. It refers to that which spans across the disciplines, runs between the disciplines, and exists *beyond* and outside all disciplines. It transverses all possible disciplines, crisscrossing and zigzagging laterally among them (Nègre, 1999; Nicolescu, 1997). The objective of the transdisciplinary approach is to understand the present world in all of its complexities, instead of focusing on one part of it (Nicolescu, 1997). Indeed, transdisciplinary research is conceptualized as both (a) a specific kind of interdisciplinary research involving scientific and non-scientific sources or practice and more excitingly (b) a new form of learning and problem solving involving cooperation among different parts of society, including academia, in order to meet the complex challenges of society. The knowledge of all participants is enhanced through a new mutual learning that collectively devises solutions to intricate, interwoven societal problems (Regeer, 2002). Out of the dialogue between academia and other parts of society, new results and new interactions are produced that offer a new vision of nature and reality (Nègre, 1999).

Transformative Practice: New Pathways to Leadership

Creating a Transdisciplinary Knowledge Base

This new way of thinking and learning results in a new kind of knowledge—transdisciplinary knowledge—that complements traditional, mono-disciplinary knowledge. A new intellectual space is formed and within that space lies a gradual cross-fertilization based upon the convergence of different paths in the spirit of conviviality and celebration (Lattanzi, 1998). This type of knowledge is globally open, and it entails both a new vision and lived experiences. It also offers a path to self-transformation that is oriented toward the knowledge of the self, the unity of all knowledge, and the creation of a new art of living (Nicolescu, 1997).

Four very compelling pillars underpin this new knowledge: learning to know, to do, to be with, and to be (Nicolescu, 1997). Although this may sound very familiar, those advocating for the transdisciplinary approach define these four pillars differently than we conventionally understand them. Very briefly, *learning to know* implies that we should train students to always question underlying assumptions and to build bridges that continually connect beings. *Learning to do* certainly refers to acquiring a vocation, but it specifically demands that we do so within the context of a profession that authentically weaves together several competencies while creating a flexible, inner core. The latter encourages students to be an apprentice to creativity or, more specifically, to create one's own potential. *Learning to be with others* means not only that we learn to respect others but also that we foster a new attitude that permits us to defend our own convictions. This new attitude makes a space for

Transformative Practice: New Pathways to Leadership

both open unity and complex plurality, instead of placing these two values in opposition to each other. Finally, *learning to be* does not mean simply existing. To learn to be, one must discover how we have been conditioned, note whether there is any tension between the inner self and the social life, test the foundations of our convictions, and question, always question. We have to ask ourselves "Where am I?" because things change and so do we. To state the obvious, this new knowledge is profoundly different from other types of knowledge that are generated through traditional approaches to research and practice.

Lattanzi (1998), writing for UNESCO, suggested that the latter type of knowledge should be referred to in terms that include departments of knowledge, distinct bodies, or autonomous branches in order to distinguish the more traditional knowledge forms from the holistic awareness that is the foundation of transdisciplinarity. From this stance, Lattanzi argued that knowledge from distinct disciplines is valuable first-step knowledge that helps us to understand problems from one perspective. The transdisciplinary knowledge base, on the other hand, is the better resource for addressing problems that should not be treated in "disciplinary isolation." Such problems include human aggression, harmonious distribution of resources, development of anthropocentric or human centered worldviews, and the realization of human empowerment and potential through education.

This methodology explains why transdisciplinarity is described as a process that is characterized by the integration of efforts among multiple disciplines to address issues or problems with global implications. In this context, integration implies a removal of the boundaries and obstacles that exist between disciplines. This open atmosphere among all disciplines can then foster the creation of something new and permanent through a synthesis and harmonization of ideas and perspectives. Indeed, many questions of fundamental importance to our society could not even be posed within the domain of one discipline. Issues of freedom and self-determinism span many, many disciplines. It is also of significance that Lattanzi (1998) believed an inquiry into a simple issue should not stop just because a satisfactory explanation had been found. Transdisciplinary inquiry demands that we dig deeper, that we seek to understand how the underlying complexities of daily reality can create issues of global importance, e.g., pollution, population growth, war and unrest, or unsustainability.

Intellectual Outer Space

Some professionals needlessly fear that the transdisciplinary approach may eclipse the importance of individual disciplines. Lattanzi (1998) proposed that disciplinary knowledge is *intellectual inner space* and transdisciplinary knowledge is *intellectual outer space*. Although it is easy to chuckle at this imagery, the argument is a very convincing one. The pursuit of understanding relies heavily upon individual disciplines, along with the possibility for new disciplines. It also requires a space for the integration of credible knowledge into a new whole where fresh insights can emerge.

Transdisciplinary Concepts, Metaphors, and Patterns

François (2002) developed an intriguing notion that,

Transformative Practice: New Pathways to Leadership

although we have interdisciplinary teams, we need transdisciplinary concepts to unify the knowledge that is formed across traditional disciplinary boundary lines. These concepts then become the building blocks of the bridge between disciplines that is referred to in the first sentence of this chapter. As these transdisciplinary ideas continue to evolve, they provide a mechanism that enhances our understanding of the interwoven structures and functions that complex social issues are built upon. François explains that we need to look for *isomorphies*. Those trained in the field of living systems will recognize this term as one that describes an analysis of common, predictable patterns instead of separate ideas. Following this lead, Wheatley (1999) urged us to look for patterns in nature because nature is replete with similar forms (the Greek meaning of iso-morph).

Patterns help us to move away from the disparate semantics of individual disciplines toward a purer language, a set of concepts that is not influenced by each discipline's opinions and prejudices. These patterns provide a template for us to find similarity among disciplines that are not alike.

Part of this process involves the use of metaphors as tools to help us make analogical leaps from the familiar to the unfamiliar. Metaphors can be conduits or passageways to help people learn new, abstract concepts. They help us to extend our familiar knowledge of the world into a region that we have not yet experienced. From a transdisciplinary perspective, this region is very complex. It is composed of many interconnected parts, and it is difficult to understand because of this intricacy. Metaphors simplify and augment our joint

learning process, giving us a temporary common language while we navigate the space between the disciplines. Metaphors give us new degrees of conceptual freedom, releasing us from the chains that bind us to our root discipline. They are useful tools for conveying multifaceted, complicated ideas (Judge, 1991).

Nourishing the Fertile Middle Ground Between Disciplines

To use another metaphor, we do not want to build a bridge *over* the space between disciplines because transdisciplinarity holds that everything happens *within* the space between the disciplines. This happens because the conduit is seen as full and vibrant rather than empty. Transdisciplinarity manifests itself in this fertile space because it is nourished by disciplinary work and vice versa. Newtonian physics tells us that the space between disciplines is empty. The classical Aristotle and logic of dualities says that there is no middle ground. In practice, this means that people from different disciplines often find that they cannot talk to each other; hence, there can be no integration or generation of new knowledge. One of the pillars of the transdisciplinary approach, however, is that there *is* middle ground (Nicolescu, 1997, 2001) if we accept that different people have different perceptions of things. However, it is impossible to find new knowledge in this fruitful middle ground until everyone's ideas are heard. Each individual's point of view defines the truth until that point of view encounters something else, like another person's ideas or another discipline's perspective (Enigl, 2003). Because such encounters are so frequent here, it is within this abundant, productive space that transdisciplinarity fully blooms.

Transformative Practice: New Pathways to Leadership

A powerful new leadership theory developed by Andrews, Mitstifer, Rehm, & Vaughn (2001) demonstrates the transdisciplinary principle of uniting knowledge in the space between the disciplines. The authors worked in that fertile middle ground between disciplines, crisscrossing between authentic leadership, quantum physics, chaos theory, and living systems theory to create a new leadership model. Reflective Human Action theory suggests, for the first time in the home economics/family and consumer sciences profession, a way to see ourselves as leaders shaped by the principles of the new sciences. As is the intent of transdisciplinarity, this leadership theory helps us to confront the educational, political, social, economic, cultural, and spiritual arenas with authenticity, reflection, and an appreciation for the order inherent in chaos. If people can move about in the middle ground, come into contact with one another, and get motivated, an energizing force is generated and a synergy is created. A sense of community and belonging is nurtured and this sense tells us that we are a part of something bigger than each one of us, yet each individual is a new and different person in each relationship. The strength and potentialities that emerge are life giving and transformative. To engage in professional practice using this leadership model would allow us to free-float in *intellectual outer space* instead of staying pinned down in our traditional, safe disciplinary space.

Complexity, Emergence, and Multiple Realities

Couple the acceptance of a viable middle ground between disciplines with a deep respect for complexity, then add to

that the acceptance that several realities can coexist, and we can form a space wherein profound new knowledge about the world can be created (Nicolescu, 2001). Transdisciplinarity draws its notion of complexity from the new sciences of quantum physics, chaos theory, and living, adaptive systems. From this perspective, a complicated situation differs from a complex one. Although both complicated and complex problems are hard to solve because they are intricate and detailed, a complex problem demonstrates the additional feature of *emergence*. Emergence is the process of deriving some new and coherent structures, patterns, and properties. These patterns begin to appear as a result of the web of relationships between people.

Imagine the progress that could be made if researchers transitioned away from solving static problems alone to working together with disparate colleagues from different disciplines. Many new insights would materialize from the dynamics inherent in such collaborations, because a set of constantly adapting relationships lies at the heart of the process and makes solving complex problems a very meaningful experience. Within this scenario, a participant cannot operate outside of the whole; therefore no one individual can control the space (Wikipedia, 2004a). In addition, information brought to this productive space between disciplines is modified as it is passed from one person to another within these changing relationships so that information truly becomes *in formation*. Because energy and knowledge are continuously being formed, the "fertile space between the disciplines" is in constant flux. Not only is the space

Transformative Practice: New Pathways to Leadership

changing but also the people, their relationships, the nature of shared information, and the energy flows.

If we accept that reality is a coherent whole comprising several layers, we must be constantly aware of all layers if we are to understand any one layer in particular. This realization prevents us from studying a single aspect of a problem in isolation. Instead, we must entertain the role of the invisible particle layer; the material layer; the biological (ecological), social, and psychological layers; along with the economic, political, and technological layers of any complex problem. We must accept the challenge to never lose sight of the whole as we deal with complex social issues. From this perspective, it is easy to see why transversing across disciplines is so necessary if we are to solve the problems facing contemporary society. To operate effectively, we must develop a robust intellectual outer space that incorporates many disparate disciplines that are nevertheless able to live and work together to create integrative, embodied knowledge (Aerts, 2001).

Attaining a deeper understanding of the world is a hallmark of the transdisciplinary approach. To accomplish this goal, scholars must move beyond imagery to seek a more profound awareness of the differing realities that contribute to the world's complexity (Nicolescu, 2001). This deeper understanding can evolve if we operate within a nourishing space that is open to several realities. One of those realities is the sacred: an irreducible, impossible to simplify presence in the world. Students of transdiciplinarity cannot overlook this concept, because it is highly significant when one assumes that there are

several layers of reality (Voss, 2004).

Nicolescu (2000) defined the sacred as a zone of nonresistance to perceptions, a place where one's concept of reality can stretch beyond known experiences. Within this zone, individuals allow themselves to cross through the veil of rationality to arrive at a deeper reality. Imagine the doors that would open if researchers assumed that independent realities concurrently exist and that they manifest themselves to us through our interactions with them! We would never cease to wonder and to seek far-reaching solutions to the world's pressing problems. The depth of our understanding of the world would be greatly enhanced if humanity embraced this mind-set, even when the results run counter to what common sense suggests.

In this state of mind, we see information both as coming from outside us and as being transformed by us. As we step through the veil to other realities, our flow of consciousness corresponds to the flow of information from others in this fertile space. We move from seeing things in dualities to seeing things more complexly in open unity. If we take the quantum world into our mind-set, then we say that solving problems is associated with a substance-energy-information-space-time *complex* (Nicolescu, 2000). These are difficult concepts, but there is nothing simple about gaining a deeper understanding of the world.

Copyleft in a Virtual Creative Commons

A final example of a very novel concept germane to transdisciplinary inquiry is that of the Internet-generated model of *copyleft*, as opposed to

Transformative Practice: New Pathways to Leadership

copyright. A copyright bestows the right to restrict reproduction of an original expression. Copyright does not grant a monopoly right to do something; it merely allows the holder to prevent the unauthorized actions of others. Copyleft provides the opposite. It refers to the expectation that, within an accepted set of terms, anyone who wants to modify a work can do so. This system leads to the successive improvement of an original expression by a wide range of contributors. Novel ideas that are generated in the fertile space between and beyond disciplines are nurtured and expanded upon because there is continuous feedback and input. Under copyleft, the author grants irrevocable permission for free, unlimited use, modification, and redistribution of new material that flows from the original. In fact, it is expected that these derivative works will be shared, and that they will be copylefted in turn. The result is a creative commons, an intellectual outer space on the Internet where useful changes tend to be merged and other changes are maintained only to the extent that they are useful for solving the complex problem at hand (Nicolescu, 1997; Wikipedia, 2004b).

The Transdisciplinary Charter

In 1994, a transdisciplinary charter was struck at the First World Congress of Transdisciplinarity in Portugal (15 articles). The charter states that transdisciplinarity does not strive for the mastery of several disciplines, but opens all disciplines to that which they share and to that which lies beyond them. The key to this approach is that new knowledge is generated when people crisscross back and forth between disciplines and go beyond where they were when they entered the dialogue. Notions of zigzagging and going beyond known boundaries are hallmarks of transdisciplinarity, because transdisciplinary work cannot be done in isolation. It has to include academia, the arts, literature, poetry, civil society, and spiritual experiences. By association, this means that education must come to revalue the role of intuition, imagination, emotional sensibility, and body in the transmission and creation of knowledge. Information shared through dialogue and discussion should lead to a shared understanding that is like a fruit ripe with (a) rigor to avoid distortions, (b) openness and acceptance of the unknown, the unexpected, and the unforeseeable, and (c) tolerance of ideas and truths different from one's own. Inherent in the transdisciplinary approach are an individual's oneness with nature, an economy that puts people first, an open attitude toward myth and spirituality, and the earth as our home because we are all transnational beings instead of human beings (de Freitas, Morin, & Nicolescu, 1994).

Transdisciplinarity in Practice

To bring transdisciplinarity into professional practice, we must embrace an exciting, deep, mind shift so that we

- accept that our ultimate intent is to *understand the world as a complex whole* rather than to understand problems about parts of the world.
- move beyond the development of interdisciplinary teams toward the creation of new transdisciplinary concepts whose patterns are central, because these patterns provide a template for us to find similarity between disciplines that are not alike.

Transformative Practice: New Pathways to Leadership

- create space for people to reach their potential and find hidden possibilities in such a way that they can work in dialogue to understand the world as a complex whole.
- use new metaphors to illustrate the complexity of social problems and draw comparisons that enable people to make analogical leaps from the familiar to the unfamiliar.
- resist the impulse to stop once a satisfactory solution to a problem has been reached and instead dig deeper through dialogue and perspective sharing.
- acknowledge that the space between disciplines is full and fertile, rather than stagnant and empty.
- respect information obtained from separate disciplines as important first-step knowledge while working collaboratively to unite the knowledge gained by interacting in the fertile margins.
- work to form a new intellectual space that inspires gradual cross-fertilization of ideas while respecting disciplinary work.
- continually search for fruitful alternatives to the obvious response.
- create an intellectual space where disparate ideas can be merged into new insights, even when the individual concepts appear to be irrelevant or have nothing in common.
- reconfigure our collection of concepts to increase the flow or fluidity of the insights that emerge, are cross-fertilized, and become integrated into larger patterns.
- pay tribute to our imaginations and examine issues in context instead of being enamored by concrete numbers and abstract analyses.
- acknowledge that it is irresponsible to simplify our view of reality in order to simplify our work. We

Transformative Practice: New Pathways to Leadership

must embrace the complexity of life and erect permanent, complex structures and processes that function in intellectual outer space. Nicolescu (1997) offers a description of what these structures look like in academia.

- establish studios, workshops, or ateliers of transdisciplinary research that are free from ideological, political, or religious control. These workshops should involve researchers from all disciplines along with representatives of the arts, music, theater, poets, writers, and dancers.
- build centers of transdisciplinary orientation to expand the discourse beyond the scope of this book.
- establish a virtual creative commons and shape outer space knowledge using the principles of copyleft.
- crave new forms of learning and problem solving that involve

cooperation among different parts of society, including academia.

It may be both daunting and exciting to consider this new approach to practice, much like an intellectual roller coaster. However, if we are sincere in our desire to find solutions to complex social problems, and if we genuinely value interdisciplinary inclusiveness, then the transition to transdisciplinarity follows a natural process of professional evolution. The self-orientation tool in Appendix 1 will help readers take this next step by evaluating their position and progress along the path to a successful transdisciplinary approach.

An Example of a Transdisciplinary Experience

To conclude, my own understanding of the transdisciplinary approach was deeply informed by a recent

Transformative Practice: New Pathways to Leadership

gathering I enjoyed on the topic: *Spirit Matters - Wisdom Traditions and The Great Work* (see http://tlc.oise.utoronto.ca/conf2004/schedule.html). It was organized by the Transformative Learning Center of the Ontario Institute for the Study of Education (OISE), part of the University of Toronto. Those at this event consciously chose to call it a gathering and not a conference, and we were co-learners and active participants instead of passive attendees.

The visionaries who planned this gathering grounded it in Thomas Berry's (1999) *Great Work*. The intent of the gathering was to celebrate our connection with earth and each other. It was like no gathering or conference I have ever attended. The event was totally transdisciplinary, even though the word was never used at the conference (the organizers used the word transformative). There were academics from many disciplines; high school, undergraduate, and graduate students; musicians; poets; videographers; film makers; writers; artists; actors; playwrights; indigenous elders and drummers; journalists; small and medium sized businesses and corporations; and NGOs and activists, both local and world famous. It was transdisciplinary in nature because we eagerly jumped from our occupational bridges onto the fertile ground between the disciplines; we literally and figuratively danced a most awesome dance for four days.

Another quantum physics principle was in evidence at the gathering (with deep thanks to Dr. Nancy Chesworth, personal communication, May 28, 2004), because the co-learners brought with them many fuzzy-edged balls of knowledge and ways of knowing. When individuals and their

Transformative Practice: New Pathways to Leadership

knowledge balls collided on the fluxing fertile field—the sacred space—fusion occurred and new outer space knowledge was created. This fusion occurred because the separate bits of knowledge and the people who carried it came together to dance, and when they were exposed to each other they moved faster than they did when they were alone. It was totally amazing. There are no words to describe the palpable energy that emanated from that gathering. I went home immersed in it. It enveloped me and held me attached to all of those people I met and all that we shared and created. I smiled for days afterwards, at peace with myself yet intellectually stimulated to write this book. I came away with a lexicon of new concepts and patterns that we worked on together and took back with us. These new concepts, detailed below, guide us as we strive to contribute a more comprehensive understanding of the world—a hallmark of transdisciplinarity.

♦ As we walk the earth, we walk on the bones of all our ancestors. On this walk, we access their stories that are not written down.
♦ When Aboriginal peoples walk the land, they listen to the earth. They hear and share the songs and stories that become part of the peoples' great narrative. People know where they are geographically when they hear the song or story! There are song lines embedded in the geography of a land. That is the essence of indigenous knowledge. We live in a landscape alive with stories that are inherently local and rural in nature, to be spoken, gestured, sung, or danced in that place.
♦ These stories and songs are a living encyclopedia of an oral culture. They are place-

Transformative Practice: New Pathways to Leadership

bound and community-based. To write these stories or preserve them is to take them from their place of origin, without which they lose their meaning. These stories are meant to be retold in the same place from generation to generation so they become embodied, literally stored in our bodies. Contemporary stories are told using telecommunication technologies over great distances, so they have become placeless and they have lost the generational power of interconnectedness.

♦ My skin and color are just a covering. They cannot tell my story. One has to come inside me and hear my stories to let me be real, and to experience my imagination, my mystery, my secrets.

♦ Our dreams are our souls speaking.

♦ Imagine God as an underground river— the common waters— and imagine that each religion or faith drills down to tap that common well. There is not one God, but a deep, common spiritual collective that is lived out through unique rituals and celebrations.

♦ The original North American natives have a relationship with the Earth that embodies a way of living, not an organized religion. Indigenous peoples give thanks throughout each day in ceremonies and rituals, while others only celebrate on special occasions. Ceremonies keep us mindful of our role in the world, but organized religions can cause us to lose consciousness so we are not continually mindful. Religion has swamped the boat of spirituality.

♦ We need emancipatory spirituality, or a globalization of spirits. We also need to experience spirituality

in public spaces (business, government, community, schools, marketplace, and NGOs), not just in the private spheres of self and home.
- Earth and women are witnesses to the conceptual meaning of transdisciplinarity.
- To trust, we need to touch.
- If you are a free spirit, you have a real understanding of who you are. Indigenous people believe that freedom was once rampant, but we are no longer free because we do not know who we are. To go is to return to your self, to find yourself. To *go* means to learn, to reflect, and to critically see. Finding yourself is an act of worship!
- One individual's liberation and freedom is inextricably tied to every other person's liberation.
- Chiefs and visionaries are responsible for keeping us off balance on purpose. We need to ask ourselves "Who am I?" The answer must be continually re-evaluated because circumstances and relationships are always changing us.
- It is significant that we call our species human *be*ings, yet we spend all of our time as humans *do*ing. We have become so busy that we cannot think.
- We only know what it means to be human when we are in touch with other sentient beings. When we lose sight of our interconnectedness, the harm we do to the earth or other species does not cause us alarm. If we think we are most important and that we know it all, we are unable to take responsibility for our actions; we are not aware of others because they are invisible.
- Finally, our species is living through a collective *dark night of*

Transformative Practice: New Pathways to Leadership

the soul. This is a sacred place of waiting, learning, and stillness. Something is waiting to be born—a sense of hope, a connection to the future.

As we imagine many local centers of hope, we envision people who are connected to the future. Eventually, they become aware that they are also connected to one another. It is at this point that we see a paradigm shift, and a space opens to accommodate transdisciplinary work.

References

Aerts, D. (2001). *Transdisciplinary and integrative sciences: Humanity's mind and potential.* Accessed May 19, 2004 at http://www.vub.ac.be/CLEA/aerts/publications/2001EncLifeSupSys.pdf

Andrews. F., Mitstifer, D., Rehm, M., & Vaughn, G. (2001). *Leadership: Reflective human action online supplemental text.* East Lansing, MI: Kappa Omicron Nu.

Berry, T. (1999). *The great works.* New York: Bell Tower.

Colins, J. (2002). May you live in interesting times: Using multi disciplinary and interdisciplinary programs to cope with changes in life sciences. *BioScience, 52*(1), 75-83. Accessed May 19, 2004 at http://www.msu.edu/user/gradschl/es/pubs/collins.pdf

Enigl, D. (2003). *Philosophy of mathematics/logic and cryptology.* Accessed May 18, 2004 at http://home.earthlink.net/~enigl/TL.htm

de Freitas, L., Morin, E., & Nicolescu, B. (2002). *Charter of transdisciplinarity.* Accessed May 19, 2004 at http://perso.club_internet.fr/nicol/ciret/english/charten.htm

François, C. O. (2002). *Transdisciplinary unified theory.* Accessed May 19, 2004 at http://www.uni_klu.ac.at/~gossimit/ifsr/francois/papers/transdisciplinary_unified_theory.pdf

Judge, A. (1991). *Metaphors as transdisciplinary vehicles of the future.* Accessed May 19, 2004 at http://www.laetusinpraesens.org/docs/transveh.php

Lattanzi, M. (1998). *Transdiscipliarity at UNESCO.* Accessed May 19, 2004 at http://www.unesco.org/philosophy/en/

transdisciplinarity/
transdoc.htm

McGregor, S. L. T., et al. (2004). *Confessions of recovering home economists.* Accessed May 19, 2004 at http://www.kon.org/hswp/archive/recovering.html

Nègre, A. (1999). *A transdisciplinary approach to science and astrology.* Accessed May 19, 2004 at http://cura.free.fr/quinq/02negre2.html

Nicolescu, B. (1997). *The transdisciplinary evolution of the university condition for sustainable development.* Accessed May 19, 2004 at http://perso.club_internet.fr/nicol/ciret/bulletin/b12/b12c8.htm

Nicolescu, B. (2000). *Levels of reality as source of quantum indeterminacy.* Accessed May 19, 2004 at http://arxiv.org/PS_cache/quant_ph/pdf/0012/0012007.pdf

Nicolescu, B. (2001). *Manifesto of transdisciplinarity.* Albany, NY: State University of New York Press.

Regeer, B. (2002). *Transdisciplinarity.* Accessed May 19, 2004 at http://www.bio.vu.nl/vakgroepen/bens/HTML/transdiscipliNl.html

Voss, K. C. (2004). *Review essay of Brsarab Nicolescu's manifesto of transdisciplinarity.* Accessed May 19, 2004 at http://www.esoteric.msu.edu/Reviews/NicolescuReview.htm

Wikipedia. (2004a). *Complex system.* Accessed May 19, 2004 at http://en.wikipedia.org/wiki/Complex_system

Wikipedia. (2004b). *Copyleft.* Accessed May 19, 2004 at http://en.wikipedia.org/wiki/Copyleft

Wheatley, M. (1999). *Leadership and the new science.* San Francisco: Berrett-Koehler.

Transformative Practice: New Pathways to Leadership

Appendix 1: Transdisciplinary Self-Orientation Tool

Nuances of the transdisciplinary approach	I have never heard of it	I am aware of it	I can explain it to others	I use it in practice
The ultimate agenda is to **understand the world** in all of its complexities instead of in bits and pieces. To reach this level of understanding, people who know about the bits and pieces work and learn together.	☐	☐	☐	☐
Someone **initiates collaborative work** and explains that it will happen in the fertile space between and beyond the disciplines. The walls between the disciplines are removed to allow the fertile space to expand. People from different walks of life then grow together, moving beyond separate disciplines to reach a new collective space and mind-set.	☐	☐	☐	☐
People from more than one discipline meet with non-academics to solve complex, intricate problems. The melding of people from **different walks of life** is what makes this approach unique. Academic minds are different from the minds of artists, poets, dancers, or musicians. The differences in the ways we see the world generate patterns of similarities that ground the work. Diversity brings eventual unity.	☐	☐	☐	☐
The nature of this mutual learning is unique. It involves questioning assumptions and building bridges instead of separate paths. It demands that we seek the factors that condition us to be the way we are. Students of the transdisciplinary approach work on how to be with others while trying to find their own potential and inner core. They strive for shared creativity instead of hoarding personal knowledge.	☐	☐	☐	☐
Conversations and contributions are brought to the fertile space by each person and are put forth knowing that they will be melded with all of the				

Appendix 1: Transdisciplinary Self-Orientation Tool (continued)

Nuances of the transdisciplinary approach	I have never heard of it	I am aware of it	I can explain it to others	I use it in practice
others. There can be no ownership of separate bits of information. People must become comfortable with letting go of intellectual ownership, perhaps by creating a website where they can share their ideas freely as they evolve. This creation of "outer space knowledge" is called a **virtual creative commons** or **copylefting**.	☐	☐	☐	☐
Problems that are dealt with in this space involve a rich weave of societal structures and functions that cannot be studied as a single entity. For example, pollution, disease, population growth, and lack of peace are all linked together. It is not enough to address one component in isolation.	☐	☐	☐	☐
The property of emergence describes the difference between a *complicated* problem and a *complex* one. New insights bubble up as conversations simmer and perk over time. Because people change within an interactive set of relationships, the energy flow also changes. Solutions to problems emerge grounded in embodied knowledge, or knowledge that people take into themselves. Participants see the world through new lenses, and they have different stories to tell, shared stories. They have learned new dance steps and new patterns.	☐	☐	☐	☐
Inquiries into social issues do not stop with the first *best* answer because researchers appreciate that individual issues are profoundly complex and are linked to other issues of equal complexity. They dig deeper and dance longer in unison, knowing that collaborative efforts pay off. They create dialogue about the many layers of social issues that gradually unfold while never losing sight of the issue's wholeness. The result is new, embodied, outer space knowledge that can be applied to solve the many layers of a social problem.	☐	☐	☐	☐

Transformative Practice: New Pathways to Leadership

Appendix 1: Transdisciplinary Self-Orientation Tool (continued)

Nuances of the transdisciplinary approach	I have never heard of it	I am aware of it	I can explain it to others	I use it in practice
People who come to these meetings are equipped to solve problems, and to create a new space for integrating credible ideas into a new whole. For this to occur, participants must leave their zone of resistance and enter a common zone of acceptance. From then on, those involved do not see *her idea versus my idea*, because they are no longer in their safety zone. They have entered the fertile space that is constantly in flux and sound footing is no longer available. Instead, they must work in uncertainty with trust that a result will emerge that all can support, that will support all involved.	☐	☐	☐	☐
If participants come from different disciplines and from civil society, they may have no way to talk to each other. They have to respect the power of metaphors through narratives, stories, dance, and so on. They must be open to using metaphor to create a temporary language that will help everyone to navigate the unfamiliar space between their respective disciplines.	☐	☐	☐	☐
Those attending problem solving or posing sessions must accept that what they think is true will change when they encounter someone else's interpretation. Openness to different realities prepares the way for a shared truth to emerge in the fertile working space.	☐	☐	☐	☐
People working (dancing) in the fertile space have to move beyond temporary teams and toward the concepts that form the foundation of the dance floor. These ideas are formed when participants actively search for patterns to form a common language for expressing themselves as they work in the fertile space. Although the people who develop these concepts came to the fertile space with ideas from their respective disciplines or activities, all of these old ideas will eventually be altered.	☐	☐	☐	☐

Transformative Practice: New Pathways to Leadership

Appendix 1: Transdisciplinary Self-Orientation Tool (continued)

Nuances of the transdisciplinary approach	I have never heard of it	I am aware of it	I can explain it to others	I use it in practice
People working in the fertile space appreciate the strength of patterns as grounding concepts. Imagine a pattern for making a dress. Many people make different dresses using the same pattern, so there are similarities because the foundation is the same. A pattern can also be defined as an activity that is done without thinking. After working in the fertile space, participants develop patterns of relating to and learning with one another that become second nature. This strengthens their ability to understand the complexities of the world.	☐	☐	☐	☐
As people work together in this space, they weave ideas back and forth until the original yarn of the contributions is left behind and a new fabric takes shape. This new fabric offers a richer approach to solving social problems and brings everyone closer to understanding the world as a whole. Many new pieces of cloth are created; eventually even the yarn changes because new concepts become the starting point! To continue with the dance metaphor, people weave back and forth in the dance as they work together in this space, changing partners until the original contributions are left behind and new patterns and partners emerge. New dances with new steps and new patterns emerge continually.	☐	☐	☐	☐

Transformative Practice: New Pathways to Leadership

Chapter 4: Sustaining the Life Energy of the Profession: Insights from the Holomovement Principle

There is general agreement that the field of home economics/ family and consumer sciences, like so many others, has evolved into a fragmented discipline. North American, European, Australian, African, and Middle Eastern professionals all state that this field has been broken down into too many isolated components, and that the disparate specializations that remain appear to have little in common. Brown (1993) maintained that professionals who do not see the world holistically have a mind full of little islands with no bridges between them (p. 109). This is a compelling image that calls to mind a collection of experts in food, clothing, housing, consumption, and family dynamics—each practicing on an individual island with no way to talk to or work with one another. Acceptance of this fragmented system as the norm for the profession makes practitioners complicit in perpetuating this unhealthy pattern in the larger world.

Those who study home economics/family and consumer sciences do little good for individuals, families, or humanity by embracing a fragmented view of the world. This attitude merely leads to more isolation and disconnectedness at a time when the complex problems of contemporary society require cooperative relationships that foster harmonious co-existence. Both internal and external forms of fragmentation must be overcome. An individual might feel internal fragmentation through feelings of

Transformative Practice: New Pathways to Leadership

personal loss due to fear, anxiety, stress, misguided self-interest, and the disintegration of the social norms that govern behavior, thought, and social relationships. External fragmentation refers to the real or artificial boundaries that affect families and society, the economy, the political system, and the ecosystem. Fragmentation is also evident in the self-imposed boundaries that are erected between expert micro-specializations and in the many different names that practitioners apply to the field as a whole. Professionals perpetuate fragmentation by observing a strict separation between fields of expertise while avoiding agreement on a guiding philosophy to unite the distinct components.

Thank goodness human thinking has evolved beyond the dominant paradigm of Newtonian science that describes the disparate component pieces of the universe as isolated, disconnected, and unrelated, much like balls on a pool table. We can now learn many lessons about being holistic, creative, and complex from the new sciences of chaos theory, quantum physics, and living systems (Wheatley, 1999). One of those concepts is the holomovement principle (Bohm, 1980). *Holo* stems from the Greek word *holoteles* for wholeness or undividedness, often applied to mean entirely, completely, or perfectly. When *holo* is combined with *movement*, it indicates a profession that is not comprised of bits and parts from many individual areas of expertise but is instead an undivided wholeness in flowing movement without borders. This is the new fabric of our professional reality. Instead of visualizing the field as a collection of separate parts, we can conceive of the profession

Transformative Practice: New Pathways to Leadership

as an undivided whole that exists in perpetual, dynamic flux. From this perspective, the profession is a collection of different aspects of one whole and unbroken movement.

Implicate and Explicate Order

From the holomovement perspective, we can say that each facet of the profession contains the total order of the "home economics" universe, including the past, the present, and the future. Everything folds into everything else. Bohm (1980) introduced the *implicate* and the *explicate* as the two kinds of order in the universe. Implicate comes from the Latin *implicare,* meaning "to fold inward." Explicate is taken from the Latin *explicare,* which means "to unfold" (Phillips, 2004). This concept leads to an assumption that professions also display implicate and explicate order. The implicate order describes that which is implicit: the underlying whole of the profession that is invisible, yet fundamental, to the entire field. We tend to call this our philosophy, our mission, or our value system. When elements of the profession manifest themselves so that others can see them, they become part of the explicit order. This book describes a new implicit order, a new fundamental foundation for the profession. Although the implicit order is not visible, it is the undivided whole that serves as the profession's new core.

In addition to defining the implicate and the explicate, Bohm (1980) also stated that a holomovement cannot be defined or measured. There is no way to describe it or to specify it because to do so would

Transformative Practice: New Pathways to Leadership

divide it. It is only known through particular appearances, and even then only glimpses of its shadow are possible. For this reason, descriptions of potential new "parts" of the profession's holomovement indicate ideas that are made explicit. That is to say, these ideas emerge temporarily and then become enfolded back into the whole, or the implicit, invisible but fundamental order. Imagine an inert slinky, a solid object sitting motionless on a desk or in your hand. When set it in motion, the coils separate and we glimpse each segment of the whole, yet the individual coils remain connected to the whole while the entire slinky is in motion. Each part of the slinky contains the whole.

To explore this idea further, consider the difference between regular film and holographic film. Holographic film does not display an image of a photographed object. Instead, it holds a pattern of intricate, concentric circles that look like rain drops on the surface of a pond, or the wave patterns of the image (Talbot, 1991). If a piece is ripped off a regular photograph, the picture becomes incomplete because each section of the film it came from only stored information about that part of the picture. Conversely, each section of holographic film stores information about the entire image. For this reason, each holographic fragment contains a complete image of the entire object, just in lower resolution. The whole appears fuzzy but remains intact (Keepin, 1993). It is even more exciting to consider that this holograph is in perpetual movement and, like a lava lamp, every portion of the

Transformative Practice: New Pathways to Leadership

flow contains the entire flow. A lava lamp's viscous fluid is always in movement, with new things bubbling up and then falling back into the whole again. This model applies to holographic movement, as well. The whole is embedded in all of the parts, and everything is connected.

Remember that the implicate order is the foundation for everything and it is invisible. Relative to an organization or even an entire profession, the implicate comprises the paradigm, principles, philosophy, assumptions, and other underlying beliefs that shape a practical new collection of ideas. To clarify, imagine that Star Wars' R2D2 is projecting the holographic image of Princess Leah. If someone attempted to touch this holographic projection, he or she would find nothing but focused light and a handful of air, but the disturbed image of the princess would remain intact. A holographic image cannot be destroyed, even if parts of it are interrupted. The image simply becomes fuzzy or distorted until the disrupted area flows back into the whole. This book describes what a sustainable profession would look like through the prism of the holomovement concept. As individual parts are identified in subsequent chapters, consider each element to be a shadow of the whole, and remember that these components only appear to be independent (Sharpe, 2000).

Transformative Practice: New Pathways to Leadership

The Ensemble

Bohm (1980) put forward another metaphor to describe a professional holomovement. He suggested that each holomovement operates within a given context, and this context plays a key role in determining what holomovement segments come to the fore and make themselves explicit. In other words, certain holomovement contents become visible based largely upon the context of the larger whole. When we see the contents of the holomovement, we see an ensemble of parts that continues to relate to the invisible whole, wherein the ensemble is a group of complementary parts that contribute to a single effect.

Working from the notion of implicate order, it is possible to suggest that a hidden order is present in apparently random events, or simple chance. There is no single aspect of professional practice, no isolated element among the ensemble of ideas that constitutes the profession because they are all connected. No one aspect of practice can be understood without considering how it relates to the others. They cannot be separated. Picture spinning airplane blades that give the appearance of a solid disk. Separateness is an illusion that is broken by a rapid sequence of unfoldings. What we see at any point in time is actually a totality of the ensemble, with each element present together in a continual process of unfolding and folding. These parts intermingle and interpenetrate each other to create a whole.

Because only certain aspects of the holomovement emerge at any one time, not every characteristic piece will rise up at once. Furthermore, if we accept the notion of wholeness we can suggest that the

Transformative Practice: New Pathways to Leadership

profession's ensemble, or implicit wholeness, should be the same in all contexts. However, Bohm (1980) suggested that we must examine the context to accurately predict the amount of sameness we can expect. Consider, for example, whether professionals working in conflict or post-conflict zones use the wholeness that those in non-conflict zones adopt in practice. Bohm's (1980) thinking suggested that such work is based on the same implicit or invisible order. He offered the idea of *generative order*, in which the implicit order helps to generate structure for work in conflict zones. The parts of the whole that may not be manifest in this context (e.g., participatory democracy, non-violent conflict resolution, citizenship, and empowerment) are still present and are enfolded within the whole of the profession in question. These elements have a different level of visibility in a conflict zone than they do in non-conflict situations, but the implicit order or invisible foundation still shapes thinking, actions, and reflections. The profession's holomovement lies beneath the visible world. It unfolds and folds back into itself continually, and it is the invisible core that sustains each practitioner.

Perpetual Dynamism

From the holomovement perspective, certain aspects of a profession are important in any given context, while others are not. Because both the whole and all pieces of reality are constantly in process, readers may be ready to see some parts of the profession's holograph but not others. As individuals gradually adapt to this new way of thinking, they will find that additional pieces of a new professional reality are revealed. The future reality is constantly in process, or in flux, as we saw in the lava lamp metaphor. Every portion of the flow contains the entire flow and exists in a perpetual dynamism (Keepin, 1993).

In simple terms, professionals who embrace some or all of the ideas presented in this book accept the idea that no single aspect of any given field stands alone. Each facet is connected to every other. This way of thinking reflects holistic practice, and it implies a continual effort to move toward the formation of a professional whole through creative evolution. As we create this new whole, each specific manifestation of a single element (transformative learning in a classroom, for example) is simply a ripple on the surface of that whole (Keepin, 1993), reminiscent of the metaphorical raindrop on the face of a pond. As we live each day within our chosen profession, we must never lose sight of the underlying orderliness of the whole, and we must always be creative as we perpetually create this whole.

Locality and Nonlocality

Bohm's (1980) notions of locality and nonlocality can also be extended to this professional holomovement metaphor. Nonlocality simply means that everything connects with everything else regardless of proximity. The implicit order, or the invisible fundamental essence of a profession, is nonlocal and all aspects of the ensemble are interconnected. Things become local when we try to separate parts of the ensemble from one another. Local is a quantum term meaning separated. In other words, if bits and pieces of a profession's life force are used without appreciating that each is connected, the practice will not percolate up from the life energy of the profession. Instead, practice will drain energy

Transformative Practice: New Pathways to Leadership

from the profession. Further discussion regarding the effects of locality on the profession of home economics/family and consumer sciences can be found in a paper called *Confessions of recovering home economists*, which argues that the profession is addicted to the technical mode of practice (McGregor et al., 2004).

An appreciation for nonlocality, or the concept that all things are interconnected, does not rule out local influences. If, however, the local characteristics of separateness and fragmentation become universal, then people lose the ability to see things as connected. This may be what has happened in the home economics/family and consumer sciences profession, and in many others. Practitioners have not embraced the idea that the profession has a core of life energy. Instead, members have gone separate ways and have developed a profession that is not sustainable. The energy core is draining at a rapid pace, but principles from quantum physics give us hope! Because fragmented locality is less organized than connected non-locality, the professional system will strive for *extropy*. Extropy is an increase in intelligence, information, energy, vitality, experience, diversity, opportunity, and growth (Sharpe, 2000).

Complexity-Consciousness

Another idea that stems from Bohm's (1980) quantum physics theory is that of consciousness. Each individual displays an unfolding of the consciousness of his or her profession, in which a thought or idea about practice enters one's mind from the deep recesses of the professional holomovement. This holomovement is the life energy of the profession, and the thought processes

Transformative Practice: New Pathways to Leadership

of each practitioner arise from this energy. Likewise, professionals can reenter this energy force when necessary to encourage evolution and strength (Sharpe, 2000).

Bohm (1980) referred to extropy as increasing the complexity-consciousness. As a profession becomes more complex, it becomes more interconnected, more non-local. The new whole causes each individual element of the professional system to behave in a new way. People begin to relate over longer distances, even though they are not connected by immediate physical contact. Throughout history, humanity has fluctuated between separateness and complex connectedness. As an example, labor unions were initially built around a very simple structure, but as they grew they formed increasingly complex and numerous connections. In some instances, the complexity of the non-local or global movement must temporarily abate to allow for more local growth. Indeed, local action is often the first step, and it is necessary to create the elementary components needed to bring consciousness and complexity into a profession. Individual practitioners become both by-products of professional complexity and actors in perpetuating a professional expansion of complexity and consciousness. This force strives to maintain the profession's initial complexity and eventually moves beyond it (Sharpe, 2000).

Summary

To review, the reality of a profession may appear to consist of a collection of separate people and ideas on individual islands, but it has the capacity to evolve beyond this state. It can become an undivided whole that is in perpetual, dynamic

Transformative Practice: New Pathways to Leadership

flux. Talbot (1991) told us that people who possess unique qualities can still be part of an undivided whole. Although the

professional field exists as a unified, unbroken whole, each member maintains individuality, but it is difficult to determine where the professional ends and the profession itself begins. Just as eddies in a river appear, at first, to be separate entities, it soon becomes hard to distinguish the boundaries of the whirlpool from the surrounding stream. So it is with a professional holomovement. Each unique individual practitioner draws strength from the life energy that is at the core of the profession.

A profession's base reality is made from the seamless holographic fabric of the implicate order. We cannot see it, but it is the energy core that every aspect of practice is drawn from. Each day, professionals wake to enter the explicit order as they unfold from the underlying energy of the implicate order, but they never lose their connection to the core. The implicate order remains to provide a professional compass and a light to guide the way.

Today, most professions exist in a state similar to that of a photo taken using traditional film. When one piece is ripped off, the picture becomes incomplete. Contemporary challenges demand a more comprehensive approach, one that involves re-imaging or re-imagining the profession

Transformative Practice: New Pathways to Leadership

holographically. In this manner, the whole of the profession, its core goals and philosophies, becomes encoded upon each component piece and the resulting holographic image is projected outward to each practitioner and the larger world. This becomes the unfolded image of the profession that is visible through each professional's actions and interactions. The philosophical heart of the field lies at the core of this image. Each individual's self-image as a professional flows in and out of this film while remaining continuously anchored to the core. Therefore, practitioners can step in and out of the core, where they have the opportunity to constantly form and change. This is the professional holomovement—the whole moving as one (Talbot, 1991).

Conclusion

Readers who focus on the idea of a professional holomovement have a real opportunity to form the vanguard of professional practice. From this position, a field's professionals form a creative group that is active in the innovation and application of new concepts and techniques. By embracing the holomovement as a guiding metaphor, practitioners become open to the idea that the entire whole is in constant

Transformative Practice: New Pathways to Leadership

movement, folding into and out of itself as it recreates a central core of professional life energy.

To examine this idea from the perspective of a specific field, there is deep meaning in the choice of a flame as a symbol among many home economics/family and consumer sciences associations. It could be said to represent the profession's inner energy core. The flame encompasses the dance, the folding and unfolding, and the entirety of the whole moving as one. It must be stoked and continually tended if it is to burn brightly into the future. Practitioners must commit to a sustainable profession by taking care of themselves and one another and by nurturing the deep energy core of the profession as a whole.

References

Bohm, D. (1980). *Wholeness and the implicate order.* London: Routledge.

Brown, M. M. (1993). *Philosophical studies of home economics in the United States: Basic ideas by which home economists understand themselves.* East Lansing, MI: Michigan State University.

Keepin, W. (1993). *The lifework of David Bohm.* Retrieved November 27, 2004 from http://www.satyana.org/html/bohm2.html

McGregor, S. L. T., et al. (2004). *Confessions of recovering home economists.* Accessed May 19, 2004 at http://www.kon.org/hswp/archive/recovering.html

Phillips. C. (2004). *Glossary.* Retrieved December 2, 2004 from http://www.moonstar.com/~acpjr/

Sharpe, K. (2000). *A theology based on Bohm's holomovement metaphysics.* Retrieved November 27, 2004 from http://www.ksharpe.com/word/BM09.htm

Talbot, M. (1991). *The holographic universe.* New York: Harper Perennial.

Wheatley, M. (1999). *Leadership and the new science.* San Francisco: Berrett-Koehler.

Transformative Practice: New Pathways to Leadership

Chapter 5: Transformative versus Transactional Leadership

Murray (2002) predicted that the concept of leadership will develop in accordance with a number of basic principles as the 21st century unfolds. First, leadership is for everyone. It involves learning and sharing new knowledge. It is based on empowered people working in collaborative teams for agreed-upon purposes. Leadership involves communicating with people, not to people. It assumes that authority comes from what one knows and says, not from one's hierarchical position. Finally, it includes fellowship, in which some people have more responsibilities than others do but everyone learns together to achieve the mission. Committed professionals within home economics/family and consumer sciences should also be leaders. As such, each professional has a responsibility to build, pave, and maintain a path that leads to a society where individual and familial well-being and quality of life are respected and ensured. Each practitioner chooses which approach to embrace within a professional leadership role. These individual choices affect the nature of one's practice and, by extension, the future of the larger profession.

This chapter will aid readers in making this choice by elaborating on one of the newest leadership approaches, transformative leadership (TF). TF can be best described by explaining the aspects that differentiate it from the traditional transactional (TA) approach. The TF approach was chosen because it best meets Murray's (2002) predictions regarding the development of leadership in this century. From the transformational leadership perspective, one does not have to be a manager to be a leader (Alimo-Metcalfe, 2001). A leader can be anyone, regardless of formal position, who serves as an effective social change agent (Astin & Astin, 2000). In this sense, every individual practitioner has the potential to be a leader. Leadership no longer has to be relegated to any one person, committee, or working group. **A profession that embraces this leadership perspective is capable of genuine transformation**.

Transactional Leadership

The transactional (TA) leadership style has prevailed for many decades. Those who see it in action consider it good, effective, and proper management based upon techniques developed over the last 50 years. These techniques include performance appraisals, performance related pay, job descriptions, management by objective (MBO), organizational process analysis and clarification, and job grading and classifications (Bass & Steidlmeier, 1989; Stockdale, 1999).

Transactional leadership takes its name from the common definition of a transaction, i.e., an agreement that involves an exchange, in which an individual gives one thing in order to obtain another. In transactional leadership, the exchange takes place when the leader specifies the terms of the transaction by delineating what is expected. Followers are told what they will receive (or avoid) in exchange for fulfilling those expectations (Bass, 1985). For this reason, transactional leaders are power wielders who hold power over people or processes. In a power-over model, the leader

Transformative Practice: New Pathways to Leadership

directs, regulates, manages, and controls subordinates using influence and authority. These subordinates then expect to receive promotions, raises, or positive reinforcement if they do well, and criticism or sanctions if they do not do well (Alimo-Metcalfe, 2001).

Because people in transactional relationships will only perform tasks for which they are rewarded and will only avoid actions for which they are punished, the participants begin to avoid taking risks and work becomes stale, stagnated, and static (Burns, 1978). To create incentive, TA leaders use praise, recognition, and the delegation of responsibilities from the top down because people will compete for positions and seek pay raises for rewards (Stuart-Kotze, 2003). When dealing with problems, TA leaders tend to (a) wait passively for subordinates to make mistakes and then correct them, (b) take no action until a problem occurs and then hand out punishment, or (c) avoid leadership altogether (Bass & Steidlmeier, 1989; Stockdale, 1999).

Transactional leaders accumulate power and continue to use it by efficiently allocating resources so that subordinates achieve management-set goals. Under this leadership style, goal achievement requires that the subordinate follow a path prescribed by the TA leader, replete with directions and assistance. There is an explicit agreement between manager and subordinate (Hochberg, 1996). Indeed, the methods and results of transactional leaders are primarily associated with management, not leadership. TA leaders do not build on others' need for meaningful work nor do they tap into the subordinates' creativity (Brown, Birnstihl, & Wheeler, 1996).

Transformative Practice: New Pathways to Leadership

Transformative Leadership

Unlike transactional leaders, transformative (TF) leaders succeed by (a) articulating powerful change agendas, (b) encouraging people to change internally as they embrace this new agenda, (c) accepting the idea of power through people instead of power over them, (d) grounding people in a moral dimension, (e) striving for others to exceed their own expectations and reach their fullest potential, and (f) reminding people to challenge the status quo. Each of these traits is explored in detail below.

Articulate Powerful Change Agendas

As Stokes (2003, p. 1) so clearly explained,

> Transformational leaders are able to articulate clear, powerful, transformational agendas. They are able to tell us what the current reality . . . is, and they are able to outline the outcomes of our work should we decide to follow them or join them.

Leaders are people who take responsibility for change agendas; transformational leaders take responsibility for very large change agendas, so we hear their agendas for societal transformation with skepticism because they are ambitious, difficult, and uncommon. But we are also excited, inspired, and energized because these agendas draw us back to the center of our humanness, our deepest moral and ethical concerns.

The TF leader's vision for a better reality unfolds over a long period and is ever present until it becomes a reality. Indeed, change envisioned by TF leaders is often of such magnitude that it requires years to be truly embedded (Stokes, 2003). For this reason, TF leaders know that the likelihood that an envisioned change

will become a reality hinges upon its co-creation among like-minded people. Only in this way can the effort be sustained over the long term (Rodriquez & Villarreal, 2001). To this end, a TF leader must identify other leaders and potential leaders whose change agendas overlap with theirs and skillfully nurture the growth and development of those leaders. They look for leadership among those who already hold formal leadership responsibilities and among those who have not been given a formal role. Because transformational leaders want leadership at all levels, they find ways to invite leadership at the upper level, the line level, and at the volunteer level (Stokes, 2003).

Change Internal Belief Systems

Transformative leadership is not concerned with transactional exchanges. Instead, it seeks to alter the beliefs and values of others, especially in times of change (Covey, 2001). Rather than exchanging rewards for performance, TF leaders attempt to build ownership on the part of others by involving them in the process. They are able to move others from external to internal control, meaning that behaviors become internalized so that people want to perform instead of being told or threatened to act. If people value the desired outcome or future direction, they will willingly and passionately strive for that outcome and vision, leading to a more positive self-concept that is aligned with the mission of the organization, group, or profession (Scholl, 2002).

TF leaders change other people's internal belief systems by (a) becoming role models that followers want to emulate, (b) providing meaning and challenge so as to motivate and inspire commitment to

Transformative Practice: New Pathways to Leadership

goals beyond self interest and toward a shared vision, (c) encouraging new ways of thinking, new approaches to problems, and learning from mistakes, and (d) paying attention to each individual's particular needs, desires, and capabilities through mentoring (Bass, 1985). These four behaviors are referred to as the "Four I's" of transformational leadership. They are idealized influence, inspirational motivation, intellectual stimulation, and individualized consideration. Put another way, transformational leaders coach people to take on greater responsibility for developing and improving upon their own personal performance. They encourage people to rethink ideas or problems from a fresh perspective, challenge them to increase their awareness, and push them to question tried-and-true methods and assumptions. TF leaders communicate their vision in compelling ways so that people embrace it and make it their own. TF leaders also give up the desire to know everything, because they do not need to position themselves as experts. Instead, they hunger for the insight and input of others.

Other people who wish to embrace the envisioned agenda of the TF leader must unlearn, relearn, and become life-long learners while the TF leader creates opportunities for this process to unfold. TF leaders realize that creating and facilitating this drive for learning is important, because a critical mass of leaders must be reached to advance any organizational or societal transformation. TF leaders hold the broader welfare of families and the community as their core responsibility (Rodriquez & Villarreal, 2001).

TF leaders see large human problems that need to be solved. These

Transformative Practice: New Pathways to Leadership

problems often align with the leader's own central, unresolved issues in some deep way. As TF leaders make a commitment to solve other people's problems, they make a commitment to their own emergence and to an internal change in their belief systems. As more leaders experience personal transformation, the world itself is transformed (Stokes, 2003).

Power Through People

Transformational leaders manifest power through other people instead of over them. On a personal level, they appeal to an individual's higher sense of morality, ethics, and values. At an organizational level, they change the culture by introducing new beliefs and goals and by changing how group members define their roles (Bensimon, 1989; Liontos, 1992). TF leaders help people to (a) enlarge their vision, insight, and understanding, (b) clarify their purpose, (c) make their behaviors congruent with the envisioned future's beliefs, principles, and values, and (d) bring about changes that are permanent, self-perpetuating, and momentum-building. They accomplish these objectives by adapting their style to suit group members' ability, maturity, competence, and commitment (Covey, 2001).

To develop power through people, the TF leader must exercise good diagnostic skills, have a large repertoire of management styles, and have the courage and flexibility required to choose the management style appropriate to the situation and its participants. The TF leader is a developer rather than a hero, a consultant as opposed to a commander, and a mentor instead of an order-giver. The TF leader does not act as a decision-maker. He or she is instead a value clarifier and an exemplar that shares power rather than retains it. This type of leader fosters collaborative rather than adversarial relationships and is someone who chooses to focus on empathy over confrontation (Covey, 2001).

Moral Dimension

Transformational leadership is based upon a foundation of action on moral principles (Goeglein & Hall, 1997). TF leaders initiate power relationships with colleagues, subordinates, followers, or clients so that each gains a greater awareness of issues of consequence. Leaders accomplish this by arguing for what they see as right or good, rather than advocating what is popular or acceptable within the established wisdom of the time. As noted before, they appeal to an individual's higher level of morality, ethics, and values (Alimo-Metcalfe, 200; Bensimon, 1989; Gronn, 1995; Liontos, 1992). Transformational leadership is grounded in moral foundations that emancipate individuals from externally imposed forms of authority and control—the status quo and prevailing ideology (Bass, 1997; Bass & Steidlmeier, 1998). TF leaders are concerned with unearthing people's core issues and potentialities and with raising people's consciousness regarding deep ethical and ideological issues. The TF leader's moral obligations are grounded in the broader needs of individuals within their communities, not their own self-interest. When the leaders themselves are morally mature, those they lead display higher moral reasoning (Bass & Steidlmeier, 1998).

Motivate People to Reach Potential

Instead of expecting people to follow rules and

Transformative Practice: New Pathways to Leadership

fulfill pre-established expectations, TF leaders design and redesign jobs to make them meaningful and challenging. This is done to enable people to realize their full potential (Brighouse, 2003). TF leaders engage and involve others, changing peoples' beliefs about themselves to encourage more positive expectations and more creativity (Alimo-Metcalfe, 2001). TF leaders motivate others to do more than they intended (and more than they ever thought possible) and to move beyond self-interest to focus on the larger goals of the group, organization, or society (Bass, 1985; Brown et al., 1996).

Challenging the Status Quo

To bring about transformative change, TF leaders foster the end values of justice, equality, and human rights (Bass & Steidlmeier, 1998; Jahan, 2000). These are the very values that are usually trampled upon by today's prevailing ideology and agendas. Transformative leaders critically assess asymmetrical power relationships and facilitate practices that engender solidarity, democracy, liberation, and hope (Dantley, 2002). TF leaders succeed in cultivating other people's ability and determination to challenge established views and in encouraging them to question the leader's opinions as well (Andras & Erdos, 2001). This propensity to transcend the status quo is possible because people undergo a personal change when they accept the envisioned future state communicated by the TF leader (Hochberg, 1996). Transformational leaders find ways to inspire people to want to lead themselves and to become leaders who continually critique the status quo. Transformational leaders are willing to stand in the center of new ideas and amass energy around them

(Dantley, 2002; Stokes, 2003). They embrace uncertainties and ambiguity instead of concentrating their efforts on maintaining the status quo (Alimo-Metcalfe, 2001).

Conclusion

Transformational leadership begins with self-development and extends to others through coaching and development. In this way, TF leaders enable others to become agents of change in the larger society. Transformative leaders help others to clarify their own worlds, develop a commitment to democracy and emancipation, and have the courage and desire to work for the empowerment of all people (Dantley, 2002). TF leaders engage others in a commitment to long-term change. They are pioneers who pave the way for others to make the journey with them. Many will call these leaders troublemakers and rebels and will be eager to marginalize and isolate them (Townley, 1999). As a counter point, Heifetz and Laurie (1997) tendered the term *creative deviants* to capture the courage of transformative leaders as they challenge existing protocols. These leaders confront the status quo and help superiors, peers, or subordinates to become energized and focused on a shared vision. It bears repeating that engaging in transformative leadership increases the chance for a few members of the profession to convert others into transformative moral social agents. The few then become the many, and this leads to the transformation of professional practice as a whole.

References

Alimo-Metcalfe, B. (2001). Transforming leadership. *Developing People Newsletter*, 45 Retrieved February 7, 2004 from http://www.roffeypark.com/newsletter/dp45winter01/backpage.html

Andras, P., & Erdos, G. (2001). *Management, leadership and charisma.* Retrieved October 1, 2003 from http://www.staff.ncl.ac.uk/peter.andras/charisma.ppt

Astin, H., & Astin, A. (Eds.). (2000). *Leadership reconsidered.* Battle Creek, MI: W.K. Kellogg Foundation.

Bass, B. M. (1985). *Leadership and performance beyond expectations.* New York: Free.

Bass, B. M. (1997). *The ethics of transformational leadership.* Retrieved February 7, 2004 from http://www.academy.umd.edu/publications/klspdocs/bbass_p1.htm

Bass, B. M., & Steidlmeier, P. (1998). *Ethics, character and authentic transformational leadership.* Retrieved February 7, 2004 from http://cls.binghamton.edu/BassSteid.html

Bensimon, E. (1989). Transactional, transformational and "trans-vigorational" leaders. *World Wide Web Edition of Leadership Abstracts, 2*(6). Retrieved February 7, 2004 from http://www.league.org/publication/abstracts/leadership/labs0489.html

Brighouse, T. (2003). *Transformational and transactional leadership.* Retrieved February 7, 2004 from http://www.bgfl.org/services/leaders/files/leadship.pdf

Brown, W., Birnstihl, E., & Wheeler, D. (1996). Leading without authority. *Electronic Journal of Extension, 34*(5). Retrieved February 7, 2004 from http://www.joe.org/joe/1996october/a3.html

Burns, J. M. (1978). *Leadership.* New York: Harper & Row.

Covey, S. (2001). *Transformational vs. transactional leadership.* Retrieved February 7, 2004 from http://www.sportscareers.com/insiders/archived_articles/archivedDetail.asp?id=104

Dantley, M. (2002). *Transformative leadership and its intersection with Cornel West's interpretation of prophetic spirituality.* Retrieved February 7, 2004 from http://www.units.muohio.edu/eduleadership/FACULTY/DANTLEY/DOCUMENTS/prophetic_spirituality.pdf

Goeglein, A., & Hall, M. (1997). *Systems, values and transformative leadership.* Retrieved October 1, 2003 from http://sysval.org/Impact31.html

Gronn, P. (1995). Greatness revisited: The current obsession with transformational leadership. *Leading and Managing 1*(1), 14-27. Retrieved February 7, 2004 from http://staff.edfac.unimelb.edu.au/

Transformative Practice: New Pathways to Leadership

david_furr/482-707/fronn_95.html

Heifetz,, R. A., & Laurie, D. L. (1997). The work of leadership. *Harvard Business Review*, January-February, 124-134.

Hochberg, H. (1996). *Journeyman leadership* Retrieved from February 7, 2004 http://www.coxegroup.com/articles/leader.html

Jahan, R. (2000). *Transformative leadership in the 21st century*. Retrieved February 7, 2004 from http://www.capwip.org/resources/womparlconf2000/downloads/jahan1.pdf

Liontos, L. B. (1992). Transformational leadership. *ERIC Digest, 72*. Retrieved October 1, 2003 from http://www.ericfacility.net/ericdigests/ed347636.html

Murray, J. (2002). *21st century leadership*. Accessed July 16, 2004 at http://www.manage2001.com/21l.htm

Rodriquez, R. G., & Villarreal, A. (2001). *Transformative leadership in Latino communities*. Retrieved February 7, 2004 from http://www.idra.org/Newslttr/2001/Jun/Rosana.htm

Scholl, R. W. (2002). *Leadership style*. Retrieved February 7, 2004 from http://www.cba.uri.edu/scholl/notes/leadership_approaches.html

Stockdale, P. (1999). *Psychology of employee relations: Leadership*. Retrieved February 7, 2004 from http://www.siu.edu/departments/cola/psycho/psyc323/chapt16/tsld001.htm

Stokes, G. (2003). *A call for transformational leadership*. Retrieved February 7, 2004 from http://www.movethemountain.org/transform_leadership/articles/leadership_assessment.cfm

Stuart-Kotze, R. (2003). *Transformational vs. transactional management* Retrieved October 1, 2003 from http://managementlearning.com/ppl/burnjam.html

Townley, A. (1999). *Creating a peaceful school community: The role of transformative leadership*. Retrieved October 1, 2003 from http://www.westernjustice.org/pdf/wjc_rpt1.pdf

Transformative Practice: New Pathways to Leadership

Chapter 6: Reflective Human Action (RHA) Leadership Theory

A discussion of Reflective Human Action (RHA), a powerful new leadership theory, is critical to any discussion of a changing professional paradigm. In 1995, prominent scholars at Kappa Omicron Nu (KON) published a reflective theory of leadership that leads to authentic, ethical, and spiritual action by encouraging people to share information, respect chaos, embrace vision, and develop relationships. Although KON has developed strong, comprehensive materials on RHA, this chapter provides a précis that will inform our broader thinking (Andrews, Mitstifer, Rehm, & Vaughn, 1995, 2001; Stratton & Mitstifer, 2001).

RHA theory is a synergy between Margaret Wheatley's (1999) work on leadership and the new sciences and Robert Terry's (1993) work on authentic leadership. The following material, drawn from McGregor (2001, 2004), sets out the seven features typical of any action taken by humans. Discussion then turns to the features that characterize authentic leadership, or human action that is reflective, and goes on to describe the principles that shape that action, drawing upon quantum physics, chaos theory, and living systems theory.

Features of any human action

Whether individuals are aware of it or not, every action a person takes possesses seven distinct features: mission, meaning, existence, resources, structure, power, and fulfillment. Table 1 briefly outlines the essence of these features (Andrews et al., 1995). Succinctly, any human activity is inherently shaped by a larger

Transformative Practice: New Pathways to Leadership

purpose, has meaning for the person, happens within a historical context, is affected by the level of available resources, involves plans and strategies, and requires a commitment of power and spirit to see it through to completion.

Table 1: Overview of seven features of any human action (Andrews et al., 1995)

Mission	What is the ultimate purpose of this action? What expectations drive the expenditure of energy?
Meaning	Why am I doing this? To know why an action is being undertaken places the mission in context and helps people to make sense of their actions. Meaning expresses the significance of an action, legitimizes the action, and places boundaries around the process of taking action.
Existence	What is the history of this action, event, or situation? Why does the individual feel a need do something now? What are the limiting factors, the forces within and beyond control, and the rituals that limit taking action?
Resources	What elements, including tangible and intangible resources, are available to aid in performing the action?
Structure	What plans and processes can be used to accomplish this action? What arrangements, schedules, strategies, methods, and designs are at hand or could be found?
Power	What energy is expended, and what level of commitment exists to follow through and accomplish the action? In RHA theory, power is not just the ability to exert one's will upon another, it is also energy that can be released and focused upon attaining fulfillment.
Fulfillment	What did this action accomplish? Did expectations, resources, power, structures, meaning, and mission converge to create a fulfilling and complete action?

Transformative Practice: New Pathways to Leadership

Table 2: Relationship between seven features of human action (adapted from Terry, 1993)

If one of the features below presents Itself:	Deal with It by working on....
Mission (What are you working toward?)	Meaning (Why are you working toward it?)
Meaning (Why are you working toward it?)	Existence (What is the history of the need to take action? What is the current situation)
Existence (What is the history of the need to take action? What is the current situation?)	Resources (What assets can you use to take action now?)
Resources (What assets can you use to take action now?)	Structure (Through what processes can you take action?)
Structure (Through what processes can you take action?)	Power (How much energy and commitment is there to take action?)
Power (How much energy and commitment is there to take action?)	Mission (Toward what are you working?)

All of this should lead to fulfillment or completion of the initiated action

Terry (1993) provided a powerful approach to help us understand the synergy between these seven elements. Table 2 profiles his ideas for dealing with leadership issues based upon which of the six human action features is the central problem (the seventh feature, fulfillment, is the reason the other six features exist).

As an example, problems related to structure should be addressed by exploring power issues, or issues related to commitment levels and the energy people put into their tasks. If people in an organization report problems like "things are not well organized," "I don't know what my job is," or "I don't know who to report to," then the

111

organization *appears* to be facing structural challenges. However, the leader should address these concerns by focusing on power, or people's sense of powerlessness because people who feel they do not have a say in the arrangement of their work world feel powerless, complain of structural issues, and fail to commit to or put enough energy into their job. Rearranging the work environment will not solve the problem but realigning power relationships will. In other words, the leader should focus on the underlying symptoms instead of the apparent ones. Andrews et al. (1995, pp. 17-20) provided excellent examples of the other relationships identified in Table 2.

Features of Reflective Human Action

Again, *any* action a human takes is comprised of seven features that are present whether the person knows it or not: mission, meaning, existence, resources, structure, power, and fulfillment (Table 1). Three additional features relate to any human action that is reflective. They are (a) *authenticity*, or being true to one's own self; (b) *ethical sensibility*, or being ethically, intellectually, and morally responsible; and (c) *universal human capacity for passion and purpose*, or acting with spirituality (Andrews et al., 1995). This part of the RHA theory draws from Terry's (1993) work on authentic leadership.

Reflection

To be reflective, one must be able to step back from the immediacy of the situation to examine beliefs, attitudes, values, and behavior in a dispassionate manner (Jackson, 1990). van Manen (1995) identified three types of reflection. Thinking about what has happened is called retrospective reflection,

Transformative Practice: New Pathways to Leadership

thinking about what may come is called anticipatory reflection, and stopping to think while doing something is called contemporaneous reflection. Schön (1987) differentiated between *reflection on action* and *reflection in action*, where the former refers to analysis that occurs after the fact and the latter refers to scrutiny that happens concurrently with the action. In other words, reflection in action occurs when the individual is aware of the process and is able to reflect upon it as the problem, situation, or action unfolds.

Reflection comprises five steps (Dewey, 1933). First, one experiences perplexity, confusion, and doubt due to the nature of the situation. The second step involves conjecture, anticipation, and tentative interpretation of the current state's component elements. During this stage there is an examination of the meanings and consequences that the situation holds for the person who is reflecting, or for those affected by future actions. Third, one explores and analyzes the situation in order to clarify and define the problem. During the fourth step, the questioner forms and elaborates upon strategies for dealing with the situation. The fifth step is the decision to do something in order to attain the desired result—that is, to take *reflective action*.

Kolb (1984) tendered a similar set of stages that characterize the reflective process. First, an individual has some sort of an experience. Afterward, it is brought to the forefront of one's mind to consider the feelings, ideas, and behaviors associated with the experience, often in dialogue with others or one's self through journals. This process of in-depth reflection leads one to generalize across

113

experiences and to scrutinize the individual insights and principles revealed. The cycle then begins again in a new situation.

Reflection helps people to engage in observation, questioning, speculation, and self-awareness (de Acosta, 1995). To be thoughtful about one's practice is to be reflective, whereas self-reflection is designed to foster a deeper knowledge of one's self. Augmenting self-knowledge with technical knowledge enables a reflective practitioner and leader to develop the choice rules (or heuristics) needed to deal with the unpredictability of real-world problems. Reflective practitioners and leaders gain courage to act in situations of uncertainty. They also learn to value conflict and to take responsibility for their actions (Schön, 1987).

Bolton (1998) identified three paradoxes that arise when one learns to be a reflective practitioner. First, one must let go of certainty and become comfortable with uncertainty in order to acquire confidence from reflection. Second, one must trust the reflective process while looking for something, even when one does not know what it is one is looking for. Third, one has to begin to act before one knows how to act. For this, an individual must trust that he or she knows the area of practice well enough to be reflective about that practice. To that end, Andrews et al. (1995) maintained that human action that is characterized by reflection consists of authenticity, ethical sensibility, and spirituality, *as well as* the seven features that are characteristic of any human action as set out in Table 2. Following is a description of the three features unique to reflective action.

Transformative Practice: New Pathways to Leadership

Authenticity

Authenticity, or a commitment to be true to one's self, personality, spirit, and character is an intriguing component of RHA. Authentic leaders engage in the profound task of avoiding self-deception and revealing hidden agendas, because doing so unveils what is really going on and illuminates expanded possibilities. To be authentic is to be genuine, trustworthy, and reflective. Authentic leaders are courageous, passionate, and hopeful because they face reality as it is, look for common ground among diversity, and embrace the fact that life can be difficult and full of uncertainties. Authentic individuals examine both themselves and their relationships within the community of other human beings. By acting authentically, one can strive for a more humane future for the world and its citizens (Andrews et al., 1995).

Andrews et al. (1995) set out seven C's of authenticity as a way to judge if one is being authentic within a leadership role:

1. *Correspondence* — Authenticity is only achieved when the intention to act is followed by tangible action.
2. *Consistency* — "Walk the talk" captures the element of consistency, which indicates that action is connected to meaning. Those who are authentic do what they say others should do. They also mean and live what they say.
3. *Coherence* — Coherence describes actions that are effectively, synergistically combined. In other words, one action is linked to others in a way that ensures internal consistency.
4. *Concealment* — All aspects of an action, whether positive or negative, must be revealed to achieve

authenticity. Bad news cannot be concealed.
5. *Conveyance*—Authentic leaders communicate and transmit thoughts and actions in a way that assures openness and depth in each future exchange of ideas. They take responsibility for their dialogue through conveyance.
6. *Comprehensiveness*—To embrace this element of authenticity, one's frame of action must be expanded by embracing the full depth and breadth of the meaning that is taken from dialogue.
7. *Convergence*—Authentic leaders seek common ground, making it easier to bridge differences.

A lack of authenticity in leadership can emerge for several reasons. First, people may feel disconnected from others and from important social institutions like community, church, school, and work. Second, they may question the societal validity of institutions like the economy, government, organized religion, and even the family. Third, people who invent their own reality instead of facing the truth of daily life cannot be true to themselves and are therefore incapable of being authentic. This type of virtual reality and escapism is especially prevalent now, made possible by the advancement of computer technology, consumerism, telecommunications, and transportation. Fourth, a shift away from people-based activity toward information-based activity leads to inauthentic leadership, as does a tendency towards relativism, which is the fifth factor that mitigates authenticity (Andrews et al., 1995). Relativism indicates that one values functional information and accepts or conforms to societal norms and standards without critiquing them. It

Transformative Practice: New Pathways to Leadership

involves a desire for short-term advantage and a quick fix and leads people to shun responsibility for their actions. People who do not hold themselves accountable tend to seek immediate gratification and strive for self-interest at the expense of their peers and their environment. Relativism teaches that everything is relative and only useful for a moment. It gives everyone license to do their own thing and to value individualism over collectivity (Schneider, 1994).

Leadership cannot happen without action, nor can it happen unless the person who is acting is doing so authentically. Several key factors prevent people from being authentic: disconnection from the organization and its members; questions about the viability of the organization; frailty or weakness of shared purposes; a tendency towards relativism, or judging things based upon internal prejudices rather than objective qualities; and living in an invented reality instead of facing the reality of daily life without hypocrisy or pretense. An authentic community has an enduring future that features shared mutual respect, shared power in dialogue over collective interests, equitable and adequate distribution systems, adequate resources, and ecological diversity and survival. One must be empowered to be authentic, and one must engage in personal growth and development by attempting to understand oneself, by using wise judgment, and by understanding others through active listening.

Listening authentically can affirm the legitimacy of another's way of viewing the world, and can help others to let go of the defenses that protect their worldviews. A leader must be open to changing his or her own

Transformative Practice: New Pathways to Leadership

point of view to take this approach. Additionally, one has to let curiosity guide listening instead of being guided by an effort to find fault or errors. Authentic leaders must accept that there are no built-in, expected answers. They must also hone the critical thinking skills that are necessary to identify facts, ideas, and relationships between them. This skill differs greatly from that needed to seek others' values, opinions, and positions on a given issue. The latter requires strong value reasoning to facilitate active listening.

Ethical Sensibility

To be sensible is to take action marked by awareness, reason, perception, good judgment, and prudence. To be ethical means to act in accordance with principles of good or right conduct. Ethical sensibility, then, refers to leadership and actions that embrace responsibility and accountability, justice and fairness of process, freedom (potential and possibilities), and an attention to and care of one's existence and situation (Andrews et al., 1995).

Andrews et al. (1995) described the difficulty involved in attaining reflective human action and leadership shaped by sensible, ethical actions. They explain that it "takes tremendous courage to choose to act based on principles of human dignity and respect, to be honest with yourself, to recognize rationalizations that keep you from living true to yourself, to stand up for the principles in which you believe, and to act for the common good" (p. 33). Ethical sensibility obviously involves a concern for ethics in the form of right versus wrong, duties and obligations, rights and responsibilities. One's behavior is judged ethical

Transformative Practice: New Pathways to Leadership

if it adheres to the following five principles:
1. **Value for life**—One's actions must unfold in a way that does not harm human life;
2. **Goodness or rightness**—One's behavior must adhere to the principle of the greatest good for the greatest number;
3. **Justice or fairness**—One must assure equality of treatment and fair distribution of benefits and burdens;
4. **Truth-telling or honesty**—One must base action on truth; and
5. **Individual freedom**—One must assure the right of self-determination (Mitstifer, 1989).

To be sensitive to the ethical right or wrongness of one's behavior, one must act with courage. This means facing hardship resolutely, with unwavering and unshakeable firmness. An ethically sensible leader takes action based on principles of human dignity and is honest with his or herself. Ethical sensitivity allows leaders to recognize rationalizations that are designed to keep one from being "in the gap," and it gives people the strength to stand up for their principles and to act in public places for the common good.

Spirituality

Individuals whose authentic leadership is grounded in courage believe that each of their actions will contribute to increased well-being and improved quality of life for all those they meet, touch, and serve. This sense of spirituality is the component of RHA leadership that helps each person to feel connected to the world and other people, and it fosters the call to contribute to something larger than one's self (Andrews et al., 1995). It challenges people to take

119

Transformative Practice: New Pathways to Leadership

responsibility for themselves in concert with others as they build a global commonwealth worthy of the best that humans have to offer each other and nature. Spirit is the element that ties each person to the larger world (Terry, 1993).

To clarify, one's soul is personal and one's spirit is universal. This distinction is important because one pre-requisite for being a reflective leader is respect for and faith in one's inner self (Bolton, 1998). In order to engage in authentic, ethical, and spiritual leadership for the betterment of all, each person must consciously recognize the soul and the non-physical dimensions of being human. The soul is one's personal substance, or the essence of one's inner self beyond the material and physical dimensions of life. Those who come to terms with their inner selves become empowered to expand their compassion and energy to the needs of others (Zukav, 1989). A healthy, individual human spirit enables leaders to meet professional goals and to practice using reflective human action. In other words, authentic leaders engage in a spiritual form of leadership that strives to better the human condition worldwide.

Leadership Lessons from the New Sciences

Andrews et al. (1995) also drew from Wheatley's (1999) work on the new sciences of the 21st century, specifically living systems, chaos theory, and quantum physics. In fact, insights from Wheatley's musings are the foundations for the principles of RHA (Andrews et al., 1995). The information in the next section comes from McGregor (2004).

Living Systems

Wheatley (1999) utilized a living systems approach

Transformative Practice: New Pathways to Leadership

as she challenged readers to stop each day while in a natural environment to ask, "What is it that a ____(fill in the blank) can teach me about leadership?" It could be a stream (pp. 17-18), an anthill, a spider web, a bird, a hornet's nest, a tree, or a rock. She offered an interpretation of how leadership looks from a living systems perspective. She argued that we need more openness because today's world is impossible to pin down. Ironically, this openness leads to more order. She continued with the profound and discomfiting insight that chaos is a necessary place to dwell.

We must trust that new insights will appear in this chaotic state, and we must believe that we are self-organizing beings capable of change. A stable but open state is a concept that is foreign to the old science, which assumes that everything wears down, the center cannot hold, and all processes grind to a halt. In the new science, an ability to remain steady while open is born from a deep stabilizing center where we know who we are, what we need to do, and where we are confident that we are not acting alone. As we mature and develop self-knowledge, we become more adept at this deeper core stability. Over time, the internal dynamics of the system begin to dominate instead of the outside influences. Because we are partners with the system, we gain personal autonomy from the system. The more freedom we have to self-organize, the more order we have. The system and persons co-evolve over time. Persons leading from this science strongly believe in keeping themselves off balance so that they can change and grow through an open exchange with the world. It is then that leaders can defy normal expectations and move people to new states of disequilibrium,

Transformative Practice: New Pathways to Leadership

confident that a deeper stability serves as their foundation.

Chaos Theory

In the old science, chaos and disorder are seen as signs of deep trouble in the system. Not so in the new sciences. Wheatley (1999) explained that chaos theory proposes a new relationship between order and chaos where the two are mirror images of each other. Order is created through chaos, through the processes of fluctuation, change, and disturbance. To illustrate, imagine two floor mirrors facing each other. As one mirror reflects off the other, disturbances occur that lead to growth, as evidenced by the dance between the two images. Neither mirror is the dancer that leads the dance because they are both necessary for the existence of the dance. What follows are invisible footsteps on the floor between the mirrors. These footprints in dust are the patterns that reflect order. Chaos theory is all about patterns and complexity. It appreciates that autonomous interactions, like those that occur between dancers, lead to complex structures. The shape that chaos takes comes from the familiar processes of input and feedback, creating newness and potential. This is a powerful way for someone to approach leadership. Chaos is order without predictability, and this concept is very different from that of the old sciences, which perceived order as predictable, controllable, and consistent.

This new science perspective does not create order through organizational charts and job descriptions. These tools are perhaps analogous to the wooden frames of the mirrors in the previous example. Instead, we take direction from the self-growth that occurs while dancing the

Transformative Practice: New Pathways to Leadership

dance. The wooden frame's style may change over time as new organizational charts or job descriptions are implemented, but the dance remains constant as it yields new patterns, partners, and discoveries. We find order in the chaos. We come to welcome chaos because we know it will lead to personal growth, evolution, and a new order.

In summary, change creates chaos defined as a lack of order or regular arrangements. We self-organize, or reorganize, when we accept chaos and seek solutions to the lack of order. This reorganization leads to renewal. We do not try to maintain the old order but instead enter into trustful, sharing relationships with others who possess the same vision and relevant information; together we create a new order.

The metaphorical footsteps in the dust are the evidence of personal change that results from the dance through chaos to order. We cannot engage in this dance without relationships, because it takes energy to dance. The new science explains that power is energy, or more precisely, power is the capacity to generate energy through our relationships. We cannot have power without relationships; because power is energy, it needs to grow. Whether the power we generate is negative or positive depends upon the nature of the relationships. This is also a powerful insight for leaders. It means that leaders must manage relationships in such a way that there is always positive energy for the dance, because this energy leads to personal growth, potential, and more change.

Quantum Physics

Quantum physics allows us to see that everything is connected. As individuals engage in these power dances, these relationships, it becomes obvious that each single act of leadership is invisibly connected to another set of dancers. The entire dance floor is full and all are part of one dance. Leaders can take courage from knowing that the impact of an act is not equivalent to its size but to the collective impact of all of these acts. "We work where we are, with the system we know, the one we can get our arms around" (Wheatley, 1999, p. 44). We each act independently, yet we have a collective impact on the system. This is not the same as incremental change. It is called a quantum leap, and it is the abrupt and discontinuous change through which the entire system invisibly creates visible conditions.

In conclusion, Wheatley (1999) discussed life's capacity to change, adapt, and grow. She suggested that (a) participation is the nature of our reality, (b) we have to focus on relationships, and (c) information is the basis for participatory relationships. (d) This information must have meaning for us, and it must be free to circulate and find new partners and (e) we have to be free to use information in a way that makes sense to us, so we can do what needs to be done. As we do all of this, (f) we will be self-reflective and reach new levels of insight and growth. We will find order in the chaos and be freed.

Principles of RHA Leadership

In light of this rich description of living systems, quantum physics, and chaos theory (Wheatley, 1999), Andrews et al. (1995) developed the following four principles for RHA leadership:

1. *Accept chaos*—Despite new and chaotic information, we have an unerring ability to

Transformative Practice: New Pathways to Leadership

find order, leading to the personal ability to change and renew;
2. *Share information* — People need to share information to find creative, consensual solutions. Information embodies the invisible workings of creativity, the primary life force of the universe. It must be shared, not hoarded;
3. *Embrace vision* — Leaders derive clarity, purpose, and a sense of direction from shared values and a vision; and,
4. *Develop relationships* — Leaders grow and construct themselves through relationships because nothing is known except in relation to persons, ideas, and events.

In summary, order will come from chaos for those who stay with their commitment to sharing information, developing relationships, and gaining consensus of vision.

New Understanding of Chaos

To elaborate, change creates chaos, defined as a lack of order or regular arrangements. Chaos is perceived as messy confusion, the turmoil of cluttered disarray, and a snarled and scrambled disorganization; yet, chaos is a recognizable step in the transition to a new state. By accepting this notion with confidence and a firm belief in one's own power, each individual can reach new levels of understanding. This is especially true for those who stop looking at the component parts and, instead, stand back to watch the system unfold over time. These individuals expect and embrace chaos instead of being surprised when disorder emerges. It is also important to accept that organizations are not permanent structures, and to know that sometimes people must change in order to function within the emerging structure. To

Transformative Practice: New Pathways to Leadership

transform, each person must let go and pass through the darkness of chaos, confident in the knowledge that chaos leads to order.

New Understanding of Information

Because information is a source of order, it must be shared, not hoarded. Information nourishes an organization because it has the power to aid adaptation and development in an ever-evolving setting, and because it leads to creative, consensual solutions. Withholding information leads to distrust, lack of resiliency, and an inability to participate. A sense of community and belonging can be nurtured when information is handled correctly, wherein persons sense that they are part of something bigger. The strength and potentialities that emerge are life giving, and a vision grows out of the ongoing conversations. For the vision to fully flourish, however, each participant must believe that everyone else has something to contribute to these conversations.

Leading in the Moment

Leadership requires a willingness to "be in the moment," along with consciousness of the gap between being stimulated by something and responding to it (see Table 3). Leading happens in the gap. Those who are aware of their own behavior while in "the gap" can see who they are being as they are being it. In part, this awareness stems from knowing one's value system. Such knowledge enables participants to differentiate between authentic commitments and things they are merely interested in doing if it is convenient. An awareness of principles helps individuals to know whether their commitments are in line with their value system — is it interesting or is it a

Transformative Practice: New Pathways to Leadership

commitment? If it is the former, participants can become distracted and the action's completion can be sabotaged. Commitment is required in order to act authentically as the genuine, unquestionable "self" free from pretense or hypocrisy.

Indeed, authentic leaders must notice who they are "being" in a given situation and ask, "Am I acting like the person I really want to be?" Framing an issue is central to authentic leadership, so leaders must continually ask, "What is really going on?" Each person must frame the issue instead of blaming or finding fault with an issue or person. We must become rich resources to one another; so shutting others out is not the answer. Once the issue is framed, the intervening solution becomes automatic (see Table 2). From an RHA

Table 3: Stimuli, the gap, and a response—Leading happens in the gap

Stimuli	The Gap	Response
Things that prompt and encourage a response.	♦ Your potential ♦ Your spirit ♦ Your imagination ♦ Your conscience ♦ Sense of rightness and decency ♦ Your self-awareness, perception, and consciousness; taking into account, noting, observing ♦ Your independent will ♦ Power (free from influence) to make choices, set goals, and act upon them firmly, in spite of opposition or difficulty	Something spoken or written, or an action that is taken in reaction to a stimulus.

Transformative Practice: New Pathways to Leadership

perspective, we must be able to think in different ways about the same thing, at the same time. We need others to help us, because leading in the gap is difficult.

Self-Knowledge

Leadership calls for authentic action "in the commons." Each leader must engage in reflective action in public places while living in the gap and being who he or she wants to be at all times. Taking action as an RHA leader means having obligations, and one of the most significant of these obligations is self-knowledge. Why do you behave as you do? What are the roots of your behaviors, and how do these influence your current actions, values, and beliefs? What are your strengths and weaknesses? What makes you unique? Are your actions in line with your values and guiding life principles? Do you have a vision, and do you live it based on your values? Have you formed a mental image of what and how you want to be? What is your unique purpose in this life? Are you satisfied at the end of each day? Do you see yourself alone or in relation with others?

Creativity

Finally, RHA leadership requires creativity and innovation, each of which arises from ongoing circles of exchange where information is not just accumulated and stored but created. Knowledge is generated anew from connections that were not there before, and these connections evolve through continuing interaction with others in the organization or profession. Information is shared and created jointly rather than stored or hoarded for future use and personal gain. The more this happens, the more numerous the possibilities and the more creative the results.

Transformative Practice: New Pathways to Leadership

As human beings, we must be creative by expressing ourselves through forms of art, dance, stories, and other outlets that develop external, concrete forms to represent the inner soul. RHA would have us take time to stop, notice our thoughts, and engage with them. Stretching the imagination by forming mental images can lead to surprise and discovery. We must also pay attention to the things, people, and ideas that perplex, intrigue, and attract us to know if we wish to pursue them further by engaging more deeply. Often, this engagement leads to insights that solve dilemmas. This focus comes during the creative pause, and it often leads to innovative, vanguard actions.

Final Thoughts

Transformative practice involves fostering personal, internal changes so that practice can change. The RHA approach provides a profound model for leadership that is genuine and sustainable. This approach to leadership focuses on relationships, a respect for the power of information, and new understandings of chaos and order as it pushes thinking beyond the boundaries of the old sciences. New metaphors define a different way to practice that involves reflection, authenticity, and ethical sensibilities. Leaders are urged to stand in *the gap* between a stimulus and a response and to know, deep inside, that this is where true leadership happens. Leadership hinges on potential, spirit, consciousness, and autonomy.

Individuals must find a new respect for the place of spirituality in their leadership in order to see themselves as self-organizing leaders instead of relying on outside sources to tell

Transformative Practice: New Pathways to Leadership

them what to do, when, and how. RHA leaders find a level of comfort in being kept off balance, because they know that is how things change. They understand that disequilibrium is all right because they are solidly grounded in their inner stability, or their self-knowledge, spirituality, and ethics. RHA leaders do not shy away from uncertainty because they know that chaos leads to order. They do not rely upon organizational charts for direction. Instead, they foster the self-growth that stems from patterns, partners, and the new discoveries derived from trusting and sharing relationships. Such leaders strive for power through people, appreciating that power is energy that must be continually renewed.

RHA leaders draw strength from the knowledge that the impact of one act does not equate to the size of the act. Instead, it correlates to the collection of many single acts, and to the strength of working together. RHA leaders are committed to actions because they are in line with their value systems. Finally, RHA leaders have a deep respect for many ways of knowing because more creative and innovative modes of practice stem from this approach to leadership, which is truly a transformative approach to practice in the profession.

References

Andrews, F., Mitstifer, D., Rehm, M., & Vaughn, G. (1995). *Leadership: Reflective Human Action - A professional development module*. East Lansing, MI: Kappa Omicron Nu.

Andrews, F., Mitstifer, D., Rehm, M., & Vaughn, G. (2001). *Leadership: Reflective Human Action online supplemental text*. East Lansing, MI: Kappa Omicron Nu. Available at http://www.kon.org/rha_online_files/rha_online2.htm

Bolton, G. (1998). *Writing as a reflective practitioner with wisdom* [Online]. Available:

Transformative Practice: New Pathways to Leadership

http://www.shef.ac.uk/uni/projects/wrp/rpwrite.html

de Acosta, M. (1995). Journal writing in service-learning. *Michigan Journal of Community Service-Learning, 2*, 141-149.

Dewey, J. (1933). *How we think*. New York: Heath and Co.

Kolb, D. A. (1984). *Experiential learning*. Toronto, ON: Prentice Hall.

Jackson, O. R. (1990). *Dignity and solidarity: An introduction to peace and justice education*. Chicago, IL: Loyola University Press.

McGregor, S. L. T. (2001). *Leadership for the human family: Reflective human action for a culture of peace*. Retrieved February 22, 2005 from http://www.kon.org/leadership/peace.html

McGregor, S. L. T. (2004). Leadership and the new science. *International Journal of Consumer Studies, 28*(3), 312-313.

Schneider, R. (1994). Ideology and family change. *Canadian Home Economics Journal, 44* (1), 5-7.

Schön, D. A. (1987). *Educating the reflective practitioner*. San Francisco: Jossey Bass.

Stratton, S., & Mitstifer, D. (2001). *Reflective human action: Introduction and course syllabus* at http://www.kon.org/rha_online_files/rha_online.htm

Terry, R. W. (1993). *Authentic leadership*. San Francisco: Jossey-Bass.

van Manen, M. (1995). On the epistemology of reflective practice. *Teachers and teaching: Theory and practice, 1*(1), 33-50. (see also http://www.phenomenologyonline.com/max/epistpractice.htm

Wheatley, M. (1999). *Leadership and the new science*. San Francisco: Berrett-Koehler

Zukav, G. (1989). *The seat of the soul*. New York: Simon & Schuster (Fireside).

Transformative Practice: New Pathways to Leadership

Transformative Practice: New Pathways to Leadership

Chapter 7: Leadership Responsibilities of Professionals*

Dorothy I. Mitstifer

This chapter introduces a leadership development model that raises the question: Leadership for what? Leadership is about going somewhere—personally and in concert with others in an organization.[1] Although leadership, especially position (elected or appointed) leadership, is often discussed in terms of leader qualities and skills, the matter of leadership as a responsibility of each professional receives little attention. Organizations and programs do not flourish with one leader in a group. Thus, more attention has to be paid to the definition of leader as anyone willing to help (Wheatley, 2005). Leadership is not about position only, but about taking responsibility as a member of a group (whether 2-person or 60-person) to share leadership for the organization's well-being.

Despite the investments in time, money, and energy, leadership development programs in many organizations are piecemeal, focused on aspects in isolation (Ready, 2004). They may offer the latest competency program, an up-to-date performance management system, a sophisticated assessment instrument, the latest electronic learning package, and/or a program built around available speakers and facilitators known to the leadership development committee. These approaches can focus on local issues to the

---

*Earlier version published in *Human Sciences Working Papers Archives*, http://www.kon.org/hswp/index.html.
[1] Footnotes for Chapter 7 begin on page 158.

133

Transformative Practice: New Pathways to Leadership

exclusion of broad, sweeping issues of importance to the organization's national or international perspective. Then, too, we live in a world that is different and changing so fast that earlier approaches just don't serve the current and future needs of organizations.

Each organization needs to learn how to grow its own leaders, but it needs a theoretical framework to accomplish this worthy objective. The South American poet Machados declared, "The road is your footsteps, nothing else" (Wheatley, 2005, p. 43). The leadership development model described in this chapter is intended to guide your footsteps in a direction that clarifies your personal and professional journey and shares responsibility among colleagues for the well-being of your organization. The following sections will discuss the basic components of a leadership development model, a leadership theory, issue framing, and a concluding section that ties everything together to form a comprehensive approach to leadership development.

Basic Components of the Reflective Human Action Leadership Development Model

If the premise is accepted that an organization cannot succeed without position leadership and group members sharing leadership responsibilities, it is then incumbent upon each organization to establish an intentional program to develop leadership skills at all levels. Presently, both pre-professionals and professionals experience leadership development in a haphazard manner. In some ways, leadership of a profession is more important than content to carry on its mission and practice. The proposed Reflective Human Action (RHA) Leadership Development Model (Figure 1) focuses on (a) strength-

Transformative Practice: New Pathways to Leadership

ening self-awareness, (b) developing relationships and teamwork, (c) understanding alliances and political realities, and (d) understanding the elements of a promising future of the organization, coupled with (e) Reflective Human Action (RHA) leadership theory as its foundation and (f) framing as a communications tool. It is hypothesized that the model will enable individuals to assume leadership responsibilities as professionals. At its base this model states the philosophy that underlies leadership; the next level includes the basic components of leadership development that are coupled with theory and with competency in framing—all leading to the overall objective: organizational leadership. The following section explains the four basic components of the Model.

Organizational Leadership

with Framing as a Communications Tool

| *Principles:* Accept Chaos; Share Information; Develop Relationships; Embrace Vision | *Core Features:* Authenticity; Ethical Sensibitlity Spirituality; Features of Action |

Coupled with
Reflective Human Action Theory

| Strengthening Self-Awareness | Developing Relationships & Teamwork | Understanding Alliances and Political Realities | Understanding the Elements of a Promising Future |

Focus on Basic Components

Leadership is not about position only, but about taking responsibility as a member of a group to share leadership for its well-being. Focus is on a belief in people—their capacity, energy, creativity, and committment; on coherence, not control; and on taking action.

Figure 1: Reflective Human Action (RHA) Leadership Development Model. © 2005 by Dorothy I. Mitstifer. Used by permission. All rights reserved.

Transformative Practice: New Pathways to Leadership

I. Strengthening self-awareness

People live in their own, often untested, world of self-generating beliefs (Ross, 1994). These beliefs are the product of past experience and inferences from observations. Argyris (1990) labeled this phenomenon the "ladder of inference," a mental pathway based upon observable data and experiences and composed of the data selected, the meanings assigned, the assumptions made, conclusions drawn, beliefs adopted, and actions taken. If all of these components are unquestioned and untested, these inferences may lead to misguided beliefs. But one's self-awareness can be strengthened by reflection (becoming more aware of one's own thinking and reasoning), advocacy (making one's thinking and reasoning more visible to others), and inquiry (inquiring into other's thinking and reasoning) (adapted from Ross, 1994, p. 245).

From abstract to concrete – Self-awareness can be defined as the ability to become the object of one's own attention, to evaluate the self. It requires the ability to reflect—to step back and take a hard look at one's information, perspectives, assumptions, conclusions, beliefs, and actions. Writing or journaling may be useful in getting in touch with self, as can mental imagery, which offers the opportunity to see oneself as seen by others. Another method involves entering a quiet natural setting or following a guided discovery process to free one to look inward. Feedback from someone with whom you have an open, trusting relationship could also be helpful. The metaphor of a lens might be beneficial in looking at self. What lens am I using to look at self? A telephoto lens could help to pick out a few more elements, or a

Transformative Practice: New Pathways to Leadership

wide-angle lens could help me see the big picture. Some questions might include: what influences do my style and habits exert on others? What more information could I gather? What are alternative perspectives and assumptions? What impacts do additional information and alternative perspectives and assumptions have on conclusions and beliefs? How might my actions change with more insight?

Ross (1994, p. 245) suggested the following questions that can assist a group in testing beliefs:
- What are the observable data behind that statement?
- Does everyone agree on what the data are?
- Can you run through your reasoning? What is the basis of your interpretation?
- When you said _____, did you mean _____?

The ladder of inference is a tool for examining one's own beliefs and actions. It contributes to a healthy climate for reflection in organizational matters.

II. Developing relationships and teamwork

By definition, collaborative leadership within an organization requires that one's self-knowledge be applied in interaction with others to develop relationships and teamwork. Collaboration is a worthy skill because it provides many benefits: a unified approach, effective internal decision making, reduced costs through shared resources, and more creative outcomes (Weiss & Hughes, 2005). However, collaboration is not easily achieved. To improve the team's chance of success, the issue of conflict must be addressed. Differences in perspective, competencies, access to information, and strategic focus cause conflict, so acknowledgement and development of processes to manage it are necessary

137

Transformative Practice: New Pathways to Leadership

precursors to effective collaboration. By exploring all of the differences, conflict situations produce benefits by providing new insights and possibilities for improving organizational decisions and outcomes.

Effective collaboration requires both individual and network expertise. Connectivity gained through networks produces synergistic outcomes, but it has its downside as well: countless meetings can drain time and energy. For this reason, there is a "need to develop a strategic, sophisticated view of collaboration . . . ." (Cross, Liedtka, & Weiss, 2005). The appropriate degree of connectivity must be determined in order to achieve the specific results required of the organization. Some tasks will require all players while others can be assigned to specific networks, all the while maintaining openness and communication to ensure understanding and transparency.

From abstract to concrete – Teamwork relies first of all upon trust, meaning that the group must firmly rely upon the integrity, ability, and character of team members. Trust develops through

♦ **sharing**: speaking and listening about personal events and feelings;
♦ **vulnerability**: being perceived as having the capacity to err and willingness to acknowledge it;
♦ **loyalty**: making a commitment to goals and other members;
♦ **accepting others**: welcoming the uniqueness of others.

Thus team building requires time to get to know each other, in informal and fun environments (family picnics, team sports events, day-long trips) or within a more formal

Transformative Practice: New Pathways to Leadership

team-building program. Many collaborative efforts fall prey to groupthink, in which team members converge upon agreement regardless of quality. To guard against this phenomenon, the following team member roles must be functioning: knowledge contributor, process observer, collaborator, people supporter, challenger, listener, mediator, and gatekeeper.

An effective team will create strategies, policies, and structures to guide its work. It will identify vision, values, and goals to respond to the perceived need, and will develop action plans to achieve the goals, including a timetable and assignment of tasks according to expertise. Successful collaborations will also monitor and evaluate the implementation, use feedback to refine plans if necessary, communicate progress, and celebrate accomplishments. High performance is gained through shared leadership, alignment of function and purpose of the team, focus on tasks, shared responsibility, innovation and creativity, diversity of ideas and expertise, effective problem solving, open and honest communication, and responsiveness to needs and opportunities. In contrast, teams need to be aware of potential pitfalls and must prepare strategies to deal with problems if they arise. Teams can prevent members working independently or at cross-purposes by making sure that the vision and goals accomplish personal and team goals. Turf battles that slow or stop project progress may require open communication regarding the conflict and redistribution of roles and responsibilities. Negative, manipulative, or secretive interactions probably indicate the need for more attention to team-building

Transformative Practice: New Pathways to Leadership

activities as well as open communication.

Internal team leaders (appointed or elected by team members) know that you can't force collaboration, but you can expect it. Expecting collaborative behavior requires discipline and dogged persistence. When leaders "consistently ask questions that remind people of those expectations, they tend to get what they expect" (Linden, 2003, p. 47). A collaborative leader should be able to

- articulate the project's purpose in a way that excites others.
- be an effective convener: get the appropriate people to the table and keep them there.
- help the participants see their common interests and the benefits possible through joint effort.
- generate trust.
- help the participants design a transparent, credible process.
- assist the participants in win-win negotiations to meet three related interests (needs of each partner, needs of the product they are creating, and needs of the relationships involved).
- make relationship building a priority for the group.
- see that the effort has a senior champion [external leader].
- help everyone to engage in collaborative problem solving and to make creative use of their diverse viewpoints when differences arise.
- celebrate small successes; share credit widely.
- provide confidence, hope, and resilience. (Linden, 2003, pp. 42-44)

The above tasks must be accompanied by the disposition to have persistence, energy, and resolve; passion about achieving a collaborative outcome; the ability to pull others rather than push them in a collaborative direction; and the ability to think systemically and see the interconnections (Linden, 2003, p. 45).

It should be recognized that involving persons in a group activity does not make a team. Equally important is the realization that teamwork may not always seem efficient, but it is likely to be most effective.

III. Understanding alliances and political realities

Relations between and among people are often uncertain, fluid, and complex. These relationships often include alliances formed around the values and interests held by a core of like-minded individuals. Thus, an organization needs to examine the alliances in the group to find the mutual points of agreement upon which to build trust. Although these alliances may be political realities, it isn't useful to label their activities as political. So-called political intelligence, however, is needed to identify how relationships are likely to affect success (Ciampa, 2005). Political skills include the use of power and influence to enhance or protect interests. To that end, group members must be encouraged to go out of their way to help the group to be sensitive to various points of view and to be respectful of diverse spheres of interest. Efforts need to be made to ensure that interactions and group processes are transparent so that trust can build.

From abstract to concrete – Politics is the procedural dimension, the art and science of making choices about the "means to the end," in every human equation. Although the end can't justify all means, some actions dismissed as "political" might be attributable to misunderstandings or miscom-

munication. Because politics stems from a diversity of interests, it is in the best interests of the organization to explore the processes by which people engage in politics (Ratzburg, n.d.):

- Where the activity takes place—inside or outside the organization
- The direction of influence—vertically or laterally in the organization
- The legitimacy of the action—generally accepted differences or threats

Political behavior is often related to the investment individuals have in the organization, the alternatives they feel they can access, the level of trust, and their perceived efficacy in influencing the group. Ambiguous goals, scarce resources, irrational decision-making processes, and organizational change can also contribute. Limiting factors are related to open communication, reduction of uncertainty, and increased awareness of the issues and activities of the organization.

Those who effectively use political intelligence accurately "read" political currents but don't label them that way, recognize how relationships affect issues and decisions, engage others to go out of their way to help, and don't seem self-serving. Holbeche (2004) described constructive political behavior as

- establishing effective relationships
- understanding individual agendas
- creating win-win situations
- acting in a principled way
- building strong support for constructive ideas
- building a personal reputation
- treating everyone fairly
- influencing others rather than directly using power

The use of power and influence is critical in examining political

Transformative Practice:  New Pathways to Leadership

realities. Power in the form of an expenditure of energy toward action—the decision, the passion, the self-determination, and the will—is the invisible spirit behind commitment (Terry, 1993). To conduct a power audit, an organization would first check the energy level of the group. Is it lively and engaged, or is it flat and dull? Is there anger, joy, frustration, or hostility? Are participation and involvement high or low? Second, are all the critical stakeholders represented? Third, what is the capacity to make and keep decisions? Power is an essential part of action and of leadership. In order for power to be dynamic, flowing, and changing over time, it should be examined under the following themes (Terry, 1993, p. 74):

♦ Power requires a prevailing sense . . . that energy, whether individual or collective, is legitimate and appropriate.
♦ Power requires a deep sense of personal or collective self-determination.
♦ Power involves outward expression.
♦ Power translates into institutional forms such as reflection, debate, voting, and consensus making.
♦ Power requires current political information and skills in order to assess and engage in a current context.
♦ Power depends on retrospective ownership of past actions.

Positive alliances are based upon effective communication, treatment of allies as equals, professionalism, and time spent in listening and strategizing. Other behaviors that contribute to the development of alliances include (Heathfield, n.d.):

♦ producing high quality work
♦ choosing "battles" wisely
♦ keeping promises

Transformative Practice: New Pathways to Leadership

- resolving conflicts and disputes immediately
- being an ally—giving credit and support
- talking directly to an ally if you have a problem

By understanding alliances and political realities and using constructive political behavior, leaders can make things happen, unblock barriers to change, create buy-in on organizational initiatives, produce greater organizational cohesion, and speed up decision making. But leaders have the responsibility of creating a receptive environment by using persuasion constructively. "Persuasion promotes understanding; understanding breeds acceptance; acceptance leads to action" (Garvin & Roberto, 2005, p. 112).

IV. Understanding the elements of a promising future

Vision, opportunity, and risk could be called the hallmarks for establishing promising futures (Price, 2004). Vision and direction need to be well understood if organizations are to have a clear sense of where they are going, and if they are to focus attention on this vision. With vision, smart choices can be made with the end result in mind. Short-term goals are geared to the larger picture. "Vision allows for a long-term proactive stance—creating what we want—rather than a short-term reactive stance—getting rid of what we don't want" (Blanchard & Stoner, 2004, p. 22).

From abstract to concrete – When pushing the boundaries, there is always an element of risk. In this fast-paced world, we face diversity, contradictions, and complexity. How do we converge our energies to balance the opportunities and risks in the interest of a new vision and excellence? It will be important to find answers

Transformative Practice: New Pathways to Leadership

to such questions as "What is important?" "What is best?" "Who are we impacting?" "What will be the consequences?" A promising future offers these challenges; answers come from looking at current realities and visions, using the data to establish core beliefs, converting beliefs into principles, and proposing practices to implement the beliefs (Donaldson, 2000). With courage and perseverance, an organization's leaders can use these elements to define and recreate the entity for a promising future.

Various strategies or models are available to guide future planning. Scenario thinking (Scearce & Fulton, 2004) clarifies the issues, explores the driving forces of change, synthesizes the driving forces to create scenarios, develops a strategic agenda based on patterns and insights that emerged in the scenarios, and creates a mechanism to monitor shifts in the environment. This process is sometimes called scenario analysis.

Strategic planning models come in various forms. Most of them include a values audit, formulation of mission and vision statements, external scan, a performance audit, a gap analysis, strategic goals, an action plan for strategic direction, a communication process for the plan, a process for monitoring the implementation and continuous environmental surveillance, and evaluation and control (Pfeiffer, Goodstein & Nolan, 1985, 1993, 1998; McNamara, n.d.). Other models include *Preferred Futuring* (Lippitt, 1998), *Future Search* (Weisbord & Janoff, 1995), and *Open Space Technology* (Owen, 1997).

Strategic thinking has gained currency over planning because of the

latter's tendency to be "overly concerned with extrapolation of the present and the past as opposed to focusing on how to reinvent the future" (Lawrence, 1999). Leidka (as cited in Lawrence, 1999) proposed a closed circle model that incorporates both notions: current reality→strategic thinking: disrupting alignment→desired future→strategic planning: creating alignment. The following discussion describes selected salient elements in establishing a promising future.

A *mission statement* describes why your organization exists, its basic purpose. The intent is philosophical; it is a statement about ends—products, outputs, or other effects. The statement must be broad in detailing the mega-end—the difference the organization will make for its beneficiaries. Sub-ends will be developed to reach the mega-end.

Carver (1993, 1997) is unusual in promulgating short mission statements that go straight to the point. Although this approach calls for more rigor, it provides clarity in defining "what good" for "which people" in a long-term perspective. The following checklist measures effectiveness (adapted from Carver, 1993, p. 5):

- Ends, not means
- Effects, not efforts
- Outcomes (nouns), not verbs
- Brevity, not padded paragraphs
- Accuracy, not cosmetics
- Not too broad or too narrow
- Net value added, not endless summary

A *vision statement* includes a significant purpose, a picture of the future, and clear values. Because a purpose is your organization's reason for existence, it must inspire excitement and commitment in order to unleash productive,

Transformative Practice: New Pathways to Leadership

creative energy. A picture of the future should focus on a concrete end result. Clear values describe behavior guidelines for daily decisions. In order to be effective, however, the vision statement must be created through broad dialogue. It must also be communicated often, and it must be lived through daily actions.

> The purpose of a vision statement is to create an aligned organization where everyone is working together toward the same desired ends. The vision provides guidance for daily decisions so that people are moving in the right direction, not working at cross-purposes with one another. (Blanchard & Stoner, 2004, p. 23)

Environmental scanning is the exploration phase of thinking and planning for the future. It plays a significant role in defining the fit between an organization and its external environment, "in light of the mission, organization strengths and limitations, and external challenges and opportunities" (Duttweiler, 2004). Other techniques exist in addition to the commonly used SWOT analysis (strengths, weakness, opportunities, and threats). These alternatives include situational analysis, assets mapping, concept mapping, issue analysis/mapping, stakeholder/political mapping, and SPOT (strengths, problems, opportunities, and threats), among others. The task at hand and the preferences of the planning group are relevant in selecting the appropriate process.

Strategic goals to establish a promising future arise from prioritizing values and needs identified during the strategic thinking and planning process. To ensure follow-through, *action planning* operationally defines each goal: the action steps

147

Transformative Practice: New Pathways to Leadership

describe the *what* and *how*, the *resources* required, *who* is responsible, *when* each step will be completed, and *how* evaluation will be conducted. Action plans help teams to stay organized, coordinate their activities, and keep projects to implement the future on schedule. A simple Excel spreadsheet can be used to display the data. Other alternatives include a Gantt chart to show an overview of tasks. The Gantt displays tasks on one side and columns of weeks, days, or months on the other. Horizontal bars are drawn to indicate the period in which each task will be performed. A PERT chart is a flow diagram of activity boxes to depict tasks.

Although understanding the elements of a promising future is the most important of the four basic components of leadership development, this stage cannot be reached without the other three—self-awareness, healthy relationships and effective teamwork, and political skill. Accomplishing each of these is a tall order. The need for leadership is clear; each organization must decide what it is going to do about it. The four basic components of the RHA Leadership Development Model, in and of themselves, will not ensure excellence because leadership is a multidimensional and multi-layered construct. A comprehensive theory and philosophy is necessary to provide a foundation for leadership.

Leadership Theory

The previous chapter described the theoretical framework of *Reflective Human Action* (Figure 2), a leadership theory and philosophy promulgated by Kappa Omicron Nu, and authored by Frances E. Andrews, Dorothy I. Mitstifer, Marcia Rehm, and Gladys Gary Vaughn (1995). This theory was

based upon the work of Terry (1993) and Wheatley (1994). To recap—the principles for leadership practice are

♦ Accept chaos
♦ Share information
♦ Develop relationships
♦ Embrace vision

and the core features of Reflective Human Action are

♦ Authenticity
♦ Ethical sensibility
♦ Spirituality
♦ Features of action

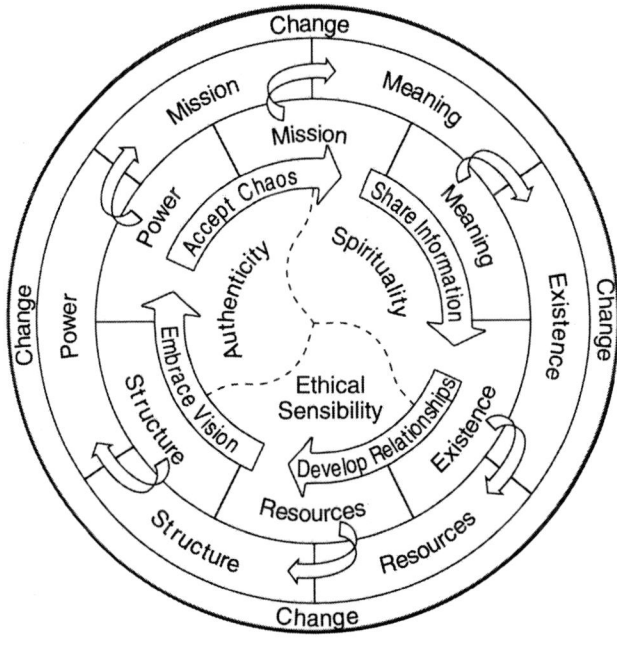

Figure 2: Reflective Human Action Model. © 1995 by Kappa Omicron Nu. Used by permission. All rights reserved.

Transformative Practice: New Pathways to Leadership

These principles and core features are themes that are present throughout the four basic components of leadership development discussed above. Hesselbine (2005, p. 4) succinctly made the case for these themes: "We need leaders who believe and embody in concept, language, and action that leadership is a matter of how to be, not how to do...."

Reflective Human Action is a state-of-the-art comprehensive theoretical framework; its action wheel is an astounding diagnostic tool for naming and framing organizational issues and determining the strategic interventions necessary to address the identified issues. A professional development module and an online free course (www.kon.org/rha_online_files/rha_online2.htm) are available to learn about the leadership theory and for use in self-managed life change.

Issue Framing with Reflective Human Action Theory

"Leadership ... is grounded in the wisdom of knowing what is really happening, which often means moving beyond fixing and managing" (Terry, 2003, p. 34). Leaders need to understand and interpret what is going on in an organization and how individuals should relate to it; these actions define issue framing. The particular means of accomplishing these two tasks has either a beneficial or a negative impact on what is done about the issue or conflict. Thus, in an effective collaborative leadership style, a core skill is the ability to name and frame issues in organizations. This requires a process to learn the concerns people have about an issue; identify the consequences, costs, and benefits associated with various options for action regarding the issue; work through

Transformative Practice: New Pathways to Leadership

inherent conflicts; and find shared direction or common ground for action. Although framing is a hot topic in political circles, it often seeks to *win* the "framing game." In contrast, this skill fulfills a powerful role in groups by evoking greater understanding of diverse perspectives, embracing a wider range of views, and finding intelligent choices about a shared future.

Terry (1993, 2003) made a significant contribution by focusing on the importance in leadership of answering the question of what is really going on. Using the RHA Action Model (Figure 2), the process of framing diagnoses the issues and identifies the interventions. In today's complex world, the deep questions of identity and meaning must be answered by engagement of spirit. Thus leadership must make a lifetime commitment to answer the tough questions of what is really going on. Terry's six features of action—mission, meaning, existence, resources, structure, and power— require the overarching skill of issue framing for fulfillment of human action. Whether or not all features of action have been attended to and are functioning well, the group is united in thinking, being, and doing.

From abstract to concrete – The RHA Action Model facilitates framing. The first step is to exame the dialogue to name and frame it, the next is to use the intervention indicated by the arrow to address the issue. Two cases follow to explain the process.

> *Case 1* - Some of the faculty members in the unit (or members of a student club) are upset. Statements such as "The decisions are already made." "Why doesn't someone just do something?" "Morale is really bad; the wrong people seem to be making decisions." "We can't get

151

Transformative Practice: New Pathways to Leadership

things done. I don't know what's happening." These are cues to the issue of POWER. The intervention should deal with MISSION. There are no shortcuts; mission work is time consuming and hard work. It must involve all members; considerable dialogue about goals—the ends—of the organization is required. What are the outcomes that this organization wants to achieve? What is it in business for? The more the involvement, the more the satisfaction with decisions about mission.

Case 2 - Mildred is a new administrator and she wants to balance the needs of her department with the greater good of the institution. She has determined that before she decides what changes are needed she will interview selected employees to get a feel for their concerns. To her surprise, there seemed to be a theme: "We can't operate; there seems to be too much red tape." "There doesn't seem to be any coordination." I don't know how decisions are made." "I think our department is poorly organized." This feedback indicates that the issue is STRUCTURE; therefore the intervention should deal with POWER—with who provides the energy for action. Examination of the power relations as discussed previously in Component III needs to involve the whole group in conducting a power audit, addressing personal and collective needs and desires, and exploring ways to share power through constructive political behavior.

"All aspects of the model [Action Wheel] are implicitly present in every act. Therefore, all features of action must eventually be addressed in any proposed action" (Terry, 1993, 91-92). Thus, the organization needs to address all features of action; a change in one affects all others. No organization is "fixed" once and for all; the dynamic nature of organizations requires continuous and productive activity to ensure viability over time.

Framing could be described as a commun-

Transformative Practice: New Pathways to Leadership

ication tool for everyone working on an issue or conflict. The objective is to redefine the perspectives, values, and assumptions about issues to become more inclusive and mobilizing to individuals in the group. The social context is created for win/win choices about direction. Communication in the form of conversation is a key element in forging organizational futures. In her book, *Turning to One Another: Simple Conversations to Restore Hope to the Future*, Wheatley (2002, p. 35) noted that

> It is difficult to give up our certainties—our positions, our beliefs, our explanations. These help define us; they lie at the heart of our personal identity. Yet I believe we will succeed in changing this work only if we can think and work together in new ways. Curiosity is what we need. We don't have to let go of what we believe, but we do need to be curious about what someone else believes.

The ability to listen without judgment needs to accompany the curious mind. It isn't the differences that divide; it's judgments that do. Listening for differences will create uncertainty, but "We can't be creative if we refuse to be confused. Change always starts with confusion; cherished interpretations must dissolve to make way for the new" (p. 37). From diversity a group can gain a rich array of ideas and possibilities for finding common ground.

Atlee (n.d.) described several additional communication strategies[2] for framing issues. In all of the processes, inclusion and engagement of diverse people and perspectives produce common ground, with underlying shared needs, spirit, and experience. Even if win/win solutions are not found, the complexity of issues will have been

Transformative Practice: New Pathways to Leadership

uncovered, and participants will have gained an appreciation for the difficultly involved in making some decisions.

Bringing It All Together

The professed intention of this chapter was to describe the RHA Leadership Development Model for developing professional leadership. After the four components of the model were explored and juxtaposed with Reflective Human Action theory, the overarching skill of issue framing was discussed as a communication tool for mobilizing leadership action. When responsibility is widely shared, leadership efforts are successful for at least ten reasons (adapted from Terry, 1993, pp. 286-287):

♦ A consensus is formed around desired outcomes.
♦ No one loses.
♦ Ownership is pooled.
♦ Fear and hope combine to motivate cooperation.
♦ People make things happen.
♦ Non-positional leaders fill key roles.
♦ Reliable information is gathered.
♦ A flexible system of self-direction is used.
♦ Individual talents are tapped.
♦ Individuals with initiative and entrepreneurial spirit are involved.

The RHA Model focuses on a belief in people—their capacity, energy, creativity, and commitment; on coherence, not control; and on taking action. Organizations depend upon these factors to ensure future endurability and viability. Most importantly, organizational endurability depends upon having a model to follow in organizing its leadership development process and upon inviting broad participation and engagement in rethinking, redesigning, and restructuring the organization to achieve

Transformative Practice: New Pathways to Leadership

its mission. Taken together, leadership and broad participation can create a sense of community.

The natural instinct for community, however, does not necessarily lead to organizational strength and endurability. Indeed, various cultures (particularly professional cultures) are increasingly creating specialty islands to protect themselves from difference. Wheatley (2001, 2005) held that this phenomenon could be traced to the mistaken assumption that organizations are machines. For example, the language of *tool, build, drive,* and *reengineer* is characteristically mechanical. A different ideal is surfacing to replace this old model, based upon a view of organizations as adaptive, flexible, self-renewing, resilient, learning, and intelligent. These attributes are found in living systems—self-organizing systems.

Organizations need to adopt characteristics of a self-organizing system and to erase all traces of mechanistic command and control.

> Self-organizing systems have what all leaders crave: the capacity to respond continuously to change. In these systems, change is the organizing force, not a problematic intrusion. Structures and solutions are temporary. Resources and people come together to create new initiatives, to respond to new regulations, to shift the organization's processes. Leaders emerge from the needs of the moment. (Wheatley, 2005, p. 33)

It is the nature of self-organizing systems to be disturbed by outside information, not directed by it. The sense-making capacity comes from within the system. "This explains why organizations reject reports and data that others assume to be obvious and compelling" (p. 37). Thus,

155

Transformative Practice: New Pathways to Leadership

the system (organization) has to develop its own identity—a coherent center and clarity about what sustains the organization through turbulent times. The organization's identity is formed through clarity about vision, mission, and values and a current interpretation of its history, present decisions and activities, and its sense of its future. Such clarity of purpose then enables the organization to reach out to its customers, partners, and others to gather information, develop effective relationships, and demonstrate that its identity truly directs its actions.

When an organization self-organizes as a living system,

> . . . it develops shared understanding of what's important, what's acceptable behavior, what actions are required, and how these actions will get done. It develops channels of commun-ication, networks of workers, and complex physical structures. And as the system develops, new capacities emerge. Looking at this list of what a self-organizing system creates leads to the realization that the system can do for itself most of what [position] leaders have felt was necessary to do to it. (Wheatley, 2005, p. 66)

Lest there is an implication that there is no place for the position leader, organizations do need a chief leader to create a receptive environment for creative thinking and experimentation, support self-organizing responses, provide information and resources, create connections, and keep the focus on what the organization wants to be and what it wants to accomplish. Position leaders also need to coach and develop people, keep the team vision alive, energize with a positive outlook, insist on transparency, make hard decisions

Transformative Practice: New Pathways to Leadership

when necessary, probe and question, inspire risk-taking, and celebrate to recognize contributions (Welch, 2005).

The new worldview of organizations as living systems affects position leaders in profound ways (Wheatley, 2001, pp. 15-19). The following principles guide their work:

- Meaning engages creativity – if we want people to be creative we must uncover meaningful issues.
- Depend on diversity – a mosaic of perspectives comes from identifying differences.
- Involve everybody who cares – the only way to know what will work is to invite everyone into the design process.
- Diversity is the path to unity – a group can come together as it recognizes its mutual interests.
- People will always surprise us – people come together through the act of listening.
- Rely on human goodness – the impossible can be done through creativity, caring, and human will.

The better nature of humans rises, according to Wheatley, because we are beginning to give up treating people as machines.

> We *are* our only hope for creating a future worth working for. We can't go it alone, we can't get there without each other, and we can't create it without relying anew on our fundamental and precious human goodness. (2001, p. 20)

In summary, then, the RHA Leadership Development Model is intended to bring it all together by choreographing the interaction among layers—the philosophy that underlies leadership, the basic components of leadership development, leadership theory, and issue framing—to offer a comprehensive approach

157

Transformative Practice: New Pathways to Leadership

to leadership development. A model is only a beginning for organizational leadership. You are invited to join your colleagues on the journey—one footstep at a time.

Footnotes:

[1]Organization in this chapter refers to all kinds of informal and formal groups: neighborhoods, communities, agencies, professions, institutions, corporations – even families.

[2]Additional communication strategies for framing issues:

National Issues Forum (NIF) and Study Circles – The NIF and Study Circles techniques employ deliberative sessions based on issue books or discussion guides developed in advance by leaders who produce briefings that are unbiased and engaging. These briefings describe the context, some of the underlying issues within the issue, three to five approaches to the issues, arguments pro and con, and notes on the values and trade-offs associated with each approach. When participants can find their own values in the approaches, they can better listen to each other's perspectives and are less likely to be stuck in narrow opinions. See www.nifi.org and www.studycircles.org.

Negotiation and Mediation – Conflict is framed in terms of interests. A moderator helps people clarify and agree on legitimate interests so that the group can work on searching for solutions to embrace all interests. Fisher and Ury's "Getting to Yes" is explained at www.colorado.edu/conflict/peace/example/fish7513.htm.

Nonviolent Communication – Conflict is framed in terms of unmet needs. A facilitator works to clarify the unmet needs through questions, empathic imagination, and reflective listening. See www.co-intelligence.org/P-nonviolentcomm.html.

Dynamic Facilitation – A choice-creating process of framing and reframing evolves dynamically during conversation. Attacks are resolved through questions such as "So, what's your concern?" "What do you think should be done about that?" The conversation continues by charting concerns, possible solutions, problem statements, and data. Framing unfolds through interaction that follows the group's energy and evolving understanding. See www.co-intelligence.org/P-dynamicfacilitation.html.

Consensus Process – An issue is framed and reframed until a new collective frame emerges

from the group. Special attention is paid to ensure that everybody's concerns are adequately addressed. Through this means a final decision will have more wisdom and broad support. See www.co-intelligence.org/P-consensus.html.

References:

Andrews, F. E., Mitstifer, D. I., Rehm, M., & Vaughn, G. G. (1995). *Leadership: Reflective human action - A professional development module*. East Lansing, MI: Kappa Omicron Nu.

Argyris, C. (1990). *Overcoming organizational defenses*. Needham, MA: Allyn & Bacon.

Atlee, T. (n.d.). *Framing issues for battle and collective intelligence*. Retrieved February 26, 2005 from The Co-Intelligence Institute website: www.omplace.com/articles/tom_atlee35.html

Blanchard, J., & Stoner, J. (2004, Winter). The vision thing: Without it you'll never be a world-class organizations. *Leader to Leader, 31*, 21-28.

Carver, J. (1993). Evaluating the mission statement. *Board Leadership, 5*, 1,4-5.

Carver, J. (1997). *Boards that make a difference*, 2nd. ed. San Francisco: Jossey-Bass.

Ciampa, D. (2005, January). Almost ready: How leaders move. *Harvard Business Review Special Issue, 83*(1), 46-53.

Cross, R., Liedtka, J. & Weiss, L. (2005, March). A practical guide to social networks. *Harvard Business Review, 83*(3), 124-132.

Donaldson, G. A. (2000, April). A promising future for every student: Maine invests in secondary school reform. *NASSP Bulletin*.

Duttweiler, M. (2004). *Environmental scanning principles and processes*. Cornell Cooperative Extension. Retrieved June 5, 2005 from http://www.cce.cornell.edu/admin/grogram/documents/scanintr.htm.

Garvin, D. A., & Roberto, M. A. (2005, February). Change through persuasion. *Harvard Business Review, 83*(2), 104-112.

Heathfield, S. M. (n.d.) *Why you need allies at work*. Retrieved June 5, 2005 from http://humanresources.about.com/cs/workrelationships/a/workallies_2.htm

Hesselbine, F. (2005, Winter). *Leader to Leader, 35*, 4-5.

Holbeche, L. (2004). *The power of constructive politics*. Horsham, UK: Roffey Park.

Lawrence, E. (1999). *Strategic thinking: A discussion paper*. Retrieved on June 5, 2005 from http://www.psc-dfp.gc.ca/research/knowledge/strathink_e.htm

Transformative Practice: New Pathways to Leadership

Linden, R. (2003, Summer). The discipline of collaboration. *Leader to Leader, 29,* 41-47.

Lippitt, L. L. (1998). *Preferred futuring.* San Francisco: Berrett-Koehler.

McNamara, D. (n.d.) *Strategic planning (in nonprofit or for-profit organizations).* Retrieved June 5, 2005 from http://www.managementhelp.org/plan_dec/str_plan/str_plan.htm

Owen, H. (1997). *Open space technology: A user's guide.* San Francisco: Berrett-Koehler.

Pfeiffer, J. W., Goodstein, L. D., & Nolan, T. M. (1985). *Understanding Applied Strategic Planning: A Manager's Guide.* San Diego: University Associates, Inc.

Pfeiffer, J. W., Goodstein, L. D., & Nolan, T. M. (1993). *Applied Strategic Planning: How to develop a plan that really works.* New York: McGraw-Hill.

Pfeiffer, J. W., Goodstein, L. D., & Nolan, T. M. (1998). *Applied Strategic Planning: An Introduction.* NewYork: Wiley.

Price, K. (2004, November). Viewpoint. *Bridge Builder.*

Ratzburg, W. H. (n.d.). *Defining organizational politics.* Retrieved June 5, 2005 from http://www.geocities.com/Athens/Forum/1650/htmlpolitc01.html?20054

Ready, D. A. (2004, December). How to grow great leaders. *Harvard Business Review, 82*(12), 93-100.

Ross, R. (1994). The ladder of inference. In P. M. Senge, A. Kleiner, C. Roberts, R. B. Ross, B. J. Smith. *The fifth discipline fieldbook: Strategies and tools for building a learning organization.* New York: Currency/Doubleday.

Scearce, D., & Fulton, K. (2004). *What if? The art of scenario thinking for nonprofits.* San Francisco: Global Business Network.

Terry, R. (1993). *Authentic Leadership: Courage in Action.* San Francisco: Jossey-Bass.

Terry, R. (2003, Winter). Leadership in a shifting world. *Leader to leader, 26,* 32-37.

Weisbord, M. R., & Janoff, S. (1995). *Future search: An action guide to finding common ground in organizations & communities.* San Francisco: Berrett-Koehler.

Weiss, J., & Hughes. J. (2005, March). Want collaboration? Accept—and actively manage—conflict. *Harvard Business Review, 83*(3), 93-101.

Welch, J. with Welch, S. (2005, April 4). How to be a leader. *Newsweek, CXLV*(14), 45-48.

Wheatley, M. J. (1994). *Leadership and the new science.* San Francisco: Berrett-Koehler.

Wheatley, M. J. (2001, Spring). Innovation means relying on everyone's creativity. *Leader to Leader, 20,* 14-20.

Wheatley, M. J. (2002). *Turning to one another: Simple conversations to restore hope to the future.* San Francisco: Berrett-Koehler.

Wheatley, M. J. (2005). *Finding our way: Leadership for an uncertain time.* San Francisco: Berrett-Koehler.

Transformative Practice: New Pathways to Leadership

Transformative Practice: New Pathways to Leadership

Chapter 8: Transformative Change Agents

The goal of this chapter is to help professionals assume the role of a transformative change agent. Those who do not perceive themselves as change agents will not *be* change agents, at least not intentionally (Fischer, 1998). Because change has to happen at the societal level (Lerner, 2000) to assure individual and familial well-being, it is incumbent upon professionals to learn the skills involved in being change agents. Change agents deliberately bring about innovations; they are conscious architects of events. Change agents must exert power and influence to accomplish broader desired ends by impacting human political systems or altering people's entire social reality.

Nature of Social Change and Transformation

Social transformations address the root causes and systemic nature of social problems and issues. Successful change efforts transform worldviews and the institutions that embody those worldviews. Every aspect of society is affected when society is transformed: culture, consciousness, technology, politics, and ecology. Social transformation alters the balance of power in ways that make it easier to create positive changes in the future. It also leads to the evolution of higher levels of consciousness while fostering development, human capacity, and sustainable futures (Earley, 2004).

Social transformation is meant to identify, leverage, and even create new underlying principles and new sources of power (United States Department of Health and Human Services, 2005). Change results in structural and fundamental

modifications that impact society and its citizens. These transformations often occur over the long term and involve multiple phases and stages of change. In addition, the "rules of the game" change along the way, impacting players, signposts of success, values, and norms (Haines, Aller-Stead, & McKinlay, 2004).

Importance of Self-Knowledge for Change Agents

Before discussing strategies for conducting social change, this section will address the profound importance of professionals knowing who they are and what they believe. Bennet (2000) submitted that individuals who wish to become change agents must know themselves before they can affect change. They must be aware of their own biases, perceptions, capabilities, limitations, prejudices, assumptions, motives, beliefs, values, expectations—all of the baggage and jewels they carry around with them. Those who are unaware of their inner selves run the risk of misunderstanding or misinterpreting the external world they encounter. If failure to correctly understand the situation leads to harm for individuals and families, professionals are behaving unprofessionally and irresponsibly. *Self-knowledge* can mitigate such damage and ensure that professionals are accountable both to themselves and to the public at-large.

Role of Mental Models

Self-knowledge involves awareness of the mental models each person uses to understand both personal daily reality and the reality experienced by others. Mental models are developed over time and are deeply entrenched in the psyche. They include assumptions, beliefs, and worldviews (paradigms) that allow one to make rapid decisions to adapt to

Transformative Practice: New Pathways to Leadership

changing conditions. Concomitantly, outmoded, inaccurate, or misleading mental models can be very dangerous. For example, McGregor et al. (2004) posited that home economics/family and consumer sciences practice was negatively affected by heavy reliance on the outdated technical mode of practice. Because the world is characterized by constant, relentless change, old mental models may not be relevant. Professionals must recognize the deep importance of reviewing and revising their perceptions, assumptions, and paradigms so that they are consistent with their lived realities (Bennet, 2000). It is not acceptable for change agents to be out of touch with reality.

Forgetting, Learning, and Mind Viruses

Most people encounter a powerful wall when they reflect on changing mental models to maintain current and effective practices. They must overcome this obstacle as they struggle to learn new things while forgetting old learnings. Letting go of old modes of thinking is a prerequisite for creating new models of perception and thinking. This is a very difficult thing to do, however, because it threatens self-identity and can even shake an individual's belief system to the core (Bennet, 2000). To lessen this threat, people build defense mechanisms to protect themselves from being exposed. Without a solid, unquestionable belief system, people struggle and become afraid—hence the resistance to change.

Defense mechanisms keep the assumption and biases one believes to be true tucked away in the background of the mind so that life appears to be "business as usual." Brodie (1996) suggested that *mind viruses* invade the psyche when persons are exposed to elements

of a paradigm that are different from the currently prevailing view of the world. Professionals could embrace this analogy to lighten the tension of letting go of mental models that are outmoded. Brodie explains that mind viruses divert attention from the role of certain interests and power relationships in the social agenda. They cloud the future, distort the past, and support the agendas of special interests, thereby preventing persons from *knowing what is really going on*. The spores of the mind virus push buttons, reinforce stereotypes, entrench biases, and insinuate themselves into people's minds, making it very hard to forget what they have already learned in order to make room for new perspectives, assumptions, and belief systems.

Symptoms of the virus at work include getting tired when reading something that does not resonate with one's truth, getting confused, seeking distractions, even getting angry as one listens to an idea that is unsettling. The virus is entrenched and it is very protective of ideas that may be stolen away, so any attempt to change mental models triggers strong emotion. Life and work may become less meaningful, unfocused, and stressful for those who find themselves in this position. They often feel that something is wrong but they cannot localize the source of the problem. These reactions pass, however, as people ride them out, and this process leads to a new view of the world along with engagement in social change for the future of humanity (Brodie, 1996).

Indeed, critical reflection and collegial dialogue about disorienting dilemmas can bring awareness of the threatening thoughts, fears, and feelings that comprise these viral mental defenses. Once the

Transformative Practice: New Pathways to Leadership

inner viruses that impede change in mental models are properly understood, the defense mechanisms dissolve because they no longer serve any useful function (Richmond, 2005). A personal example below illustrates a change in mental models and describes my shift in views regarding consumers in the marketplace. To make this change I had to purge the mental viruses of consumerism, neoliberalism,[1] and free-market ideology.

The neo-liberal free market ideology was chosen as the example on the following page for several reasons. Markets have always existed as a place where citizens gather for the exchange of goods and services, and they are supposed to exist to serve society. The values of a market include competition, profit, wealth, and growth. Over the past 100 years, however, the value system of the market has become the value system of society itself and a *market society* has emerged. With the exception of a short period between the 1930s and the 1970s when Keynesian economics gained popularity, society has been restructured in

---

[1] The doctrine of neo-liberalism emerged from the thinking of Friedrich von Hayek (early 1930s) and his students, like Milton Friedman (University of Chicago), in the early 1970s. It was to take the place of economic thinking championed by John Maynard Keynes (1930s). Neoliberalism is an economic ideology that embraces privatization, decentralization, deregulation, and individualism as basic tenets of the market. It is implemented via economic policies that facilitate the freer movement of goods and enterprises in an effort to find cheaper resources while maximizing profits and efficiency. Neoliberalism has now come to represent an economic, social, and moral philosophy that can be found around the world. Although the term is rarely used in the U.S., the conservative push for a "trickle-down" or supply-side economic model, combined with industrial deregulation and free trade, is reflective of the neoliberal ideal that allows the market itself to be the final arbiter in determining the validity of public policy.

Transformative Practice: New Pathways to Leadership

A Life Example: Purging the Mental Viruses of Neoliberalism and Consumerism

The unconscious represents all that is unknown about ourselves (Richmond, 2005). It was not until I started reading the peace and social justice literature, the alternative press, and the literature of progressive thinkers that I realized that the way I was teaching consumer studies was perpetuating the status quo. I did not know that I had a virus and that I was perpetuating and entrenching the neoliberal agenda by teaching students how to get out of debt, how to get the best value for their dollar, how to gain power over business, how to make sure government policies protect them, how to serve their own self-interest in the marketplace, and how to assert their rights. This agenda comprises privatization, decentralization, deregulation, individualism, free market and trade ideology, competition, corporate-led globalization, success and profit, wealth, and growth. Translated into policy, this agenda recognizes the rule of the market, cuts public expenditure for social services, and eliminates the concept of the public good. A compliant and unenlightened consumer propagates this agenda. I was unaware that this approach to consumer studies precluded

- seriously considering the stressful impact of living in a consumer society. These stresses include competition, individualism, survival of the fittest, success, getting ahead, work ethic, materialism, selfishness, the onslaught of lending, marketing and advertising, and commodification (McGregor, 2003). For example, members of a consumer society who are bankrupt or in arrears find themselves subject to significant stress, yet they are seen as failures or deviants who need to be rehabilitated or fixed because they are unable to meet the societal norm of managing credit.
- understanding that best value for the dollar often means buying products made under oppressive and unjust labor conditions, especially by women and children;
- knowing that focusing on power *over* business diverts attention to power *with* those who make the goods and services and with nature (solidarity and ecological integrity);
- realizing that government protection mitigates personal responsibility for accountability and creates dependent consumers rather than vigilant citizens;
- appreciating that self-interests divert attention from mutual interests; and,
- recognizing that asserting rights distracts people from concomitant responsibilities as global, human citizens (McGregor, 2005).

I was able to purge this mental virus by becoming open-minded and willing to acknowledge emotions attached to mental discomfort and angst, and also by talking with like-minded others, reading widely with a critical lens, and writing. I framed new courses and let them unfold, not knowing how I was going to field questions and challenges to the status quo but trusting the healing process. I teach courses on consumerism, globalization, and the human spirit; creating peace in a consumer society; peace, human rights, and citizenship education in the context of a consumer culture; and socializing consumers in a global economy. My new focus embraces citizenship, global education principles, non-violence, inner power and sustainable self-empowerment, cultures of peace versus consumerism, justice in the marketplace, challenges to the prevailing neoliberal ideology, and transformative inquiry. I still teach consumer studies but now have a new mental model. I consider my work akin to that of a change agent.

Transformative Practice: New Pathways to Leadership

such a way that citizens have become servants of the market.

Under the ideology of a neoliberal free market, society is governed by rules that favor deregulation of businesses, privatization of public services, decentralization of government power, and extreme individualism (especially in the form of consumerism). The market forces of liberalization do not take the fulfillment of social needs under consideration. Additionally, trade is not perceived to be useful unless it serves the needs of the elite, therefore the more resourceful elites manipulate the forces of the market to their benefit regardless of the impact on the remainder of the populace. People are expected to adapt and to pay their own way, regardless. Those who cannot are considered failures who are unworthy of support or assistance from the more productive members of society. The end result is a pervasive loss of self-reliance, self-initiative, and self-esteem for the majority of the world's citizens.

Although it is certain that the world still requires markets, these markets must serve society and the common good. This type of market produces results that are very different from a free-market, neoliberal economy. Change agents can work to design markets that enrich community and human resiliency, foster ecological integrity, and ensure human rights and social justice. Alternate approaches to markets can be mindful of the human condition, the human spirit, and human security. Instead of globalizing neo-liberalism, architects of economies can use the localization model to create economic systems. New strands of economic thinking can employ

concepts put forward by eco-economics, feminist economics, and behavioral economics. Change agents have access to a wide range of alternative approaches as they work to create mindful economies of care.

Judicious consideration also must be given to the pace of change and whether this pace reflects a balance with stability. Commentators frequently observe that the pace of social change accelerated during the 20th century (Rudel, 2005). Changes to any social institutions can have unintended consequences. Changing "what is wrong" could worsen quality of life, not make it better. To offset any long term disruptive fallout from social change (appreciating that initial resistance is a natural part of change), those affecting the transformation have to appreciate that lasting success is a long-term process, not a one time event. The intent is to reach ordinary citizens and, ultimately, the policy powerholders who are in a position to change the institutions. This sustainable pace of change can be achieved through the promotion of a participatory democracy, a focus on social justice, rather than a vested interest, and by using non-violent, transformative means (Moyer, 2005).

The transformation of human systems and institutions is a delicate, complicated, and challenging endeavor. To further the analysis of these complexities, this chapter has described the primacy of self-knowledge, the notion of current mental models, the analogy of mind viruses, and the challenges of updating paradigms and personal belief systems so that the lived realities of individuals and families can be respected and augmented. The journey of self-change underpins the ability to facilitate

Transformative Practice: New Pathways to Leadership

external change. The next section provides some ideas for how to be a change agent.

Strategies for Social Change

In order to facilitate social transformation, agents of change have to understand the existing power structure and determine whether it is oppressive, unjust, or inequitable. They must question the existing assumptions and underlying decisions that shape society, and they must be aware of manipulation by others. By necessity, change agents engage in the exercise of power, politics, and interpersonal influence (Imel, 2000). To enable readers to hone these necessary skills, this book covers paradigm shifts, critical science, intellectual curiosity and skeptical thinking, discourse analysis, and perspective transformation—all of which enhance our understanding of power and influence. The role of change agents is discussed next.

Change Agent Roles

Gamage and McLennan (1997) suggested that change agents have to

- stimulate the desire for critical self- and world-awareness,
- develop cohesion and solidarity by creating a structure to bring people together,
- support people as they gain the necessary skills to affect change,
- act as intermediaries in linking like-minded people,
- help people deal with issues of power and vested interests,
- strengthen their capabilities, and
- widen the range of methods and solutions for change.

To affect change, there must be a collaborative relationship between the change agent and those who will benefit from the

change. This relationship serves to establish problem-solving infrastructures and processes. This paradigm assumes that persons must participate in their own re-education toward self-awareness, self-understanding, and self-control. Change involves both the individual and the kinship and friendship networks that may also require re-education. The focus is on creativity and critical reflection as requisites to coping with, adapting to, and affecting change (Gamage & McLennan, 1997).

It is important to note that there is a difference between managing an issue and affecting social change. If professionals work outside the system to fix problems that are symptomatic of larger social ills, they are *managing issues*. From a transformative perspective, it is not enough to help people manage change outside the system so they can cope with or adapt to what is happening in society (Baldwin, 1991). If, however, professionals work from *within the* system to change or transform values while challenging the ideologies that shape policy and trade decisions, they should be able to create conditions more conducive to family well-being and quality of life. That is, professionals can be transforming agents in shifting societal values toward family as a social institution (McGregor, 1996). Human betterment should be the goal.

Change Agent Mindset

Fischer (1996, 1998) and Markham (2000) provided a comprehensive array of strategies and mind-sets employed by effective change agents. Change agents should

♦ embrace continuing change instead of predictability, order, and stability (see chapters 6 and 7);

Transformative Practice: New Pathways to Leadership

- recognize that turbulence can be a frightening fact of life, but it can also be an opportunity for growth and transformation;
- focus on the daily, external realities lived by individuals and families in today's complex world instead of focusing solely on their own practice;
- call upon professionals to make a positive difference in the world;
- maximize opportunities for self-learning and for facilitating learning and development to encourage appropriate roles in social change;
- foster leadership of potential leaders (see chapter 5). Be patient with failure and celebrate progress; social change takes a long time;
- share information and insights and expect others to do the same (see chapters 16 and 17);
- maintain a high sense of urgency for challenging the present social and political order without resorting to intimidation or rushed judgments to impress upon people the need to engage in change. The former approach is less fearful and more empowering;
- gain comfort in working with people who have different ideas and values by diffusing their fears about confrontation, loss of influence, and being left behind;
- learn to balance the nature and pace of social and political change so that it is sustainable, renewing, and rewarding;
- frame the proposed change so that people sense they are separating the present from the past without clinging to the past;
- project inspired urgency, passion, composure, and confidence so that others will join and not shy away from change;
- transcend the personal effects of the stress

Transformative Practice: New Pathways to Leadership

inherent in social and political change;
- present and hold the "big picture," the vision for what the future will hold if the desired political or social change transpires;
- be consistent and portray an image of continuity—stand for something and stay with it. Avoid fads, opportunism, and expediency because opting for these causes can taint one's influence; and finally,
- remind people that the work of being a change agent does not always yield visible, immediate results but that it is an important component of transformative professional practice.

Change Agent Questions and Process

Diaz, Massialas, & Xanthopoulos (1999) posed a series of questions to (a) shape the process of taking a position on a social or political issue, (b) form the appropriate political and social actions to advance one's position, and (c) follow up to ensure success of future initiatives relative to change in societal relations or political arrangements. These questions help change agents to gain insight into how the system works so they feel confident in their ability to change it. Efficacy is key, because it involves the possession of a quality or virtue that gives a person the inner power to bring about a desired result. Power comes from fostering the feeling that people are an inextricable part of the world and have the right and responsibility to act on their worldviews.

- Do your observations confirm others' shared reports, narratives, stories, and memories?
- What positions do you support with respect to what has to change, why, and how?
- Can you find others who support your position? How would

Transformative Practice: New Pathways to Leadership

you mobilize their support for your proposal? Who else could you contact and recruit?
- What proposals for action can you make (and to whom) to alleviate the problem as you view it? (See chapter 10).
- On what critical thinking grounds would you support your proposal?
- How would you organize the actions you and your supporters would take to bring about change and resolution of the problem? (See Wollman, Lobebstein, Foderaro, & Stose, 1998).
- Who are the decision makers, and what are their positions?
- What would you gain or lose by taking your position to these decision makers (or to one versus another)?
- How would you go about negotiating or arranging various ways to resolve the issue with respective decision

makers in such a way that it does not damage your cause by losing too much ground?
- How can you bring your position to a vote or ensure that it is considered appropriate by all concerned?
- What actions have you taken so far to make sure your change results will be sustainable?
- How successful were you? Did you affect the political or social change you desired? What actions were not successful and why not?
- If this round was unsuccessful, what do you need to do now to ensure future success on this issue? If you achieved success this time, how will you maintain the current success?

Assertive Relationships

As evidenced in the above social change processes and questions, building relations is a central role of change agents.

175

Transformative Practice: New Pathways to Leadership

Effectiveness truly depends on forming and nurturing a wide range of relationships in networks. Professionals who affect social change have to be non-threatening, low key, and supportive, and they must convey their intention to assist others in forwarding the cause. They have to show that they can be trusted. Most significantly, they have to be assertive rather than arrogant. This may sound fundamental, but assertiveness means standing up for oneself while not stepping on the rights of others (Powers & Simon, 2003). It means having a strong belief in the cause without being arrogant. Arrogance plays out in behavior that conveys a sense of superiority over others, an overbearing presence, and a deep sense of self-worth and self-importance. Arrogant people sometimes fail to see that others even exist or that their interests merit attention on the political and social stage.

Assertiveness, in the form of boldness and self-assurance, happens when one states a position on an issue positively, with conviction. People communicating assertively are not afraid of speaking for themselves or influencing others but do so in a way that respects personal boundaries. They are also willing to defend themselves when people cross their boundaries in order to mitigate undue influence or having their position sidetracked in some way. Transformative social change is highly dependent on assertive relationships (Powers & Simon, 2003).

Social Change as Waves on an Ocean

As noted earlier, political and social change are delicate, complicated, and challenging endeavors. Cooley (1897) likened social change to an ocean wave or a combination of waves. He described

Transformative Practice: New Pathways to Leadership

modern society as an interrupted ocean, upon which the waves of social and political change meet with no obstacles except one another. These waves roll as high and as far as the impulse that created them can carry them. If professionals embrace this mental image, they can view themselves as initiating a wave of change that will only go as far as their will and professional work take it. See the description in the sidebar for an illustration of this powerful analogy.

Transformation or change should lead toward maturity, autonomy, and responsibility (Brown & Paolucci, 1979). Restructured and reorganized institutions such as schools, religion, government, judicial and legal systems, the marketplace, workplace, and community should place a higher value on families (Vaines, 1988). Professionals must assume that these institutions are capable of

---

Example of home economics as a wave of social and political change

In the late 1800's, founders of the home economics profession initiated a change in the education system so that work related to the family and the home gained respect and influence. They did this in response to the Industrial Revolution that was overtaking and collapsing the earlier Agricultural Revolution. University programs were put in place, school curricula were developed and taught, teachers were prepared, career paths opened up, and government legislation entrenched funding for the discipline. The wave gained momentum and strength as it rolled out over the ocean of society.

This home economics-initiated wave of social and political change to benefit individuals and families grew in momentum until it encountered the capitalistic, neo-liberal, competitive paradigm (a powerful wave in its own right) that now presses upon the home economics/family and consumer sciences wave so that it is in perpetual threat of drowning.

Sometimes waves of social and political change are so powerful that they are termed shock waves or juggernauts, defined as overwhelming forces that crush everything in their path. They can even be called tidal waves or killer tsunamis. Corporate-led globalization and consumerism are often regarded as juggernauts.

If we accept that waves go on until they meet another opposing wave, then it is time for the profession to initiate *another wave of transformative social and political change*, one that helps society to revalue families as a social institution and becomes society's *raison d'etre*. This new wave will crash into the corporate globalization wave and dissolve it completely.

being rearranged and re-composed so that families are emancipated and empowered to be independent and self-forming. Home economics had this vision of social change.

Challenges in Meeting Today's Needs

Ideally, professionals listening to the needs of the day and then determining new ways to meet those needs will result in people and institutions that are transformed through social change (Markham, 2000). These changes will encompass community, relatedness, connectedness, security, truth, justice, spirituality, and meaning. However, enacting social change to meet these needs is challenging in today's postmodern world, because contemporary society is characterized by

- disconnection and alienation,
- self-serving individualism,
- cynicism, or an attitude of scornful or jaded negativity, especially a general distrust of the integrity or professed motives of others,
- self-focused greed,
- a plague of disbelief that infringes upon the pursuit of truth,
- questions about the veracity of authority, and
- despair and lack of connection with the future (hopelessness).

Markham (2000) asked people to identify when they last experienced a sense of connection, relatedness, and community in their work and lives. She then had them identify instances of alienation and disconnection and followed that with a dialogue on building linkages across the gaps. She encouraged people to articulate the bold actions that they could initiate to make a significant difference. She also asked professionals to ponder what forces could stop

Transformative Practice: New Pathways to Leadership

them from taking social action. Melson (1980) suggested that this approach instituted change rather than adaptation, although in some instances adaptation is a necessary skill.

Summary and Conclusion

Any proposed social change should have a well-articulated vision and justification for need and should anticipate how people will fit into the changed situation. It should have a strategy for implementation and evaluation. This entire process requires leaders who view themselves as change agents to be committed to a better way and a better world, and to have the courage and commitment to challenge existing power bases and cultural norms, even in the face of uncertainty, resistance, and possible failure. Such leaders will not wait for someone else to take the lead but will exhibit initiative, break bottlenecks, think outside the box, and reframe setbacks as learning opportunities. They will be able to motivate others to the cause and inspire them to build and sustain momentum. Change agents will enable others to find their inner power and innate capabilities, along with the fortitude to stay with the cause over the long haul. Finally, but not exhaustively, these leaders will know how to keep a low profile until or unless it is appropriate to do otherwise. Politically astute and socially sensitive change agents find ways to work in less visible, even covert ways without sacrificing transparency and accountability (Baker, 2005; Blewett, 2000; Tearle, 2003; Wesley, 1996).

Political and social change is a transformative stance for a profession. This chapter illustrated a connection between self-knowledge and commitment to social change (Ettling, 2001). It also acknowledged that every person is an agent of change to some degree, though some people assume more passive roles (Schaller, 2002). Indeed, Imel (2000) clarified that the role of change agent is not appropriate in every situation and that not all practitioners will be comfortable with the role. The intent of the chapter was to introduce professionals to the imperative of social change and to the need to identify with the role of change agent. Through this better understanding, practitioners can persevere in taking transformative action that can change the world. Transformed professionals know that the learning curve is steep and that the process is complex, but they are also aware that the results of social change are worth the effort because they benefit well-being and quality of life.

References

Baker, M. (2005). Effective change leaders. *Corporate Social Responsibility News and Resources*. Retrieved June 21, 2005 from http://www.mallenbaker.net/csr/CSRfiles/effective.html

Baldwin, E. E. (1991). The home economics movement: A "new" integrative paradigm. *Journal of Home Economics, 83*(4), 42-48.

Bennet, A. (2000). *Knowing: Self as a change agent*. Retrieved June 21, 2005 from http://www.au.af.mil/au/awc/awcgate/navy/knowing/knowing_selfaschange.htm

Blewett, V. (2000). *Workers changing work*. Unpublished Dissertation, University of Adelaide, Australia.

Brodie, R. (1996). *Virus of the mind*. Seattle, WA: Integral Press.

Brown, M., & Paolucci, B. (1979). *Home economics: A definition* [mimeographed]. Alexandria, VA: American Association for Family and Consumer Sciences.

Cooley, C. H. (1897). The process of social change. *Political Science Quarterly, 12*, 63-81. See also http://spartan.ac.brocku.ca/~lward/Cooley/Cooley_1897b.html

Diaz, C. F., Massialas, B. G., & Xanthopoulos, J. A. (1999). *Global perspectives for educators*. Needham Heights, MA: Allyn and Bacon.

Earley, J. (2004). *Conscious action*. Retrieved June 21, 2005 from

Transformative Practice: New Pathways to Leadership

http://www.earley.org/Conscious_Action/home.htm

Ettling, D. (2001). Leadership for action: Wedding adult education and social change. *Proceedings of the Adult Education Research Conference*, East Lansing, MI. Retrieved June 21, 2005 from http://www.edst.educ.ubc.ca/aerc/2001/2001ettling.htm

Fischer, T. F. (1996). *Five principles to facilitate change*. Retrieved June 21, 2005 from http://www.ministryhealth.net/mh_articles/042_five_principles_of_change.html

Fischer, T. F. (1998). *Twenty-one marks of a pastoral change agent*. Retrieved June 21, 2005 from http://jmm.aaa.net.au/articles/8228.htm

Gamage, N., & McLennan, K. (1997). *Change agents (1)*. Retrieved June 21, 2005 from http://www.caledonia.org.uk/change.htm

Haines, S., Aller-Stead, G., & McKinlay, J. (2004). *Enterprise-wide change*. New York: Wiley.

Imel, S. (2000). Change: Connections to adult learning and education. *ERIC Digest No. 221*. Retrieved June 21, 2005 from http://www.cete.org/acve/docgen.asp?tbl=digests&ID=106

Lerner, M. (2000). *Spirit matters*. Charlottesville, VA: Hampton Roads Publishing.

Markham, D. (2000). Spiritlinking: From dreams to reality. *Keynote delivered at the Heartland III Conference*, Omaha, NE. Retrieved June 21, 2005 from http://www.creighton.edu/Heartland3/markham.html

McGregor, S. L. T. (2005). Sustainable consumer empowerment through critical consumer education: A typology of consumer education approaches. *International Journal of Consumer Studies, 29*(5), pp. 437-447.

McGregor, S. L. T. (1996). Embracing values: A home economics imperative. *Canadian Home Economics Journal, 46*(1), 3-7.

McGregor, S. L. T. (2003). Postmodernism, consumerism and a culture of peace. *Kappa Omicron Nu FORUM, 13*(2), online at http://www.kon.org/archives/forum/13_2/mcgregor.html

McGregor, S.L.T., et al. (2004). A satire: Confessions of recovering home economists. *Kappa Omicron Nu Human Sciences Working Papers Archives*. Retrieved June 21, 2005 from http://www.kon.org/hswp/archive/recovering.html

Melson, G. F. (1980). *Family and environment: An ecosystem perspective*. Minneapolis, MN: Burgess.

Moyer, B. (2005). Seven strategic assumptions of successful social movements. In L. Slattery, K. Butigan, V. Pelicaric and K. Preston-Pile (Eds.), *Engage: Exploring Nonviolent Living* (Part Four, Resources). Oakland, CA: Pace e Bene Nonviolence Service.

Powers, M., & Simon. J. (2003, June). *Key role: The change agent.* Retrieved June 21, 2005 from http://www.nasconsulting.biz/pdfs/TCA.pdf

Richmond, R. L. (2005). *Unconscious defense mechanisms.* Retrieved June 21, 2005 from http://www.guidetopsychology.com/ucs.htm

Rudel, T.K. (2005). Is the pace of social change accelerating? *International Journal of Comparative Sociology, 46*(4), 275-296.

Schaller, L. E. (2002). *The change agent.* Nashville, TN: Abingdon Press.

Tearle, R. (2003). *The role of a change master.* Cape Town, South Africa: Change Designs. Retrieved June 21, 2005 from http://www.changedesigns.co.za/The_role_of_a_change master.htm

United States Department of Health and Human Services. (2005). *Transformation.* Washington, DC: Author. Retrieved June 21, 2005 from http://www.samhsa.gov/matric/mhst_manuscript.doc

Vaines E. (1988). The reflective professional: Reflecting on helping for the 21st century [Theme booklet]. *People and Practice: International Issues for Home Economists (PIPHE), 1(1)*, University of British Columbia.

Wesley, D. (1996). *Are you the person to lead a change?* Lakeland, FL: ChangeCraft© Corporation. Retrieved June 21, 2005 from http://www.changecraft.com/Articles/perslead.htm

Wollman, B., Lobebstein, M., Foderaro, M., & Stose, S. (1998). *Principles for promoting social change.* Ann Arbor, MI: Society for the Psychological Study of Social Issues. Available at http://www.spssi.org/ppsc.pdf

Transformative Practice: New Pathways to Leadership

Chapter 9: Typology of Styles*

Author's Note – While this chapter was written to address professional styles found within the home economics/family and consumer sciences profession, practitioners from other fields are likely to find that the styles presented here have parallels that are applicable across professions.

All practitioners of the home economics/family and consumer sciences work in areas that are encompassed by or related to the profession founded as home economics, even if they do not consider themselves *home economists*. It is significant that not everyone demonstrates the same passion and commitment to the field or to related professional associations and initiatives. Respect for this diversity is of paramount importance in appealing to the widening scope of emotional attachment levels among professionals, and this broad appeal must be attained in order to develop a transformative future for this particular profession. The premise of this chapter is that typological styles influence each practitioner's outlook, predisposition to the field, beliefs about the profession, and role within it. This collection of beliefs has profound implications for professional leaders, because it confirms that each individual has something valuable to contribute, even though each will relate to the field somewhat differently. The following discussion relates a new typology of styles that will enable professionals to understand each other better. It will also provide leaders with an incentive

---

*Earlier version published in *Human Sciences Working Papers Archives*, http://www.kon.org/hswp/index.html.

to be more inclusive by exploring the different preferences individuals express in self-identifying as members of the field.

Typologies Explained and Justified

Although typologies are not as important to the field as leadership theories, there is still space in the professional dialogue for a discussion of types. The challenge lies in not succumbing to an effort to get along with one another at the expense of forgetting to learn together (Dorothy Mitstifer, personal communication, February 8, 2004). By including both typologies and theories in the dialogue, practitioners can mitigate that possibility. Furthermore, typologies are assured a place in the social sciences through the three types of social science data: attributional data, relational data, and ideational data. The last is used to describe the meanings, motives, definitions, and typologies of things. Typological analysis, or the analysis of data to create types and styles, is an intellectual strategy for developing theoretically significant, meaningful categories of observed phenomena. The result is a collection of types or styles that is useful because it simplifies and codifies distinctions between complex examples of various phenomena (Scott, 1991). In this case, the complex phenomena are the different approaches that individuals take to professional practice.

Typology theorists examine individual differences in how people view and relate to the world. Typologies are not developmental, interactive, or cognitive in nature, meaning that (a) they do not assume sequential movement through the types, (b) they do not deal with the way types interact with one another, and (c) they do not illuminate what people

Transformative Practice: New Pathways to Leadership

think about. They do, however, capture innate individual differences in mental processing and perceptions. In other words, typologies seek to describe the way that individuals see and interact with the world around them (Brown University, 2004).

Typologies are useful instruments for exploring the challenges and opportunities inherent in relating to and leading a diverse group of practitioners. Typologies utilize a classification system that categorizes items or people into "general types" according to shared attributes or dispositions. Although separating things into distinct categories does not seem to promote an appreciation for interrelationships, it can function as a first step in identifying relationships and patterns. This chapter therefore assumes that the recognition of unique, unconnected categories can eventually lead one to appreciate each category in context and in relationship to the whole. Professional types are offered accordingly. Readers are invited to read the postscript at the end of the chapter for further elaboration on this point.

Those who wish to benefit from this chapter should avoid trying to identify their own characteristics in each description. Instead, each individual should progress through the concepts objectively and with an open mind. This strategy will offer professionals a platform from which to get to know one another better. In this way, solid, respectful working relationships are formed and practitioners can take the first step toward learning together as a community of practice.

Overview of Myers-Briggs Model of Personalities

Many typologies mirror the familiar Myers-Briggs (MB) model, which

185

provides a framework for understanding personality types. Because the discussion of typology that follows is modeled on a similar approach, and because application of personality types to other topics is a widespread practice, a brief overview of the MB typology is pertinent. The MB types will not themselves be part of the typology proposed in this chapter; they will merely be described to the extent that readers will be better able to appreciate the overall approach.

The Myers-Briggs personality model is based on four preferences that people hold regarding how they direct their energy, process information, make decisions, and organize their life. The assumption is that everyone's personality includes variations of all four, but that differences in emphasis among the components are manifest over time to reflect one's true preference or personality. Each person tends to favor one style over the others, and this preference becomes particularly apparent when one is either under stress or enjoying a situation (Team Technology, 2000b).

To elaborate, the first preference indicates whether one prefers to direct personal energy inward through thought and emotions or outward via activity and the spoken word. Those who display a preference for the former are referred to as introverts, whereas those who exhibit tendencies toward the latter are called extroverts. The second preference determines one's favored approach to processing information. It involves either (a) sensing, or using facts and familiar terms to focus one's senses on the present reality, or (b) intuition, or finding patterns and relationships by using a larger viewpoint to imagine

potentials and possibilities for the future. The third preference describes one's decision-making style, which can entail either thinking things through logically and objectively or basing decisions on principles, values, and personal feelings. The final preference indicates one's favored method of life organization. Some prefer a great deal of structure, organization, and control (this approach is referred to as judgment). Others are flexible and spontaneous, and they are open to discovering life and everything it presents (this approach is called perception) (Team Technology, 2000b).

To provide a simple example, the author's MB test reveals a combination of extrovert, intuition, thinking, and perception (ENTP). This result indicates a person who likes to

- explore new ideas and challenge the status quo;
- spot new patterns and relationships between ideas, fostering a deeper understanding of a key issue;
- present ideas that are contradictory to accepted conventions and use logic to analyze patterns in an attempt to identify underlying principles not evident to others; and
- continue to learn more about a topic rather than come to a final conclusion, so ideas can continue to evolve (Team Technology, 2000a).

Drawing Insights from Other Typologies

The following section presents an overview of two spiritual typologies that the author discovered by chance during recent research for a paper (McGregor & Chesworth, (2005). Posterski (2002) and Ware (1994) offer two typologies that may provide transformational new insights for professionals.

Transformative Practice: New Pathways to Leadership

Posterski's (2002) Four Spiritual Types

In drawing insights from the Myers-Briggs approach, Posterski (2002) used extensive factor and cluster analyses to evaluate the results from a survey of Canadians that questioned whether they attended church weekly or monthly. He determined that there are four spiritual styles or types: charismatic, traditional, divergent, and tolerant. Like the personality types found in the Myers-Briggs model, these spiritual types differed on several factors such as resistance or acceptance of various family forms, importance of faith in day-to-day life, level of concern for spiritual well-being, and several others. As with all typologies, Posterski illustrated the intent to categorize according to common attributes or dispositions.

More insight into the nuances of these four types will follow, but a short example offers a useful starting point. Posterski (2002) characterized charismatics as those who were intensely resistant to non-nuclear family forms, convinced that religious faith is central to daily life and very concerned about spiritual well-being. Divergents, on the other hand, are the respondents who were open to many different family structures, least likely to say that faith plays an important role in day-to-day life and unconcerned with spiritual well-being. Yet, all attended church weekly or at least monthly. Posterski makes the significant and compelling case that spiritual leaders need to be aware of these four different styles because each implies a need for different leadership initiatives. If a spiritual leader wants to reach an entire congregation, he or she simply cannot assume that one approach to spiritual leadership will work for everyone.

Transformative Practice: New Pathways to Leadership

Ware's (1996) Four Types of Spirituality

Ware (1994) also conducted research into spiritual types, suggesting the existence of four other types of spirituality. She concluded that each of these types (head, heart, mystic, and kingdom) experiences and imagines God differently. Some utilize thoughts in their experience of the divine while others rely upon feelings. Some picture God in a concrete manner where other people's perceptions are more abstract. Ware's four quadrant Spirituality Wheel Selector helps people to identify their predominant spirituality, their spiritual alignments, and those types of spirituality that are foreign to them. Those who identify with the Head style learn through Bible study groups, Sunday School, traditional worship and hymns, and listening to sermons. The Heart style seeks to experience God in any living moment and does this through group fellowship, evangelistic preaching through the promotion of God's message, and contemporary worship that uses music and other mediums that reach today's culture. Mystic spirituality involves listening to God through private meditation, spiritual retreats, and renewal initiatives. Those who follow this approach feel that they are on a journey that requires quiet and solitude. Finally, followers of the Kingdom spirituality type utilize a visionary, even missionary, form of spiritual expression. Those who belong in this group are likely to be tireless in their actions to foster peace and social justice, and they typically seek societal transformation through community projects such as Habitat for Humanity or local food banks.

Toward the Creation of a New Typology

This section explores insights that can be gained

from bringing these two spiritual typologies to bear in the transformation of home economics/family and consumer sciences practice.

Bringing Posterski's (2002) Model to Home Economics/Family and Consumer Sciences

Table 1 illustrates Posterski's (2002) typology as applied to home economics/family and consumer sciences, where four styles are suggested using Posterski's labels: Charismatic, Traditional, Tolerant, and Divergent. Although a unique factor analysis would pose benefits over borrowing from an existing set, this typology lends a new perspective on the profession's journey into a transformative future.

As is the convention with the MB model, these four types vary based upon several factors: (a) emotional attachment and commitment to the profession, (b) sense of inclusion and acceptance by others, (c) propensity to affiliate and identify with other types, (d) level of involvement and attendance at events, (e) likelihood of recruiting people to or promoting the profession, and (f) length of time one has been in the field. Each professional will likely fall into one of these four categories, and it is important to note that no style is any better or worse than another.

Table 1 also reflects Posterski's (2002) suggestions that attendant leadership challenges and opportunities are dependant upon which type is being considered. Columns two and three reflect his ideas but they also ring true for home economics/family and consumer sciences professionals. As an example, the president of a professional association wants to make sure she reaches each member to ensure engagement and involvement. She must pay close attention to the

Table 1: Typology of home economics/family and consumer sciences types with leadership challenges and opportunities
(adapted from Posterski, 2002)

Home Economics/FCS Type	Leadership Opportunities	Leadership Challenges
Charismatic professionals: • are exuberant about the profession • are extreme in their actions • want to help others see the relevance of the profession • walk the walk • are sustained by ancient and old ways while remaining open to new experiences • are zealous – they jump in to tasks head first • anticipate working as a professional all the time, regardless of the setting.	• bring life to the profession • bring renewal • bring energy • are vital to the profession	• may provide too much effusive enthusiasm, which can sow seeds of division
Traditional professionals: • are committed to their values • meet occasionally with other professionals • avoid charismatic types, oppose them, and aren't afraid to say so • hold earnest and strong beliefs about the profession • remember becoming a professional • will talk about the profession if asked to • form the oldest group of practitioners	• are loyal • are dependable • are faithful • provide the solid cornerstone of the profession • give many years of life expecting little in return	• are hard to budge because they are cornerstones • resist change • like the way things have been • feel there is no room for them in the future
Tolerant professionals: • will not get pulled into a debate about the profession • feel it is up to each person to decide how to "be" a professional • are not interested in pressuring others to be a professional • are middle aged • don't object to other professional types • are moderate/modest in expressing professional values • display fairly open-minded tendencies	• build bridges • are even-handed • display a conservative, yet open-minded approach • act as advocates for the divergents • are inclusive and welcoming	• can provide too much bridge building and get co-opted for another group's agenda • can be inclusive to the detriment of the whole by overly embracing external professionals
Divergent professionals: • form the youngest group of professionals • could take the profession or leave it • do not get involved in professional events often, and the events they do attend are large • wonder why they are in the field, but they do find parts of it satisfying • can take or leave the charismatic practitioners • demonstrate the lowest rate of involvement and attendance at events • do not hold conventional beliefs regarding professionals, partly because they don't know what to believe • are nonplussed, perplexed, and at a loss for what to say, do, or believe; they often know what they don't want but do not know what they do want • are the present and the future	• are vocal and truthful when present • desire to be a professional but don't know what they want that to mean • can be professionals when it comes to the crunch	• can despair • can become frustrated • have often given up and abandoned the profession • are sometimes chronic complainers with no solutions • are very hard to please because they do not know what they want

Transformative Practice: New Pathways to Leadership

dynamics that emerge as she tries to bring all four types into play. As a Charismatic type, she needs to appreciate that too much untempered enthusiasm can sow deep seeds of division among the other types, either because she is likely to suggest too many options or because she is simply too energetic. If she is not sensitive to the more Traditional members, she may run into unexpected obstacles. Conflicts could arise, since professionals of this type are adverse to change and do not feel there is a place for them in the future of an evolved association. The Divergents, on the other hand, may resist the fictitious president's ideas because they do not know what they want; hence, they are very hard to attract initially and they become hard to please as the project progresses. It is difficult to reach people who are frustrated and have given up on the organization's goals. The Tolerants have to be guided or they may spend too much time building bridges with other organizations. As they attempt to mitigate the tension created by their charismatic leader, the tolerants can be lost to the group completely as they become drawn away to other projects and causes.

From a more positive standpoint, the association's leader can work concurrently with all four different home economics/family and consumer sciences types by building on the opportunities for leadership that present themselves through factors that shape each type. As a charismatic, she is eager to bring life to the profession. By counting on the traditionals to remain loyal to the profession regardless of what happens, she can counter their inherent resistance to her overzealous style. She can further this aim by engaging a tolerant to build bridges. At the

Transformative Practice: New Pathways to Leadership

same time, the tolerants can be an advocate for the hesitant and perplexed divergents, who can be guided to see themselves as professionals when the critical moment arrives.

Making space for variations in professional styles opens a door of opportunity for leaders in the field to try to capture every member and to respect each individual's needs and contributions. As with Myers-Briggs, although each personality is composed of parts of all of these types, there is usually one type that is dominant and informed by the others.

Bringing Ware's (1994) Model to Home Economics/Family and Consumer Sciences

This section discusses Ware's (1994) spirituality types and explores their function in creating four more types. Her ideas have been extrapolated to the profession and the labels have been reworked to reflect a less spiritual focus. Thus, the four types carried forward become: thinking, feeling, reflective, and visionary, which correspond with Ware's head, heart, mystic, and kingdom types. Just as Ware's types relied upon two factors (ways of experiencing God and ways to form mental images of God), this model's types utilize two similar factors: (a) favored mode of self-expression and professional development and (b) favored construct for professional self-image.

- ♦ The **thinking style** describes those who learn best through written text or by listening to inspiring verbal presentations. Those who favor this style are intellectuals who enjoy and receive nourishment from studying articles and books and from attending thought-provoking lectures. People who favor this style rely heavily upon content and the written

193

word because they value order, logic, and consistency. They also desire an inner congruency that stems from agreement between their thoughts and beliefs.

♦ The **feeling style** indicates that an individual seeks personal transformation and learning through art, music, stories, songs, narratives, and camaraderie. Those who exhibit this style rely heavily upon emotional expressions and deep feelings, and they achieve personal renewal by being "in the moment" with others. They appreciate the fellowship of small groups and revel in the present with a keen awareness of the events happening around them.

♦ The **reflective style** refers to people who focus on the inner self. Individuals who prefer this style often appear to be on a quest or a perpetual journey. They may feel that they do not fit into the busy pace of everyday life because they tend to engage in a deeper, quieter way of knowing. They enjoy walking the labyrinth and are often meditative, contemplative, introspective, and intuitive because they value "being" as highly as "doing." Reflective people are concerned with enriching life's journey and they are mindful and observant as they move forward along this path, often turning to retreats to achieve revitalization.

♦ The **visionary style** encompasses action-oriented, socially aware individuals who strive to work through unified groups that focus on justice and peace issues. They are active creative thinkers who, like the reflective types, are somewhat distanced from the mainstream because

Transformative Practice: New Pathways to Leadership

they attempt to transform the whole of society by rectifying the world's wrongs. They are tireless crusaders who support political action to establish justice in society and its institutions. Visionary types are also moralistic, and they tend to act on moral reflection in a passionate way. This courageous and sturdy idealism propels the desire for societal transformation.

Ware (1994) held that many people experience the temptation to value their own style more highly than that of others. Indeed, she suggested that

- those who favor thinking can be seen as dry, cold, academic, dogmatic, and studious;
- those who rely upon feelings are often thought to be too artsy and anti-intellectual, too introverted, and so concerned with internal thoughts and feelings that they become dissociated from reality;
- those who are reflective may be perceived as overly self-centered and flaky, removed from the real world, and lacking credibility because they are eccentric; and,
- those who prefer the visionary style are sometimes considered too involved with the world, too single minded and intensely focused, too moralistic, and too idealistic.

Many readers will identify with one or more of the categories in this typology, and many will find that they can readily place people they know into each of the categories, as well. During professional functions, an observant participant might note that others in attendance want many different things from the event. These desires can involve expert speakers and conventional academic paper sessions, group work and hands-on workshops, small reflective

groups that share feelings and perceptions, downtime for personal regrouping, sight-seeing around the host city, or political action sessions that deal with issues of social injustice and human welfare. Each of these desires reflects the four styles described above: thinking, feeling, reflective, and visionary.

A New Typology

Posterski's (2002) model is adapted to honor the old guard, the new guard, those who are on the edge, and those who are on the fence. Ware's (1994) approach provides an appreciation for those who want to think, those who want to dance, those who contemplate, and those who want to change the world. Although each of these typologies stands alone, a richer conceptual approach can be achieved by integrating them into one whole. To that end, the following represents a marriage of sorts—the amalgamation of two models into a single new typology.

Like the previous models, this typology employs the circle-quadrant format made popular by the Myers-Briggs model. There are four compass points that are reminiscent of Posterski's (2002) approach and a circle divided into four parts that is suggestive of Ware's (1994) typology. Until data can be collected to empirically verify this typology, readers must move forward on faith by assuming that this model can inform and transform professional practice. As with all typologies, some amount of each type is present within every individual, but one type typically proves dominant. Table 2 (see page 198) illustrates the proposed 16 types of home economists. The following text will elaborate on four of them, chosen because they were the ones that lined up with the first spin of the wheel in Figure 1.

Transformative Practice: New Pathways to Leadership

Charismatic/Visionary Typology

Charismatic/Visionary professionals exhibit a blend of being on the edge and wanting to change the world. They bring life to the profession through their exuberance and their desire to promote the field. This vital energy, along with an ability to renew others' energies, indicates that these individuals possess the stamina required to sustain social causes. In fact, visionaries may perceive home economics/family and consumer sciences itself as a cause as they work toward their vision of the profession's future. They value solidarity, take moral positions, and act on principle. Professionals in this category are dedicated, unwavering professionals who are prepared to work tirelessly for any cause they choose. They are sustained by the links they see between the

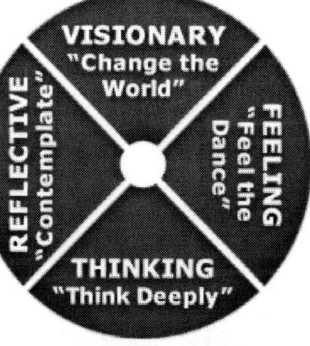

Figure 1: Typology of home economics/FCS Styles

Transformative Practice: New Pathways to Leadership

Table 2: Identity of the 16 Home Economics/Family and Consumer Sciences Types
(those highlighted are described in the chapter)

Charismatic Visionary	Charismatic Thinking	Charismatic Feeling	Charismatic Reflective
Traditional Visionary	Traditional Thinking	Traditional Feeling	**Traditional Reflective**
Tolerant Visionary	Tolerant Thinking	**Tolerant Feeling**	Tolerant Reflective
Divergent Visionary	**Divergent Thinking**	Divergent Feeling	Divergent Reflective

past, present, and future as they remain open to new experiences and trans-formative ideas. Excessive enthusiasm can sow divisions among peers, but distance from the mainstream shields visionaries and allows them to persevere. Finally, courage and idealism can contribute to a penchant for extreme actions, but each step a visionary takes is intended to advance the cause.

Tolerant/Feeling Typology

The tolerant/feeling professional sits on the fence while seeking personal transformation. Those who fit this category feel that each individual must determine for him or herself what it means to be a professional. Emotional expression and deep feelings are central to this type, as is a penchant to build bridges between other types and between aligned groups. They appreciate the fellowship of small groups where deep feelings can be expressed more freely. The tolerant aspect means that they are open-minded, welcoming, and inclusive and that they advocate for the divergent types who could take the profession or leave it. Camaraderie is very

Transformative Practice: New Pathways to Leadership

important to tolerant/feeling professionals; they are sociable and friendly. One of the pitfalls of this combination of traits is the potential for individuals of this type to be co-opted by related causes. They are also inclined to invite the perspectives of professionals outside the field. This is commendable to a point, but taken to extremes the trait can lead them to give away the purview of the field. Tolerant/feeling professionals are typically modest in expressing professional values, and this modesty may explain their vulnerable position astride the fence. Instead of joining the comfort of the professional circle, they remain in an uncommitted position and could fall either way.

Divergent/Thinking Typology

The profession's new guard is made up of divergent/thinking professionals who seek intellectual stimulation that will stir and inspire them to action. They value lectures and the written word, and they obtain this input by attending conferences and other large events. They appreciate order and consistency, and they tend to complain if these elements are missing from their lives. Divergent/thinking types are very hard to please because they do not understand that their complaints stem from not knowing what they want. On occasion, they find contentment in reading stirring new material. They find it difficult to follow through over time, however, because they are unable to maintain or recapture the original spark of inspiration. Although the thinking aspect of this personality type requires congruence between thoughts and beliefs, this agreement is often absent because the individual is unable to determine what he or she believes. The resulting frustration and despair are very unfortunate, particularly because this type encompasses the current generation of up-and-coming new professionals. If this generation lacks hope and turns away from their chosen career path, the future of the profession is in trouble.

Traditional/Reflective Typology

The profession's old guard, the traditional/reflective professionals, attempts to achieve personal transformation by reflecting upon their role within the mainstream of the field. This type earnestly holds strong beliefs about the profession, and they tend to see this stage of their career as a personal quest or journey. They remember the day they *knew* the field was their calling and they remain mindful of the impact of this realization. This core of commitment results in deeply held values that do not require regular reinforcement, although these individuals do enjoy meeting with like-minded others. They have given many years to the profession and now feel that it is time to take care of themselves. To facilitate this self-nurturing, they seek inner growth while simultaneously resisting change in the profession and seeking balance in their relationship with the whole. Finding this balance proves difficult, however, because they see themselves as outside the mainstream and they have a tendency to believe there is no room for them in the future of the profession. This sense of exclusion is ironic because these are the professionals who form the foundation of the field. The field, in turn, forms the core of the professional, whose identity is inseparable from his or her position as a member of the profession.

Transformative Practice: New Pathways to Leadership

Conclusion

Although mathematics tells us there are only 16 possible professional types, sharing just these four illustrates the power of this typology. Working under the assumption that not everyone shares the same depth of passion for the field, its professional associations, or its initiatives, it becomes obvious that diversity must be respected for the field to survive into the future. Leaders must learn to appeal to a widening scope of professional emotion, commitment, and compassion. This aspect of the profession can be better understood if we borrow from other typologies, and these ideas must be quantified to provide more rigor to the typology. In the interim, this discussion will help professionals to honor the old guard, the new guard, those who are on the edge, and those who are on the fence, along with those who want to think, to dance, to contemplate, or to change the world! By expanding the scope of our understanding of and respect for one another, it becomes clear that professional transformation is both possible and probable.

Postscript - Moving Beyond the Categories

This chapter, grounded in modernist thinking, shares the creation of styles so we can visualize ourselves in practice. The styles are not intended to be timeless and they are not intended to exist only in concept. The new typology can be seen as a collection of archetypes or the first formation of styles from which others can arise. It is a systematic ordering of things. This creation of types was intentional but is provided as *just one* way to think about professional transformation. The categories are not absolute; they are merely advanced to propose a new way of thinking about ourselves.

Transformative Practice: New Pathways to Leadership

I was chastised by one reviewer for being complicit in creating *essentialist* categories. My philosophy encyclopedia tells me that essentialism is the practice of categorizing a group of people by a few fixed characteristics while not allowing for change or variation. This is also part of modernist thinking. When people use *essential* in this context, they mean that it is essential that a person have all of the traits to fit into a style or type. If they do not, they are apart from those who do and this causes fragmentation and marginalization. My intent, however is not to isolate but to create a sense of community by illustrating the potential for unity in our diverse styles.

Another reviewer warned that these neat little slots could be interpreted in a negative way. People who have not thought deeply about their professional identities may not be able to find themselves in the typology and will therefore feel excluded. In response, I suggest that if this chapter makes people think about how they see themselves instead of doing the work with no reflection, the profession moves forward.

I do not discount the possibility that imposing a modernist typology can cause damage to professional thinking, because modernists love to place everything in categories. In fact, deconstructivism is a stream of post-modern thought that holds that none of us has the same interpretation of reality because each has different experiences, attitudes, and values (McGregor, 2003). In this light, it may be hard to understand how professionals can fit into these neat categories if no one sees his/her professional reality the same way. When I asked myself this question, I found that I *could* identify with the categories as I developed this typology. It

Transformative Practice: New Pathways to Leadership

resonated with me, but I am aware that my comfort with being able to read a description of myself can also be a trap. It has the potential to close practitioners' minds to diversity and to exclude those who live in the margins.

Post-modern thinkers would also argue that categorizing people prevents individuals from functioning in relation to each other. However, as I noted at the beginning of this chapter, I feel that this typology can represent the first step in identifying relationships and patterns between diverse members of the profession. I anticipate that distinct, unconnected categories can be identified in such a way that enables professionals to see the categories in context so the dynamic relationships, professional networks, and communities of practice become apparent.

If an imposed ordering of professionals does not sit well with some readers, I am encouraged. Discomfort implies a level of acceptance for the quantum physics tenets that describe the world as a seamless and unbroken whole, in spite of its obvious partitions and boundaries. As professionals engage in relationships with one another, transformative work becomes easier through the exploration of differing notions of what it means to *be* a professional. In this way, each single act of associating with another professional is connected, invisibly, to another set of interacting individuals. "We work where we are, with the system we know, the one we can get our arms around" (Wheatley, 1999, p. 44). We act independently, yet we have a collective impact. From this transformative perspective, the identification of separate categories does not isolate practitioners from one another because a

mechanism exists for the perception of each professional as part of an unbroken whole. This realization will allow us to create productive spaces that allow for and affirm our differences (Stevens, 2002).

References

Brown University. (2004). *Peer counselling handbook*. Accessed May 5, 2004 at http://www.brown.edu/ Student_Services/ Office_of_Student_Life/ resed/counselor_resources/ chcikering.pdf

Posterski, D. (2002, Autumn). Spiritual styles and leadership challenges. *Envision Magazine*, 2(4), pp. 2-9.

McGregor, S. L. T. (2003). Postmodernism, consumerism and a culture of peace. *Kappa Omicron Nu FORUM Online, 13*(2) accessed May 27, 2004 at http://www.kon.org/ archives/forum/13-2/ mcgregor.html

McGregor, S. L. T., & Chesworth, N. (2005). Positioning spirituality in home economics. *Journal of the Home Economics Institute of Australia, 12*(3), pp. 27-44.

Scott, J, (1991). *Social network analysis*. London: Sage.

Stevens, C. (2002). *Postmodernism*. Accessed May 27, 2004 at http://mingo.info-science.uiowa.edu/~stevens/critped/post.htm

Team Technology. (2000a). *ENTP*. Accessed May 20, 2004 at http://www.teamtechnology.co.uk/mb-types/entp.htm

Team Technology. (2000b). *Working out your Myers Briggs type*. Accessed May 20, 2004 at http://www.teamtechnology.co.uk/tt/t-articl/mb-simpl.htm

Ware, C. (1994). *Discover your spiritual type*. Herndon: VA: The Alban Institute.

Wheatley, M. (1999). *Leadership and the new science*. San Francisco: Berrett-Koehler.

Transformative Practice: New Pathways to Leadership

Chapter 10: Critical Science Approach to Practice*

The concept of critical science is constructed from the Latin root *crit* (to choose or separate) combined with the Latin *scientia* (to know). One could therefore say that the critical science approach to practice involves separating the tacit and hidden ideologies, assumptions, and paradigms that affect how persons know themselves in relation to others in the world. It is a process that requires professionals to question without taking anything for granted, and it leads to insight, growth, and the potential for emancipation from personal and external oppression. This refusal to accept the status quo is an inherent part of *transformative* practice.

This chapter relies on the assumption that professionals work in socially responsible and relevant ways to actively promote continuous social change. They do so by promoting the ideals of full citizenship participation, democracy, freedom, equality, and social justice instead of maintaining the status quo in the form of existing social, economic, and political systems. Practice that is transformative and emancipative includes not only an understanding of existing power structures but also how to resist, question, and challenge these structures and their underlying ideologies (Imel, 1999). Practice informed by the critical science perspective considers power, emancipation, and resultant individual and social change. It enables professionals to deal with the changing complexity of daily life, moving

---

*Earlier version published in *Human Sciences Working Papers Archives*, http://www.kon.org/hswp.html.

beyond the customary approach that allows people to say things like, *"I was taught this way. This is the way it has always been done. This is all I know how to do. This is what the textbook says. I will get fired if I do not do it this way. This is what the curriculum says I have to teach."* A critical science approach does not leave room for taking things for granted.

Practitioners must question the precursors of the human condition to improve daily life in ways that enhance individual and family well-being. Reflective skills must be used to analyze the sources of patterns in daily reality. By using all of these skills, professionals can work with individuals and families toward the achievement of political and personal autonomy, along with the independence necessary to be fully human (Kruger, 2002).

A critical science approach probes beneath the surface meanings of words and symbols to address the root cause of a problem instead of merely treating the symptoms. Conversely, technical mode practice creates justification for the role of experts while silencing the voice of individuals and families (Kruger, 2002). The role of the expert denies individuals the opportunity to analyze their own situation and masks society's underlying power dynamics. As a result, people become alienated and feel like objects distanced from the world they live in rather than active, critical citizens (Freire, 1984). To alleviate this problem, professionals must shift toward practice that is grounded in the principles and processes of critical science because this model promotes exploration of valued ends, critique of social conditions, and improvement of well-being for individuals, families, and society.

Transformative Practice: New Pathways to Leadership

Critical Theory and Critical Science

Gentzler (1999) discussed the distinction between critical theory and critical science. Critical theory refers to the *outcome* or the improvement in human life. Critical science refers to the *process* that professionals and others apply to obtain the desired result. Critical theory has an overt, desired result in the form of a political goal—a rational, free, and decent society (Young & Arrigo, 2000). Critical theory loosely groups work concerned with the cultural assumptions and social realities that dominate a society's policies, societal structures, and power relationships. These assumptions are known as the prevailing ideology, paradigm, or worldview. An ideology is an unquestioned set of values and beliefs held by a social group. Successful ideologies, so ordinary that they become invisible, gain prominence because they (a) explain the place of people in nature, society, and history, (b) contain beliefs and values that people perceive to be true and worthy, (c) are plausible enough to mesh with common sense understandings of social reality, and (d) are useful in serving the needs and interests of those in power and in justifying the need for them to remain in power (Duerst-Lahti, 1998).

The critical science process unites science for observation (evidence) with philosophy for analysis and criticism (reason) (Yoo, 1999), resulting in improved human conditions. Critical theory assumes that a free society mediates freedom of the individual, and freedom of the individual mediates freedom for the society. Freedom is a powerful, enlightening goal for families. To achieve it, each society needs critics to envision and *idealize* a higher order

of freedom than that which exists under the prevailing ideology. According to critical theory, freedom also requires consciousness of how an ideology reflects and distorts reality, along with an awareness of what factors influence and sustain a false perception of who is in power and how that power dominates daily life (Habermas, 1973).

For people to develop into autonomous, conscious citizens, the sociocultural milieu must encourage such development (Brown, 1993). Professionals can play a key role in this transformative, empowering development by allowing a critical science approach to inform their practice. As the critics who paint an image of more emancipated individuals and families, practitioners can help to ground citizens in their inner power and voice in order to gain external respect and legitimacy in society. To aid professionals in this process, the next section discusses the main principles and insights that comprise the critical science process. The final section will then explore how one facet of practice, specifically education, changes when professionals employ the critical science approach. The entire discussion draws heavily on the inspiring AAFCS Education and Technology Division Yearbook on the critical science approach (edited by Johnson & Fedje, 1999).

Overview of Critical Science Approach

The basic tenet of the critical science approach is that people need to improve their living conditions rather than accepting and coping with their present conditions. That improvement is contingent upon consciousness of social realities that exploit or dominate and upon liberation from these

Transformative Practice: New Pathways to Leadership

forces. If people can be taught to recognize that their condition can be improved, they are more likely to work together to achieve improvement, liberation, and freedom. Otherwise, they continue to pursue passive, dependent roles and remain blind both to their own power and to opportunities for beneficial change. Those who are unaware of the potential for improvement will continue to accept their plight and find ways to adapt through conforming (Gentzler, 1999). At the same time, professionals maintain the legitimacy of the status quo by performing as experts. This approach to practice is not liberating or transformative; no one changes, and the lived context does not change unless it worsens.

Critical science practitioners are reflective and are able to articulate the assumptions that inform their practice. They inquire into the validity of assumptions and critically analyze knowledge outside their own experience in order to broaden their understanding of and potential for transforming themselves and the world (McLaren, 1989). From this stance, professionals can awaken an awareness in others that can lead to lives of conscience. The critical science approach can help individuals to develop expectations of change. It can also help them to find the energy and cooperation needed to make change happen. Critical science is about empowerment, which is the ability to assert and regain power, vigor, influence, and sustainability on personal, social, and political levels (Wolk, 2000).

The critical science approach assumes that persons must engage in the wider world if they are to survive in it and help reconstitute it. This engagement can reveal the status quo that

supports inequalities, injustices, and abuses of power. If professionals do not take the side of the powerless, they side with the powerful by default because they contribute to the preservation of the status quo. This can lead to continuing growth in inequalities of income and wealth, inequalities in relation to cultural recognition and social diversity, and inequalities that arise from lack of access to information. Conversely, transformative practice and leadership contribute to empowerment. Transformative leaders help people to find the "me power" they need to make changes to the social, political, personal, and cultural relationships that create barriers to equality and social justice (Thompson, 2000).

Three languages of critical literacy

At its core, critical science assumes that human happiness and social autonomy can be attained if societal structures and conditions can be altered. Individual happiness can occur within the community rather than at the expense of the community. Inherent in this process is the historical context that shapes current reality; issues of race, gender, religion, colonialism, sexuality, and class are fundamental to shaping identities (Gentzler, 1999; Hones, 2002). What led to the current imbalance of power and influence in society? Uncovering this imbalance entails determining *what is* in order to decide *what could be* (Rehm, 1999).

With these insights, a critical science approach helps people to gain (a) personal freedom from internal constraints like biases, lack of a skill, or point of view and (b) social freedom from external constraints such as oppression, exclusion, and abuse of power relations. Critical science

Transformative Practice: New Pathways to Leadership

is concerned with power relationships, especially distorted power relationships that make it easy for the elite to oppress others by controlling knowledge, access to power, meanings, and daily practices. Removing these limitations to freedom and daily life defines the processes of emancipation, liberation, empowerment, and transformation (Rehm, 1999). A special kind of literacy is involved—critical literacy. The fundamental concerns in this form of literacy are difference, justice, power, and language, which are intrinsically political and complex. To address this complexity, Rehm (1999) proposed three languages of empowerment that stem from critique, possibility and potential, and action (see Table 1).

Table 1: Three languages of empowerment
(adapted from Rehm, 1999)

Language of critique (unearthing *unspoken* assumptions, values, and ideologies)

Critical consciousness

- This is a slow realization that people *do* have the power to change things that keep them down, marginalized, and exploited.

Problem posing

- Telling one's own stories and reading the stories of others can give individuals the skill to name the life problems that arise from abuse of power.

Self-reflection

- Self-reflection involves figuring out "why one is doing what one is doing in daily life." These actions, or habits, keep people down-trodden. They include self-doubt, biases, resentment, compulsions, unthinking acceptance of popular ideas, and dependence on experts, bad habits, and boredom. Reflecting on these things can lead to the creation of new labels and names for the things that happen in daily life. With this understanding, people can reframe thinking and actions.

Social critique

- Through social critique, individuals can expose the beliefs, attitudes, and actions that contribute to the subordination of most people by a very few elite individuals in a way that reveals the current power relations. This process makes it easier to challenge the patterns of domination and change the balance of power so that persons no longer buy into a false consciousness, and the interests of the elite are no longer the only ones served.

(continued...)

Transformative Practice: New Pathways to Leadership

Table 1: Three languages of empowerment *(continued)*
(adapted from Rehm, 1999)

Language of Possibility and Potential

Once people unveil the negative conditions that keep them oppressed, they can reframe thinking to illuminate the possibilities of breaking free from oppression. This is achieved through three actions:

Personal voice

- When people realize they can change inside (transform), they find their personal voice and realize that it is valid and needs to be heard in the larger discussions of what society could and should be like.

Agency

- Agency is the ability to organize future situations and resource distribution. One's capacity for agency grows as social imagination grows, as one learns how lives should be constructed so that there is no oppression or inequality. As hope (a connection with the future) is envisioned, inner power is gained and a particular future emerges.

Authorship

- To move from being objects that others manipulate to subjects who are actively involved in constructing new voices, people have to take ownership of their ideas and express them to others through authoring in collective action (see below).

Language of Action

Dialogue

- Dialogue involves talking, listening, sharing, perspective taking, questioning, responding, reframing, adapting, suggesting, and even challenging silence (which could indicate confusion, anger, discomfort, anxiety, or serious contemplation).

Consensus building

- Dialogue involves listening in such a way that other perspectives can be understood. Through dialogue, individuals can learn from the opposing view and from contradictions to their own views. This learning can then lead to the growth of social imagination when multiple perspectives are shared and assimilated based upon the world experienced by others.

Take collective action

- As a result of focusing on the negative conditions of power distortions and social contradictions, individuals form collective action to right the wrongs. This action is positive—cooperative, inclusive, and caring in nature because it involves knowing people on a deep level. It is also based upon nurturing, helping relationships. Personal worth, trust, and capabilities are fostered as power is shared, not hoarded or abused.

Transformative Practice: New Pathways to Leadership

When professionals work with citizens to gain personal and social freedoms, these citizens become willing and able to move beyond the negative distortions and oppression that are revealed through a critique of their world. In this way, they learn to explore a language of possibilities as they find hope, self-determination, potential, and dreams of a better world. More importantly, these citizens transform internally to such an extent that they employ the language of action and social agency as they take social and political action to address the inequities and oppression that exist in society.

Critical literacy gives people the tools they need to deconstruct the myths that captivate them. It enhances awareness of contradictions and leads to actions that change reality. Critical literacy empowers people to make their own decisions, name and explore issues and problems, and challenge their place in the world. This process of authentic liberation is humanizing (Freire, 1984). Coupled with critical thinking skills, reflection, and social agency, practice from this perspective enables professionals to view their work as liberating and freeing, both for themselves and for others.

Three stages of critical science practice

As professionals master and steward the languages of critical literacy, they find that critical science inspires social action to correct socio-economic and political circumstances and to satisfy unmet needs. This satisfaction is achieved through enlightenment, empowerment, and emancipation. To enable achievement of these three states, professionals need to use three phases of critical science practice.

213

First, professionals must engage in discourse with others by sharing differences in thoughts, opinions, and beliefs. Arguments are often produced during discourse, and these arguments should foster an atmosphere where truth claims are stated, examined, and challenged. The goal of discourse is to find the cause of a problem and to reach agreement that the stated cause is not merely a symptom.

The second phase of critical science practice is enlightenment through self-reflection and discourse with others about the problem(s) experienced. At this stage, people realize that they have the potential capacity to change their problematic social situation (Trojanowicz & Trojanowicz, 1998). The ultimate goal of self-reflection is social action—the third phase of critical science practice. As a result of debate, dialogue, and self-reflection, individuals reach a stage where they are motivated to take social action to change their circumstances. This action is liberating when people can freely determine the direction of their own lives by changing their own situation and the situations of others. Emancipation results both from self-reflection (revealing critical insights into power relationships) and from concomitant action in the individual's immediate context (Trojanowicz & Trojanowicz, 1998).

Critical Pedagogy in the Classroom

Critical science can be used in all venues of professional practice—education, policy, community work, and media. This section focuses on critical science in the classroom because future professionals are socialized in university settings and future

Transformative Practice: New Pathways to Leadership

citizens are prepared in the public schools. In the education system, critical science and theory are referred to as critical pedagogy, a method of teaching put forward by Freire (1984). Following are some ideas for pursuing a critical science approach in the classroom.

Teaching Broad Concepts, Issues, and Controversial Issues

The teacher begins to use critical pedagogy by teaching the nuances of broad, universal concepts (see Table 2) and then facilitates student selection of issues that can be analyzed from this

Table 2: Broad Concepts & Integrative Processes
(drawn from Hauxwell & Schmidt, 1999)

Broad Concepts		Integrative Processes and Concepts
♦ oppression	♦ accountability	♦ perceptive taking
♦ ideologies	♦ responsibility	♦ values and morals
♦ sustainability	♦ democracy	♦ critical thinking
♦ marginalization	♦ justice	♦ creative thinking
♦ exclusion	♦ freedom	♦ dialogue
♦ oppression	♦ liberation	♦ the work of families
♦ dignity	♦ wellness	♦ practical reasoning
♦ security	♦ connections	♦ value reasoning
♦ respect	♦ power	♦ three system of actions
♦ diversity	♦ risk	
♦ common good	♦ caring	♦ change management
♦ authenticity	♦ equity	♦ relevance
♦ peace	♦ conflict	♦ authenticity
♦ non-violence	♦ war	♦ spirituality
♦ agency	♦ harmony	♦ ethical and moral development
♦ prejudice	♦ open-mindedness	
♦ discrimination	♦ violence	

broader level. For example, the educator would help the students to appreciate the broader concept of exclusion (to keep from being admitted, included, or considered) and then facilitate student examination of the dimensions of the recurring problem of housing related to exclusion (homelessness, low income, gentrification, social housing, or presence of pets or children when renting). To that end, the teacher does not have a developed lesson plan for content but rather a description of the process to be used to ensure critical learning (Hauxwell & Schmidt, 1999).

The necessity of teaching controversial subjects is inherent in teaching broad concepts, issues, and integrative processes. Issues are topics with no clearly defined single outcome or answer, and they are something about which reasonable people might be expected to disagree (Lewis, 2003). Issues-based learning, or that which concentrates on controversial issues, can be empowering. It is an approach that involves differences of opinion due to deeply held viewpoints and beliefs. This is a legitimate approach to use in a critical science classroom because part of becoming empowered is engaging in discourse that reveals differences of opinions and ideas (Trojanowicz & Trojanowicz, 1998). The introduction of issues with differing views often heightens the interest of students and results in an open-ended and reflective approach to topics. Students are keen to discuss issues that have political, social, and personal impact and overtones. They want to know why? Where do they stand on the issues? Where should they stand? What can they do? Not surprisingly, issue-based learning experiences offer examples of personal and relevant subjects in which

Transformative Practice: New Pathways to Leadership

students have more than a passing interest in problem solving and decision-making. Issues often contain important moral components through which students have opportunities to consider the implications of various points of view in light of fundamental societal values (Stem Cell Network, 2004).

Issues such as homelessness, poverty, racism, working mothers, divorce, abortion, same-sex marriage, and drug addictions offer opportunities to deal with controversy. Not all issues are controversial, but those that are tend to challenge personally held values, beliefs, and worldviews. Controversies can be threatening, confusing, and distressing experiences. Nonetheless, exposing students to controversial issues enables them to develop their capacity for ethical and moral reasoning and to become critically reflective thinkers—the hallmark of the critical science approach (Flinders University, 2005).

Controversial issues have several identifying characteristics. To begin with, individuals have competing values and interests surrounding an issue such as abortion. There are often strong disagreements about the statements, assertions, and actions of others, and politically sensitive issues are likely to draw protests. In order to deal with complex issues, each person must acquire self-knowledge and a strong sense of identity, and must gain objective knowledge and differing opinions about the issue. This balanced approach should also ensure the ability to take a stance on the issue without being coerced or indoctrinated by others. Dimensions of controversial issues include history, causes of present situation, desirable ends, appropriate courses of

Transformative Practice: New Pathways to Leadership

action, and likely effects of this action (Flinders University, 2005).

There are special skills and strategies for teaching issues that are controversial. First, teachers need to establish classroom rules for ensuring a safe, non-threatening environment in which to share differences of opinion. The intent is to create a climate that accepts confusion so that students can move toward clearer ideas and independent opinions. Second, teachers must attend to classroom morale that can be affected by uncivil behavior: rudeness, prejudice, neglect of needs and voices, cheating, lack of punctuality, and the like. Third, teachers need to help students move away from a black and white thinking style in which the students cling to their own point of view and toward more sophisticated thoughts and inclusive, open-minded approaches.

Moderating over-attachment to ideas and overreaction to criticism can achieve this goal. Fourth, negative thinking and strong emotions need to be moderated by reframing negative thoughts and feelings to ensure a civil approach to controversial issues (Flinders University, 2005).

Teachers need to ensure that democratic guidelines are established and they need to become good at judging when confidentiality is being stretched too far. Teachers need to make sure that learners are exposed to balanced information on issues, including differing views, and they need to decide ahead of time how far they are prepared to go to express their own views.

Problematizing Issues

Teaching controversial issues is a powerful way to apply the critical science approach in education. Even more central to a critical

Transformative Practice: New Pathways to Leadership

pedagogy is the process of problematizing an issue. Whoever defines the issue as a problem has influence over the situation, whether it's the teacher, the student, the media, the government, or the church. In turn, the person or entity that defines the issue as a problem is influenced by underlying assumptions, beliefs, relationships, and life experiences. The process of problematizing refers to how and why certain behaviors, phenomena, or processes become a problem. When did families become an issue? When did working mothers become a problem? Who pegged globalization as a problem? Why did teaching to the test become an issue? Why did these situations become problems and others not? Individuals created these issues, named them, framed them, and presented them as problems. As they did this, they defined the identity and interests of actors and their respective positions. They reconstructed the history leading up to the issue in question and they conceptualized the situation wherein the issues are at play. In other words, they painted the picture of this reality (Pearson, 1985, editing Michel Foucault's work).

If students are to hold this influence, they must be taught to pose problems instead of just solving pre-formed problems. In problem posing, the teacher and the student work together to create knowledge in a variety of contexts. They generate and address critical questions about the knowledge they produce. The intent of problem posing is to learn about and question the traditional and accepted knowledge, information, values, and approaches that have been taken for granted or accepted as inevitable. The intent is to develop critical thinkers and

Transformative Practice: New Pathways to Leadership

critical consciousness. Through the process of conscientization, students replace inevitability with autonomy, independence, responsibility, and fuller humanity (Friere, 1984, Thompson, 2000).

Teachers begin this lesson by asking students to identify the questions they want to ask about the issue or topic at hand and to describe what they are interested in learning. With this information in hand, the educator develops learning plans as discussed in the next section. A diversity of texts and information sources are then made accessible to the students, who are urged to explore, apply, and critique via discussion, dialogue, group work, and alternative, authentic assessments. Students are encouraged to accept that there is no one right answer but that many answers are likely because there are multiple ways to arrive at solutions (Cook-Sather, 1997).

From a problem posing perspective, students need to know that they could stand in a field, office, classroom, or laboratory *forever* and no problems would appear. They have to work with others to find the issues, problematize them, and propose solutions. Critical pedagogy requires teachers to provide a mental space where students can come to realize that there is a gap in their learning that they want to fill. Students need to perceive that there is a point to learning; this is more likely to happen if they are involved in identifying the issues and posing the problems that will be explored in class. To sustain this approach, teachers set a cycle of wanting to learn to fill a gap, learning something, and then wanting to fill new gaps that are identified. In this manner, students learn to make connections between what they are learning and their lives (Klaassen, 1995).

Transformative Practice: New Pathways to Leadership

Learning Plans

When teaching from a critical science approach, teachers do not use lesson plans but rather learning plans. These plans allow students to design their own relevant, meaningful learning experiences that teach the concepts and contexts that relate to a recurring problem in society (Williams, 1999). Traditional lessons planned by the teacher perpetuate the "teacher as expert, student as empty vessel" mind-set. Lesson plans contain content and procedures designed to create specific student behavior and outcomes. From a critical science approach, the lesson is about constructing a concept rather than just transmitting knowledge/facts, which undoubtedly are needed to construct the concept. Learning plans are a means to share power and foster a sense of ownership and commitment through joint planning and participation.

Learning plans focus lessons so that they build understanding of a concept from current content standards (see the 1998 national standards for family and consumer sciences in the United States at http://doe.state.in.us/octe/facs/natlstandards.htm). These content standards define what students need to know and what they must be able to do, and this can create tension under a critical science approach designed to help learners decide what they need to know, do, and think based upon what they already know. With guidance from the teacher and families, this tension can relieved because students are given a stake in their own education by planning their own learning. This makes their education meaningful, stimulating, and a reflection of life outside of school. Thus, learning plans provide a vehicle for sharing power—a central tenet of the critical science approach. Learning plans

are plans of action for the learning process for the course. At the end of the course, students decide if they have learned. This means that normative evaluation controlled by the teacher (such as true and false, fill in the blank, or multiple choice testing) has to be supplemented with authentic assessment tools controlled by the learner. These tools might include portfolios, rubrics, project based learning, assessment mapping, service learning, student-led conferences, or alternative grading techniques (Olson, Bartruff, Mberengwa, & Johnson, 1999).

Power and Authority in the Classroom

Several other aspects of classroom interaction and expectations change when teaching from a critical science approach. First, instead of teacher-generated objectives, students and the teacher set objectives together in order to ensure that they are meaningful and relevant.

Second, assigning students to groups, giving them pre-determined questions, and telling them what issues will be addressed is alien to the critical science philosophies of relevance, personal meaning, and responsibility for one's own learning. Instead, collaborative learning strategies are used by students to pose problems, form groups, guide learning, and evaluate progress.

Third, the teacher has to relinquish authority to the students, who in turn have to be comfortable with assuming authority. This assumption of authority includes control, making judgments, dealing with power, and making and enforcing rules. Students need to see themselves as learners together in a group and must be aware of power relations and how they

Transformative Practice: New Pathways to Leadership

affect the learning environment and process. They also must learn how to give up their position power while keeping their personal power.

Fourth, the objective of teaching from a critical science approach is to have students focused upon learning, rather than teachers focused upon teaching.

Fifth, this approach enables learners to perceive how they are affected by society in addition to how they affect society. There needs to be a balance of these two power positions; collective action is not effective in the absence of reflection on how persons affect external constraints.

Sixth, the critical science approach involves three levels of questioning. Instead of just using (a) the traditional technical questions that look for cause and effect, facts, and means/ends, the educator will also use (b) conceptual questions. These help uncover how students understand something, their mental images, and how their thoughts evolved. Most significantly, the educator will ask (c) critical questions that examine the meanings, reasoning, and truths revealed from the other two sets of questions. Critical questions illuminate understandings that are taken for granted, along with those that are self-defeating, self-perpetuating, manipulative, and controlling. These phenomena may be experienced as inconsistencies, contradictions, inaccuracies, and incompleteness (Selbin, 1999).

Summary and Conclusion

The preceding discussion of critical science practice wove together ideas about the connections between critical theory and critical science, then narrowed the discussion to the latter, which aims for a rational, free, and

Transformative Practice: New Pathways to Leadership

decent society. Professionals were positioned to critique the prevailing ideologies and to strive for a higher order of freedom than currently exists. The overview of the critical science approach broached the topics of critical literacy and the stages of critical science practice. Then, the conversation shifted to the socialization of professionals and preparation of young people to be critical, conscious citizens. This section of the chapter explored how to teach broad themes, issues, and controversial topics; how to problematize issues; how to develop learning plans; and how to deal with power and authority in the classroom.

Practicing from the transformative, critical science approach prepares professionals to resist the logic and practices shaped by the prevailing ideology. Working with others using this approach sensitizes them to their ability to engage in resistance, rethinking, and reshaping of society. Critical science practice imbues people with courage, intellectual curiosity, and skepticism, and it enables them to problematize their reality so they can work to change it in their own interest. Professionals who embrace the critical science approach are more inclined to connect individuals and families with their inner constraints and with their oppressors into a unified praxis that can lead to reflection and agency. Both professionals and their clients/partners can focus on the centrality of the human being and the possibilities of a consciousness that can transform their realities. Critical science practitioners experience strength in the possibilities of emancipation and the potential to challenge the central power of the prevailing ideology that determines political and

Transformative Practice: New Pathways to Leadership

social horizons for all citizens.

Professionals who view practice through the critical science lens appreciate that overcoming one set of power relations does not preclude the emergence of new power arrangements that lead to new or reverted oppression. This is why rejection of the status quo is a fundamental requirement. A critically oriented professional is convinced that the present order should be challenged and resisted; the mechanisms and deceptive politics of representation should be exposed so that a counter-position can be developed that puts justice, peace, freedom, and security front and center.

References

Brown, M.(1993). *Philosophical studies of home economics in the United States*. Michigan: University of Michigan Press.

Cook-Sather, A. (1997). *Making connections*. Retrieved June 15, 2005 from http://serendip.brynmawr.edu/sci_edu/cook-sather.html

Duerst-Lahti, G. (1998). *Masculinism as governing ideology*. Accessed May 6, 2004 at http://www.beloit.edu/~polisci/GDL/georgiamasculinism.html

Flinders University. (2005). *Strategies for inclusive issues: Teaching controversial issues*. Retrieved June 15, 2005 from http://www.flinders.edu.au/teach/teach/inclusive/controversial.htm

Freire, P. (1984). *The pedagogy of the oppressed*. New York: Continuum Publishing.

Gentzler, Y. (1999). What is critical theory and critical science? In J. Johnson and C. Fedje (Eds.), *Family and Consumer Sciences Curriculum: Toward a critical science approach - Yearbook 19* (pp. 23-31). Peoria, IL: McGraw-Hill, Glenco.

Gur-Ze'ev, I. (2001). Review essay: Challenging the perception of leftist emancipatory education. *Pedagogy, Culture and Society, 9*(2), 279-288.

Habermas, J. (1973). *Theory and practice*. Boston: Beacon Press.

Hauxwell, L., & Schmidt, B. (1999). Developing curriculum using broad concepts. In J. Johnson and C. Fedje (Eds.), *Family and Consumer Sciences*

Curriculum: Toward a critical science approach - Yearbook 19 (pp. 91-102). Peroroa, IL: McGraw-Hill, Glenco.

Hones, D. (2002). Critical pedagogy in the education of bilingual youth. *Teachers College Record, 104*(6), 1161-1186.

Imel, S. (1999). How emancipatory is adult learning? *ACVE Myths and realities* (No. 6). Retrieved June 15, 2005 from http://www.cete.org/acve/docs/mr00021.pdf

Johnson, J., & Fedje, C. (Eds.). (1999). *Family and consumer sciences curriculum: Toward a critical science approach - Yearbook 19*. Peoria, IL: Glenco/McGraw Hill.

Klaassen, C. W. J. M. (1995). *A problem-posing approach to teaching the topic of radioactivity*. Published dissertation, PDF file. The Netherlands: Universiteit Utrecht. Retrieved June 15, 2005 from http://www.library.uu.nl/digiarchief/dip/diss/01873016/inhoud.htm

Kruger, M. A. (2002). *Empowering education*. Retrieved June 14, 2005 from http://homepage.mac.com/maktress/Documents/education.html

Lewis, S. E. (2003). *Issue-based teaching in science education*. Retrieved June 15, 2005 from http://www.actionbioscience.org/education/lewis.html

Mayo, P. (1999). *Gramsci, Freire and adult education*. London: Zed Books.

McLaren, P. (1989). *Life in schools: An introduction to critical pedagogy in the foundations of education*. New York: Longman.

Olson, K., Bartruff, J., Mberengwa, L., & Johnson, J. (1999). Assessment: Using a critical science approach. In J. Johnson & C. Fedje (Eds.), *Family and Consumer Sciences Curriculum: Toward a critical science approach - Yearbook 19* (pp. 208-225). Peoria, IL: McGraw-Hill, Glenco.

Pearson, J. (Ed.). (1985). *Discourse and truth* (six lectures by Michel Foucault). Retrieved June 15, 2005 from http://foucault.info/documents/parrhesia

Rehm, M. (1999). Learning a new language. In J. Johnson and C. Fedje (Eds.), *Family and Consumer Sciences Curriculum: Toward a critical science approach - Yearbook 19* (pp. 58-69). Peoria, IL: McGraw-Hill, Glenco.

Selbin, S. (1999). Developing questions in a critical science classroom. In J. Johnson and C. Fedje (Eds.), *Family and Consumer Sciences Curriculum: Toward a critical science approach - Yearbook 19* (pp. 167-173). Peroroa, IL: McGraw-Hill, Glenco.

Stem Cell Network. (2004). *Pedagogy and planning*. Retrieved June 15, 2005 from http://www.stemcellnetwork.ca/engage/faq/pedagogy.php

Thompson, J. (2000). *Briefing sheet: Emancipatory learning*. Retrieved June 15, 2005 from http://www.niace.org.uk/information/Briefing_sheets/Emancipatory learningmar00.html

Trojanowicz, S., & Trojanowicz,R. (1998). *The theory of community policing*. Retrieved June 15, 2005 from http://www.concentri.net/~dwoods/theory.htm.

Yoo, T. (1999). *Quality of life from the critical science perspective*. Accessed March 10, 2003 http://edu.gsnu.ac.kr/~home/new/study4.htm

Young, T. R. & Arrigo, B. (2000). *The red feather dictionary of critical social science*. Accessed March 10, 2003 http://www.tryoung.com/Dictionary/shortdict.html

Williams, S. (1999). Critical science curriculum: Reaching the learner. In J. Johnson and C. Fedje (Eds.), *Family and Consumer Sciences Curriculum: Toward a critical science approach - Yearbook 19* (pp. 70-79). Peroroa, IL: McGraw-Hill, Glenco.

Wolk, A. (2000). *Social action and critical pedagogy*. Retrieved June 15, 2005 from http://www.allkidsgrieve.org/home.html

Transformative Practice: New Pathways to Leadership

Transformative Practice: New Pathways to Leadership

Chapter 11: Perspective Transformation and Reflective Inquiry

Professionals regularly encounter difficult situations that they are not equipped to deal with effectively, so this chapter examines the processes that occur when one is confronted with a disorienting dilemma. Because these challenging situations occur so frequently, individuals must be open to shifts in perspective that enable them to cope with, adapt to, and shape the change they are experiencing. The following sections explore transformative learning theory, which identifies and explores the phenomenon of personal transformation while living, working, and learning (Mezirow 1991, 1996).

The prefix *trans* is Latin, meaning "across, over, or beyond," so transformative learning is learning that goes beyond the previous *formative* learning. Learners have a "story" (or history); they begin each day with the knowledge they have accumulated over the course of their lives (Mezirow, 1991). Perspectives change when learners have an "Aha!" experience, a profound moment of insight that enables them to see the true nature of a situation or a person. They continue to *form* as persons—transform.

Perspective Shifts

At times, a new insight (or collection of insights) is so profound that it affects the learner's entire view of the world (Robertson, 1997). The learner is personally transformed, changed in such a way that it is not possible to return to the previous worldview (DiBiase, 1998). This type of learning does not refer to an individual's accumulation of additional information or

facts; rather, it refers to a completely new, deeper understanding of life conditions and changing events. It is a totally new frame of reference or personal paradigm. As a result of this change, symbols and metaphors that are used to understand life take on new meaning or are totally replaced.

Transformative learning is a shift in consciousness that dramatically, and permanently, alters one's way of being in the world. Such a shift requires that individuals understand themselves and their self-locations. It requires learners to understand their relationships with other humans and with the natural world, and it demands an understanding of relations of power amid interlocking structures of class, race, and gender. To achieve transformative learning, one must also possess body awareness, knowledge of alternative approaches to living, and a sense of the possibilities that exist for social justice, peace, and personal joy (O'Sullivan, 2003).

If priorities or assumptions change, the learning process becomes transformative. Learners gain the ability to critically reflect on their own and others' premises that were once taken for granted without any proof. By critically reflecting on these underlying premises, specific beliefs about oneself or the world transform along with one's worldview. Transformed learners progress toward being autonomous, critically thinking individuals who negotiate their own meaning instead of uncritically acting on meanings assigned by others or doing what has always been done. As a result, learners are more self-aware, more conscious of societal conditions, and more predisposed to search for new meanings instead of

Transformative Practice: New Pathways to Leadership

merely integrating new facts and information (Barkmeier, 1999; Mezirow, 1991).

Changes to Frames of Reference

Learners make new information meaningful by incorporating it into their existing frame of reference or the paradigm produced by their formative learning. To fully understand this new information, however, they may need to alter their frame of reference. This shift creates a transformative learning experience (Barkmeier, 1999). Mezirow (1996) defined two changeable dimensions for any frame of reference. The first involves "habits of expectations" or "habits of the mind" that affect how one perceives and interprets the world. The second deals with "point of view," or the way learners judge those who are different from them. Habits of mind are routine ways of thinking, feeling, and acting that are influenced by one's assumptions. These assumptions may not have been critically examined. They are called *habits* because they cause one to act without thinking, especially without critical thinking (Taylor, 1998).

These mind habits evolve as learners integrate experiences gained from logical, ethical, ideological, social, economic, political, ecological, and spiritual experiences. Learners form a point of view that is a constellation of beliefs, value judgments, attitudes, and feelings that shape and interpret situations. Points of view can change if learners get to know others who are different from them. This process is challenging because values and deeply held beliefs or attitudes are very difficult to recognize, and they are correspondingly difficult to change. A learner's reflection on a dilemma

and how it affects the self is the key to changing an individual's point of view (Taylor, 1998).

10 Phases of Perspective Transformation

Transformational experiences are usually preceded by an emotionally charged situation, a catalyst that fails to fit one's expectations. In other words, previous learning has not prepared the learner to deal with the new dilemma. Mezirow (1991) referred to these situations as *disorienting dilemmas*, in which learners experience something that makes them completely lose their bearings. Disorientation occurs when an event unfolds or new information is learned that does not fit with an individual's preconceived notions, frame of reference, or personal paradigm. This perspective change can be triggered by an acute personal or social crisis (e.g., a natural disaster, job loss, divorce, war, or retirement) or a series of cumulative events. What is central to either instance is an experience that is so traumatic, stressful, painful, or enlightening that it threatens the very core of one's existence (Taylor, 1998).

A dilemma, even a positive learning experience, can be so disorienting that learners drastically shift their practice. Under these circumstances, events have a profound impact and the resulting reflection is so meaningful that practice changes entirely and permanently as a result. The affected individual now embraces a completely new way to interpret future learning experiences, becoming more reflective and critical of the world, more open to perspectives of others, less defensive, and more accepting of new ideas (Mezirow, 1991).

Transformative Practice: New Pathways to Leadership

Mezirow (1995) identified 10 phases of perspective transformation based on a national study of 83 women returning to college after a long hiatus from school. The women participated in an academic reentry program, followed by in-depth interviews (Mezirow 1978a, b). From the data, Mezirow inductively identified the following 10 phases of transformative learning or perspective transformation (1996, p. 50).

1. A disorienting dilemma, a difficult situation for which one is not equipped: *"I was comfortable with what I was doing but now I am not."*
2. Self-examination with feelings of guilt or shame: *"Why am I (was I) doing this without investigating the consequences?"*
3. A critical assessment of one's knowledge or sociocultural assumptions: *"I always assumed that . . . .* *Maybe this assumption was wrong. Maybe I never examined my assumptions at all."*
4. Recognition that one's discontent and process of transformation is shared and that others have negotiated a similar change in their lives: *"My friends and colleagues say they found a solution and now . . . are benefiting. I feel left behind and out of touch but if they found a way maybe I can too."*
5. Exploration of options for new roles, relationships, and actions: *"What are my alternatives here and can they improve my situation?"*
6. Planning a course of action: *"What do I need to do in order to change the situation?"*
7. Acquisition of knowledge and skills for implementing one's plans: *"What steps do I need to follow, what do I need to learn to do, or how do I think differently in order to

Transformative Practice: New Pathways to Leadership

change the system at the core of my situation?"
8. Provisionally trying out new roles, renegotiating old relationships, and negotiating new relationships: " *Now that I have adapted to this new system of . . . , it does not seem so difficult or intimidating."*
9. Building competence and self-confidence in these new roles and relationships: *"I feel really good about this decision, new direction, or new way of thinking. I really see the advantage now."*
10. Reintegration into one's life on the basis of conditions dictated by one's new perspective: *"I would not consider going back to the way things were before, even if I thought everything was fine then."*

It is heartening to know that individuals progress through a series of experiences during a difficult transformation and that there is light at the end of what can be a very long tunnel. It is important to realize that transformation can lead to inner empowerment, added confidence, and newfound respect for the stress one encounters in practice. Disorienting dilemmas can be catalysts for personal and professional change. Although disorientation involves losing one's sense of direction, position, or relationship with one's surroundings, it does not have to be seen as a negative life experience. To be sure, the first such experience is daunting, but it paves the way for a healthy respect for the curves that life can throw.[1]

---

[1] Interested readers are encouraged to learn more about transformative learning in McGregor (2004). This personal account describes one person's professional philosophy and practice, and illustrates how both changed after the disorienting closure of the Human Ecology Department. All 10 of the emotions and insights identified by Mezirow (1995) are reflected and explored as events unfold.

Transformative Practice: New Pathways to Leadership

Consciously Facilitating Transformative Learning and Leading

Because reflection is an inherent part of personal transformation and because transformed practitioners may want to create leadership and learning experiences so others might be transformed, the next section discusses reflective inquiry. Educators now have access to new ways of structuring the learning and leadership environment to ensure that this type of learning happens for other people. This is particularly evident in scaffolding the learning environment. First, however, educators need to appreciate the difference between technical inquiry and reflective inquiry.

Reflective versus Technical Inquiry

Teachers or leaders have to change personally to facilitate transformative learning in their classrooms or learning environments. Reflective inquiry and technical inquiry are two different ways for teachers to think about their teaching experiences. Technical inquiry involves accountability through teaching to the tests and an assumption there are clear-cut, formulaic right answers to any given question. Using the technical inquiry model, educators are taught to rely upon analysis of their own personal classroom experiences alone, saving the enjoyment of shared stories and peer companionship for the staff room. Those who follow the technical approach also demonstrate a belief that completion of one's education, followed by busyness within the school schedule, equates to professional responsibility (Henderson & Hawthorne, 2000).

Conversely, reflective inquiry means teaching that is respectful of diverse student needs and

235

styles. It assumes that there are no right answers—just good process, appreciates that professional interaction is required when reflecting on one's teaching experiences, and uses teacher's stories to foster collective deeper reflection. Educators who utilize reflective inquiry understand that professional development never stops and recognize that this development must have a reflective component. Where the technical approach is concerned with economy, efficiency, and effectiveness, the reflective approach is concerned with values, efficacy, personal philosophies, and belief systems. The reflective approach explores the social, political, and ethical dimensions of teaching and utilizes reflective inquiry in the interplay among teacher reflection, critical thinking, and continual learning (Henderson & Hawthorne, 2000).

Scaffolding Learning Experiences

Scaffolding refers to a temporary, short-term form of teacher or leader support that is provided until learners can figure out how to proceed on their own. A scaffold helps people to reach further than they are able on their own. The teacher/leader builds the temporary scaffold with five different planks—the 5C's of transformative teaching (see following paragraphs). Individuals learn new methods and gain new insights until they no longer need the support. The learner transforms at this stage, changing inside and growing as a student and as a person. This approach to education and leadership assumes that people can be in one of three mental states that indicate readiness to learn and perform: able to do it independently, unable to do it even with help, and able to do it with help. It is the latter

Transformative Practice: New Pathways to Leadership

state that opens a person to scaffolding and transformation. The scaffolding model is built upon a foundation of five different types (5Cs) of reflective inquiry that all learners (self and others) can engage in on a regular basis: creative, caring, critical, collaborative, and collegial (Henderson & Hawthorne, 2000).

Creative

Instead of telling others what to do and what to think, creative teachers provide events and learning episodes so others can come up with their own interpretations of the experience. The educator provides learning opportunities for others to work together to pose and find solutions to problems. In this way, learners gain the experience of being passionate, creative co-problem solvers. The essence of this type of inquiry is that learners have fun, form strong relationships, have a chance to express themselves using their diverse talents and skills, and gain repeated opportunities to see things from different perspectives.

Caring

Once activity plans are creatively conceived to structure the learning environment (see above), they must be implemented in a caring manner. Teacher/leaders must resist the "sage on the stage" impulse, encouraging learners to make their own discoveries. Doing so means giving up position power while retaining personal power and setting goals for each individual learner that will help them to envision a different, yet attainable, image of self. This new self-image will differ from the existing perception and from that which the person manifests each day within the learning environment. The role of a caring reflective teacher is to repeatedly confirm to students that they *can be* thoughtful, critically informed, democratic citizens. They do not have to be unduly influenced by the media or by marketing and advertising that tells

Transformative Practice: New Pathways to Leadership

them they are missing something in their lives. The teacher's caring is manifested through dialogue, a special type of conversation that is guided by discovery as students come into contact with different ideas. In a caring approach, these new ideas are espoused by others who have agreed to be in a reciprocal relationship and are willing to function in a collaborative environment. In this way, students have an opportunity to find personal autonomy, to explore the real, authentic self, and to become the best persons they can be. The teacher or leader functions as a caring facilitator.

Critical

Reflective learners cannot transform until they identify and confront barriers that prevent them from seeing what is really happening in the education system. Teachers and learners need to become *aware* of the visible and invisible factors that repress, suppress, and constrain them from questioning practice. Instead of accepting the status quo, learners need to engage in deep questioning of the current era, and must examine the power relationships that infringe on the system. The social-political-economic structures exert a profound influence over how, who, what, when, and where teachers teach or leaders lead. For individuals to help themselves and others to expose the layers of power and interests within the system, a learner has to explore personal and social justice issues. This means celebrating the diverse and complex nature of learners while deeply questioning the assumptions behind the current era. This process should yield knowledge that can be used to exercise personal and social power in ways that address existing biases. Stressing or affirming that students can be informed, participatory, democratic citizens is a powerful approach that can prepare them to be critical and reflective learners.

Contemplative

As teachers and leaders plan learning experiences

Transformative Practice: New Pathways to Leadership

from a creative, caring, and critical stance, they must also focus on becoming visionary educators and leaders who hold well-developed, carefully articulated ethical and political visions. Visioning deals with life beyond the classroom. It focuses on the social-cultural environment within which learning is positioned. It is significant to note that contemplation does not always lead to action because action is not always necessary. Contemplation of the ideal gives an individual space by not pressuring for action upon deliberations right away. Through contemplation, one acknowledges one's humanity, cultivates the moral and aesthetic self, immerses oneself in silence and leisure, accepts the feelings that arise from this still space, and explores visions of the ideal life. Slowing down and meditating about practice helps one to become aware of tacit or unexpressed feelings and to discover metaphors that inspire learning.

Collegial

The final C describes how individuals see themselves as responsible professionals in their learning environments and practice communities. Collegiality takes one beyond the classroom or workplace into the professional realm. Collegial leaders pay close attention to three important questions: "How do I establish pragmatic, collaborative relationships with colleagues? How do I cultivate tolerance and sensitivity among my colleagues? How do I promote an ethical and political responsibility to be reflective?" Answering these questions helps leaders to convince others that they have the ability to self-grow, to enhance the structures in which they live and work, and to improve society. Professionals with this type of leadership form an appreciation for their evolving and developing profession, and by association they feel they must evolve and develop within themselves. Working with colleagues also means convincing

Transformative Practice: New Pathways to Leadership

them that they must eventually embrace a moral position that they can articulate publicly. In this way, professionals can demonstrate that they are accountable not only "to the test," but also to an ethical and moral standard of inquiry. Collegial leaders endeavor to help colleagues strive for critically informed practice in the awareness that one's practice cannot be critically informed unless one is reflective.

Summary and Conclusion

This chapter described the essence of transformative learning experiences and provided a ten-step process for a transformative journey. The discussion concluded with an exploration of scaffolding in order to facilitate reflection and assist practitioners in developing learning and leadership experiences designed to enable others to transform. As noted,

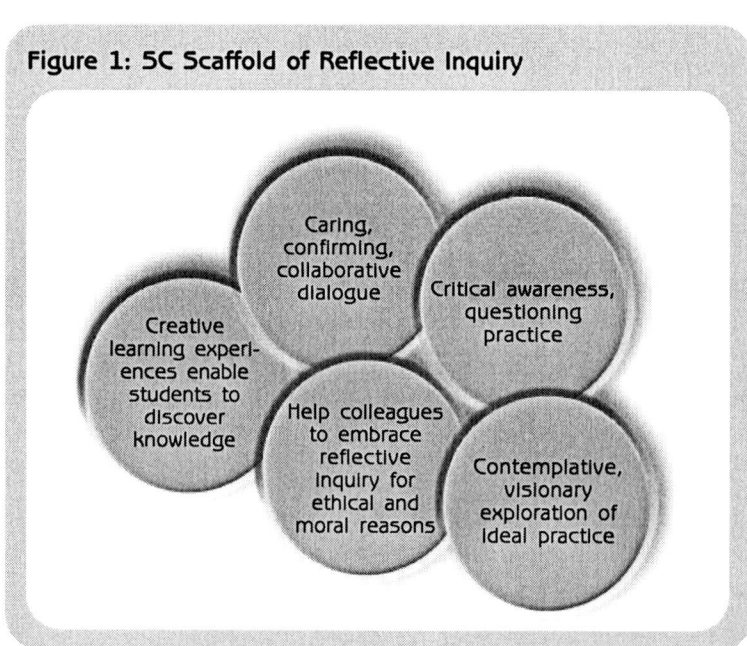

Figure 1: 5C Scaffold of Reflective Inquiry

Transformative Practice: New Pathways to Leadership

scaffolding one's practice is reliant upon the 5Cs of reflective inquiry: creative, caring, critical, contemplative, and collegial. The first four deal with what happens in the learning environment, whereas the last refers to how professionals relate to one another. Taken together, the 5Cs can lead to a transformation of the profession.

Transformative learning leads to transformed practice. Collegial scaffolding, in particular, involves helping other professionals to become responsible for the sustainability of the profession through collaboration, through tolerance of and sensitivity to diversity, and through ethical and political responsibility. This stance contributes to transformative practice because it hinges upon praxis, which is the process of anchoring theoretical knowledge to daily life. Through praxis, a theory, a concept, or a lesson being learned becomes part of a person's lived experience. Instead of teaching lessons that are simply absorbed in a static classroom, ideas are tested in the real world and are followed by an opportunity for reflection and quiet contemplation. Through this process, abstract ideas are connected directly with the real world.

The process of developing clear links between theory and practice can create disorienting dilemmas that lead to perspective shifting. Painful or enlightening connections to the real world can lead individuals to experience personal transformation. As an example, an educator may learn about the labor behind the label while preparing a unit on clothing production and consumption. This new knowledge can create an uncomfortable learning experience that leads the educator to feel a deeper level of concern for ethical consumption and social injustice. Practice will change when personal insights gained from social and political critique are linked to personal reflection (Sandlin & St. Claire, 2004).

When individuals experience a transformative moment in their professional or personal lives, the events have such a profound impact, and reflection on the event is so meaningful, that practice changes entirely. Transformed professionals embrace a completely new way to interpret future experiences as they become more reflective and critical of the world, more open to the perspectives of others, less defensive, and more accepting of new ideas. More importantly for social impact, changed practice creates a transformed profession.

References

Barkmeier, B. J. (1999). *Transformative learning.* Retrieved August 3, 2000 from http://www.usd.edu/~knorum/learningpapers/transform.html

DiBiase, W. J. (1998). *Mezirow's theory of transformative learning with implications for science teacher educators.* Retrieved December 21, 2004 from http://www.ed.psu.edu/Ci/Journals/1998AETS/s2_1_dibiase.rtf

Henderson, J. G., & Hawthorne, R.D. (2000). *Transformative curriculum leadership* (2nd ed.). NJ: Prentice Hall.

McGregor, S. L. T. (2004). Transformative learning: We teach who we are. *Kappa Omicron Nu FORUM, 14* (2). Retrieved December 21, 2004 from http://www.kon.org/archives/forum/14-2/forum14-2_article4.html

Mezirow, L. (1978a). *Education for Perspective Transformation: Women's Re-entry Programs in Community Colleges.* New York: Teacher's College, Columbia University,

Mezirow, J. (1987b). Perspective Transformation. *Adult Education 28,* 100-110.

Mezirow, J. (1991). *Transformative dimensions of adult learning.* San Francisco, CA: Jossey-Bass.

Mezirow, J. (1996) Transformative learning in adults. In *Proceedings of the Adult Learners Week Conference* (pp. 10-20). Sydney: NSW Board of Adult and Community Education.

O'Sullivan, E. (2003). *Transformative learning.* Retrieved April 30, 2004 from http://www.oise.utoronto.ca/~tlcentre/index.htm

Robertson, D. L. (1997). Transformative learning and transition theory. *Electronic Journal of Excellence in College Teaching, 8*(1), 105-125. Retrieved June 7, 2005 from http://ject.lib.muohio.edu/contents/article.php?article=138

Sandlin, J. A., & St. Claire, R. (Eds.). (2004). Editors' notes. *New Directions for Adult and Continuing Education, 102,* 1-4. (Jossey Bass).

Taylor, E. W. (1998). *The theory and practice of transformative learning: A critical review.* Retrieved April 30, 2004 from http://www.cete.org/acve/majorpubs2.asp?ID=16

Transformative Practice: New Pathways to Leadership

Transformative Practice: New Pathways to Leadership

Chapter 12: Critical Discourse Analysis*

Other chapters in this book discuss critical science, transformative learning, and authentic pedagogy. To some extent, each of these reveals the power relationships that shape society. This chapter explores transformative pedagogy, which offers a powerful strategy for helping professionals to understand the meanings of the spoken and written messages that individuals send to themselves and others. Words and language are central to conveying or hiding power. Critical discourse analysis (CDA) is used to separate and analyze written and spoken communications in order to reveal hidden assumptions, values, paradigms, and ideologies.

To gain a more personal grasp of this concept, readers can ask themselves if they have ever read something or listened to others speak and thought, "How can they even *think* that way? What are they *really* saying? Do *all* people believe *this*? What *else* could have been said?" This chapter explores the real meaning behind the spoken and written word. The insights gained can bring about more equity, justice, freedom, peace, and hope for the betterment of the human family.

Before exploring the deeper theory and strategy behind critical discourse analysis and its methodology, professionals may need to be convinced that this is a legitimate aspect of practice. The following example of a discourse (written words with overt and hidden meaning)

---

* Earlier version published in *Human Sciences Working Papers Archive*, http://www.kon.org/hswp/index.html.

Transformative Practice: New Pathways to Leadership

> **Table One: Violence in Nova Scotia schools**
>
> The researchers asked 1,800 teachers to take part. About 600 responded:
>
> ♦ 94 had been hit by a student
> ♦ 59 had been kicked
> ♦ 116 had been shoved
> ♦ 26 had either been threatened or assaulted by a student with a weapon

illustrates how unmasking the written word can bring about a different perspective and deeper understanding of the interest being served.

The Canadian Broadcasting Corporation (2003) reported a study on student violence in Nova Scotia schools entitled "Teachers facing fists, threats." To report the findings, the author cited the numbers, **not** the statistics (see Table 1).

On the surface, these numbers present the picture that the author wishes to put forward—one that depicts school violence as a workplace issue for teachers who need support in a difficult and dangerous environment. A deeper analysis can be gained by converting the numbers into statistics, but this paints a less compelling picture. Reversing the statistics describes a different scenario altogether. In the former instance, the new perspective is much less likely to result in perception of the problem as a *workplace* issue. Converting the numbers to statistics is more likely to indicate that such violence is the result of lonely, frustrated, bored, neglected, isolated children who are seeking any kind of love and attention. Specifically, a percentage perspective reveals that 15% of

Transformative Practice: New Pathways to Leadership

teachers had been hit by a student, 9.8% had been kicked, 19% had been shoved, and 4% had been threatened or assaulted with a weapon. A simple reversal in the statistics paints a different picture and message entirely: 85% of the teachers said they had not been hit by a student, 90% had not been kicked, 81% had not been shoved, and 96% had not been threatened or assaulted. The author of the report made a choice to play the low numbers and to ignore the statistics in order to depict students as a work hazard. The higher numbers were completely ignored, hiding the findings that a large majority of students are not dangerous or a threat to life at school. Whose interest was served by the words and numbers chosen? That is what this chapter will illuminate as it analyzes discourse to uncover hidden meanings, intents, and agendas.

A Tale of Power - Our Words are Never Neutral

Discourse analysis challenges people to move beyond a view of language as abstract and toward a perception of words with meanings that convey the speaker's historical, social, and political context. The words a person chooses are *never* neutral (Fiske, 1994). This is a powerful insight for professionals, who should never again speak or absorb the words of others without being conscious of the underlying meaning of those words. Words are politicized, even if the speaker is not aware of the political overtones. Words carry power that reflects the interests of those who are speaking. Opinion leaders, courts, governments, editors, even professionals, play a crucial role in shaping issues and in setting the boundaries of legitimate discourse by defining what is talked about and how (Henry & Tator,

Transformative Practice: New Pathways to Leadership

2002). The words of those in power are perceived to be "self-evident truths," and the words of those without power are dismissed as irrelevant, inappropriate, or without substance (van Dijk, 2000).

One of the central attributes of *dominant* discourse is its power to interpret conditions, issues, and events in favor of the elite. The discourse of the marginalized is viewed as a threat to the propaganda efforts of the elite. Professionals must engage in critical discourse analysis to legitimize and amplify the voice of the marginalized and to question the voice of the powerful. Such questioning can reveal the hidden agendas and ulterior motives that serve self-interests, maintain superiority, and ensure the subjugation of others (Henry & Tator, 2002). CDA clarifies the connection between the use of language and the exercise of power (Thompson, 2002).

Understanding the Theory of Critical Discourse Analysis

Discourse, the act of expressing oneself in words, is a ubiquitous way of knowing, valuing, and experiencing the world. Discourse can assert power and knowledge, and it can be used for resistance and critique. It is used to build power and knowledge, to regulate and normalize concepts, to develop new relationships between knowledge and power, and to establish or maintain hegemony, defined as the excess influence or authority of one nation over another. Given the power of the written and spoken word, CDA is necessary for describing, interpreting, analyzing, and critiquing social life (Luke, 1997).

CDA is the study and analysis of written texts and spoken words to reveal the discursive sources of power, dominance, inequality, and bias. It is also used to show how these sources are initiated, maintained, reproduced, and transformed within specific social, economic, political, and historical contexts (van Dijk, 1988). CDA illuminates ways in which the dominant forces in a society construct versions of reality that favor their own interests. By unmasking such practices, CDA scholars support victims of oppression and encourage them to resist and transform their lives (Foucault, 2000). This beneficial transformation is the central tenet of critical theory and the critical science approach (McGregor, 2003).

Stemming from Habermas's (1973) critical theory, CDA helps the analyst to understand social problems as mediated by mainstream ideology and power relationships. These social problems are all perpetuated by words used daily in personal and professional life. The objective of CDA is to uncover the ideological assumptions that are hidden in written text or oral speech in order to resist and overcome various forms of "power over." It is also used to expose situations in which a person might be exercising power over, even unwittingly (Fairclough, 1989). CDA systematically explores the often opaque relationships that exist among discursive practices, texts, and events and the wider social and cultural structures, relations, and processes. It explores how these non-transparent relationships are a factor in securing power and hegemony, and it draws attention to power imbalances, social inequities, non-democratic practices, and other injustices in hopes of spurring individuals to pursue corrective action (Fairclough, 1993).

Three central tenets

Social structure, culture, and identity are the three central tenets of CDA (Fairclough, 2000). Discourse is shaped and constrained both by *culture* and by *social structure*, which includes class, status, age, ethnic identity, and gender. For example, the field of home economics/family and consumer sciences includes professional members from across the social structure, but mainly comprised of white, middle class, women. It also has a professional culture that shapes and constrains the members' discourse. What individuals say as professionals is shaped by the professional culture, socialization, and member profiles or social structure. Discourse, or the words and language that individuals use, shapes and constrains identities, relationships, systems of knowledge, and beliefs. Thus, professional identities, social relationships, and knowledge and belief systems are shaped and constrained by the language and words espoused by professionals and by others.

Three levels of analysis

CDA unites and determines the relationship among three levels of analysis that include (a) the actual text, (b) the discursive practices, which are the processes involved in creating, writing, speaking, reading, and hearing, and (c) the larger social context that bears upon the text and the discursive practices (Fairclough, 2000). First, the text records an event's communications and its presentation of facts and ideological beliefs. The text also contains a record of the participants' identities as discussed in the communication, along with strategies to frame the content of the message (to be discussed later).

Transformative Practice: New Pathways to Leadership

Second, discursive practice refers to rules, norms, and mental models of socially acceptable behavior in specific roles or relationships that produce, receive, and interpret the message. They are the spoken and unspoken rules and conventions that govern how individuals learn to think, act, and speak within each of the diverse social positions they occupy in life (Alvermann, Commeyras, Young, Randall, & Hinson, 1977). Gee (1990) clarified that discursive practices involve *ways of being in the world* that signify specific and recognizable social identities. Persons have learned to be professionals, students, daughters, mothers, fathers, members of an ethnic group or gender, entrepreneurs, volunteers, employees, and citizens.

Third, the social context comprises distinct settings where discourse occurs. These settings might include the marketplace, classroom, playground, church, workplace, communities, conferences, and so on. There is a distinct set of conventions for each of these settings that determines the rights and obligations of each participant. These conventions outline the parameters of what each individual is allowed and expected to do. Simply put, the text becomes more than mere words on a page. It represents how those words are used within a particular social context (Huckin, 1997).

Linking text with power

As might be expected, a critical approach to discourse links the text (micro level) with the underlying power structures in society (macro, sociocultural, practice level) through discursive practices upon which the text was drawn (meso level) (Thompson,

2002). Said another way, a text that describes something within a larger social context, replete with a complex set of power relations, is interpreted and acted upon by readers or listeners depending on their rules, norms, and mental models of socially acceptable behavior. Oppression, repression, and marginalization go unchallenged if the text is not critically analyzed to reveal power relations and dominance. CDA focuses on how social relations, identity, knowledge, and power are constructed through written and spoken texts in communities, schools, the media, and the political arena (Luke, 1997). Discourse always involves power and ideologies; it is historical, meaning that it is always connected to the past and to the current context; and different individuals interpret it in unique ways because each has a different background, body of knowledge, and power position. Therefore, the *right* interpretation does not exist and analysts must be satisfied with more or less plausible or adequate interpretations (Fairclough, 2002; Wodak & Ludwig, 1999).

Discourse and language create unbalanced power relations. Portrayals of social groups appear to be commonsense, normal, and natural when in reality they are formed through prejudice, injustice, and inequity. Those who are or who wish to be in power can use nothing more than words to misdirect concern. Persistent problems among the larger systemic issues of class, gender, age, religion, and culture can be made to seem petty or nonexistent. Citizens who have not learned to debunk these words can be misled and duped into embracing the dominant worldview or ideology, even at their own expense. The term discourse may be slippery, elusive, and difficult to define (Henry

Transformative Practice: New Pathways to Leadership

& Tator, 2002), but professionals must try. When discourse is effective in practice, evidenced by its ability to organize and regulate relations of power, it is called a "regime of truth" (Foucault, 1980). It is this regime, this process by which a political system is controlled, that is revealed when people engage in critical discourse analysis. How can a profession "empower individuals and families" if it does not teach its members and families to debunk and unveil the truth behind the power?

How to Conduct Critical Discourse Analysis

Practitioners need skills to conduct a critical analysis of discourse. van Dijk (2000) acknowledged that CDA does not have a unitary theoretical framework or methodology because it is best viewed as a shared perspective that encompasses a range of approaches instead of one school. The remainder of this chapter draws upon several approaches for critically analyzing written text. A key principle of CDA states that the way people write and what they say is not arbitrary but purposeful, whether the choice is conscious or unconscious (Sheyholislami, 2001). Although CDA can focus on body language, utterances, symbols, visual images, and other forms of semiosis (signs and symbols) used as means of discourse (Fairclough, 2002), this chapter is limited to the analysis of written language.

Read, then place text in genre

Huckin (1997) recommended that critical discourse analysts first approach a text uncritically, reading it in the same way that an ordinary, undiscerning reader might. Afterward, the text can be approached in a critical manner. Price (2002) noted

that *engagement without estrangement* is to submit to the power of the text, regardless of one's own position, thereby accepting the reading and offering unquestioning support of the status quo. Wearing a critical hat and lens involves revisiting the text at different levels, raising questions about it, imagining how it could have been constructed differently, and mentally comparing it to related texts. Readers should not decipher the text word-by-word. Rather, the text should be placed in its genre and the reader should examine it critically based upon its categorization as a journal article, media piece, government position paper, public speech, manual, textbook, conference paper, or other communication.

Each genre-orientation has a style of its own and a set of characteristics that identify it—a template of sorts. Modern infomercials aside, most people can recognize an advertisement when they see one. Journal articles, technical manuals, curriculum documents, and government position papers are also easily identified. They all have different building blocks that make them unique. A scientific journal article, for example, typically includes a problem statement, hypotheses, literature review, theoretical underpinnings, sampling and method, results, analysis and discussion, and conclusions plus recommendations. Because these rules for structuring the genre belong to the institution that owns it, the genre becomes a means through which the institution extends power (Price, 2002).

Identify Perspectives

Still looking at the text as a whole, Huckin (1997) recommended an examination of the perspective being

Transformative Practice: New Pathways to Leadership

presented to identify the angle, slant, or point of view. This is called *framing* the details into a coherent whole and can be accomplished using several techniques:

- choosing specific photographs, diagrams, sketches, and other embellishments to get the reader's attention.
- using headings and keywords to emphasize certain concepts by giving them textual prominence (this is called foregrounding if the text is emphasized and backgrounding if text is there but de-emphasized or minimized).
- omitting certain things completely under the assumption that when a subject is not mentioned, the average reader will not notice its absence and therefore will not scrutinize it.
- using words that take ideas for granted as if there is no alternative, begging the question, "What could have been said that wasn't, and why not"?
- manipulating the reader by using selective voices to convey a message. Referred to as *register*, this technique presents certain points of view as more correct, legitimate, reliable, and significant, while leaving other voices out entirely based upon their position or social standing as elected politicians, corporation presidents, union leaders, bureaucrats, laborers, criminals, and so on.

Conduct Analysis

After noticing the genre of the text and examining how the message is framed, the analyst is ready to move on to a new stage that involves sentences, phrases, and words. Several CDA techniques have been developed to facilitate

Transformative Practice: New Pathways to Leadership

this level of analysis. The examples below are drawn from Huckin (1997).

- Just as text can be framed, so can a sentence. This technique is known as *topicalization*. In choosing what to emphasize, the writer creates a perspective or slant that influences the reader. For example, a media piece about peace protestors might include 11 sentences that refer to the protestors and three that refer to the officials. In this case, the text is about the protestors' actions but not about the issue that prompted the rally.
- Sentences can convey information about power relations. Who is shown holding power, and over whom? Who is depicted as powerless and passive? Who is exerting power and why? This property of the text is referred to as *agency*, and it can easily remain at the subconscious level unless it is made visible by the analyst or critical reader.
- As is true in the overall text, the omission of information about agents of power can occur at the sentence level. It is most often achieved through the process of *nominalization*, or converting a verb into a noun, and through the use of passive verbs. A headline like "Massacre of 25 Villagers Reported" does not indicate who did the killing because the verb massacre has been nominalized. The headline "25 Villagers Massacred" is an example of a passive verb that conveys agentlessness, again placing the victims in the forefront while ignoring who did the killing. Both examples involve an intentional, major omission of fact.
- Many readers are reluctant to question

Transformative Practice: New Pathways to Leadership

statements that the author appears to take for granted. This *presupposition* occurs at sentence level in the form of persuasive rhetoric that conveys the impression that an agent of power's words carry more weight. To return to the peace protest example, a demonstrator's sign that reads "Give Peace a Chance" presupposes that the government is presently **not** doing so. A government spokesperson who says, "Some of the demonstrators were a **bit more** aggressive" implies that all demonstrators were aggressive to some degree.

- *Insinuations* are another tool for gaining influence over the reader. These slyly suggestive statements often carry a double meaning, so that challenges to the author's facts or to the manner in which the facts are presented can be easily denied. The originator of the discourse simply falls back on the alternative meaning in order to escape culpability. This ability to deny any intention to mislead gives the originator a lot of power. For example, a reporter might write that a rally's 2,000-member turnout failed to match an earlier, larger turnout of 5,000. This wording conveys the message that the current rally failed somehow because the attendance numbers were lower. This insinuation takes power away from those who supported the rally, even though the rally met all of the organizers' expectations.
- Often based on the cultural knowledge of the participants, *connotations* that are associated with one word, or with metaphors and figures of speech, can convey strong meanings that influence the uncritical

Transformative Practice: New Pathways to Leadership

mind. As an example, the use of the word "protestor" instead of "demonstrator" conveys a message. A protestor is against something while a demonstrator is trying to make something evident. The media conveys a negative image of those who advocate for peace when it paints them as protesting against the government and corporate establishment.

◆ The tone of the text is set when specific words are used to convey a degree of certainty and authority. In this tactic, called *modality*, the tone of doubt or surety is introduced with words or phrases that include may, might, could, will, can, must, it seems to me, without a doubt, it's possible that, maybe, or probably. Moods of heavy-handed authority or deference can discourage the audience from challenging the speaker's positions. Simply choosing verbs or modal phrases that assert or deny the possibility, impossibility, contingency, or necessity of something can create these moods.

◆ Finally, as with the full body of the text, single words can convey *register*. Do the words ring true? Do they register? Writers can deceive readers by affecting a phony register to induce mistrust and skepticism. Register can be affected by the use of first (I, me, my), second (you, your), or third person (he, she, they). For example, a media source might directly quote a university spokesperson using first person while using third person to refer to students challenging university policy. This tactic conveys the message that the university is more

Transformative Practice: New Pathways to Leadership

objective; hence, the university's view is more legitimate than that of the students.

Discussion and Conclusion

The critical science approach holds that persons need to improve their living conditions rather than simply accepting and coping with present conditions. That improvement is contingent upon consciousness of the social realities that exploit or dominate them and the demand for liberation from these forces. A critical science perspective helps citizens to gain (a) personal freedom from internal constraints such as biases, lack of a skill, or point of view, and (b) social freedom from external constraints such as oppression, exclusion, and abuse of power relations (Gentzler, 1999; McGregor, 2003).

This chapter illustrated critical discourse analysis (CDA) methods that can be applied to debunk the hidden ideological meanings behind the written and oral word. CDA does not provide answers to the problems, but it does enable one to understand the conditions behind specific problems and the deep ideological roots of an issue (Palmquist, 1999). It can be carried out in various institutional settings or on various social, political, and critical issues by paying attention to the details of what authors/speakers actually say (van Dijk, 1999). Starting with the full text and working down to the individual word level, individuals can peel back the layers to reveal the "truth behind the regime"—the invisible power of the written and spoken word.

In plain language, CDA illuminates the way in which institutions and discourse shape us. Institutions include business, government, the media, education, health and social welfare institutions, and family as a social institution. Discourse shapes all of these institutions, and they shape it. CD analysts ask the question, "How are we *made* in our culture?" (Foucault, 2000). Professionals should consider this question in two ways: (a) how are we made as professionals and b) how do we affect the way others are made in the culture?

CD analysts assume that discourse articulates ideological interests, social formations, and movements within a field (Luke, 1997). It stands to reason, then, that discourse within a field of study is indicative of the profession's prevailing ideologies. As members of a profession examine what their language reflects about the practice and beliefs of the professional community, they inevitably discover how and why these practices and beliefs are (re)produced, resisted, changed, and transformed (Remlinger, 2002). For example, Brown (1993, 1995) discussed whether home economics/family and consumer sciences is a community of practice, raised some doubts about this, and challenged the profession to critically examine the concepts, beliefs, and values that guide its action (1993, p. 193).

Indeed, a profession's journals, newsletters, e-lists, online material, editorials, conference proceedings, textbooks, book reviews, and lecture material constitute an *order of discourse*, a network of diverse genres and discourse styles (Fairclough, 2002) that make up a profession's social practice. What would be found if professionals examined the words flowing from its professional order of discourse? What would be learned about the professional mission, values, beliefs, and philosophy relative to

Transformative Practice: New Pathways to Leadership

power relations, social conditions, equity, and justice as these impact family well-being? Are members of a profession really part of the solution or, as Brown (1993) so uncomfortably alleged, part of the problem?

The power of the meanings attached to words merits analysis of their genre by professionals. Fairclough (1995) and Wadok and Ludwig (1999) cautioned that readers might interpret text differently. Difference can be a quality for helping professionals to expose the deep meanings behind words, codified practices, and habits of language. Words are never neutral. They convey how professionals view their profession, identity, knowledge, values, beliefs, and truths—discourse permeates everything they do. Persons know themselves and others know them by the positions they reveal through discourse and practice (Rupert, 1997).

The question arises, what sort of reality and identity do professionals construct and maintain? Professionals have an obligation to uphold ethical and mature practice, something that is possible through transparency and integrity via critical analysis of language. Discourse includes representations of how things are and have been, as well as visions of how things might or should or could be. Most significantly, discourse can inculcate a new way of being, a new identity through ownership of the discourse (Fairclough, 2002). Language is central to *creating reality* as opposed to merely reflecting reality in a certain way (Bergquist & Szcepanska, 2002; Borch, 2000; Peskett, 2001). It is significant that something as simple as analyzing language can be liberating.

References

Alvermann, D., Commeyras, M., Young, J. P., Randall, S., & Hinson, D. (1997). Interrupted gendered discursive practices in classroom talk about texts. *Journal of Literacy Research, 29*(1), 73-104.

Bergquist, M., & Szcepanska, A. (2002). *Creating a common ground: Developing discursive practices.* Accessed March 6, 2003 http://www.viktoria.se/results/result_files/191.pdf

Borch, T. (2000). *Discourse in the making.* Accessed March 12, 2003 http://www.geogr.ku.dk/courses/phd/glob-loc/papers/Borch.pdf

Brown, M. (1993). *Philosophical studies of home economics in the United States: Basic ideas by which home economists understand themselves.* East Lansing, MI: Michigan State University Press.

Brown, M (1995). The concept of community. *Kappa Omicron Nu FORUM 8*(2), 7-20. Accessed March 6, 2003 http://www.kon.org/archives/forum/forum_8_2.pdf

CBC. (2003, February 19). *Nova Scotia teachers facing fists, threats* Accessed March 12, 2003 http://novascotia.cbc.ca/template/servlet/View?filename=ns_teachersurvey20030219

Fairclough. N. (1989). *Language and power.* New York: Longman.

Fairclough, N. (1993). Critical discourse analysis and the marketization of public discourse: The universities. *Discourse and Society, 4*(2), 133-168.

Fairclough, N. (1995). *Media discourse.* London: Edward Arnold.

Fairclough. N. (2000). *Language and power* (2nd ed.). New York: Longman.

Fairclough, N. (2002). *The dialectics of discourse.* Accessed March 6, 2003 http://www.geogr.ku.dk/courses/phd/glob-loc/papers/phdfairclough2.pdf

Fiske, J. (1994). *Media matters: Everyday culture and political change.* Minneapolis: University of Minnesota Press.

Foucault, M. (1980). *Power/Knowledge.* New York: Pantheon.

Foucault, M. (2000). *The Essential Works of Foucault: Volume 3, Power.* New York: The New Press.

Gee, J. P. (1990). *Social linguistics and literacies: Ideologies in discourse.* London: Falmer.

Gentzler, Y. (1999). What is critical theory and critical science? In J. Johnson and C. Fedje (Eds.), *Family and Consumer Sciences Curriculum: Toward a critical science approach - Yearbook 19.* Peoria, IL: McGraw-Hill, Glenco.

Habermas, J. (1973). *Theory and practice.* Boston: Beacon.

Transformative Practice: New Pathways to Leadership

Henry, F., & Tator, C. (2002). *Discourses of domination*. Toronto, ON: University of Toronto Press.

Huckin, T. N. (1997). Critical discourse analysis. In T. Miller (Ed.), *Functional approaches to written text* Accessed March 6, 2003 http://exchanges.state.gov/education/engteaching/pubs/BR/functionalsec3_6.htm

Luke, A. (1997). Theory and practice in critical science discourse. In L. Saha (Ed.), *International encyclopaedia of the sociology of education* Accessed March 6, 2003 http://www.gseis.ucla.edu/courses/ed253a/Luke/SAHA6.html

McGregor, S. L. T. (2003). *Critical science approach - a primer*. Accessed March 12, 2003 http://www.kon.org/cfp/critical_science_primer.pdf

Palmquist, R. (1999). *Discourse analysis*. Accessed March 6, 2003 http://www.gslis.utexas.edu/~palmquis/courses/discourse.htm

Peskett, D. (2001). *Citizenship and education II: A critical discourse analysis*. Accessed March 6, 2003 http://www.psa.ac.uk/cps/2001/peskett%20debbie.pdf

Remlinger, K. (2002). *Crossing methodological borders: Critical discourse analysis and dialectology*. Accessed March 6, 2003 http://www.joensuu.fi/fld/methodsxi/abstracts/remlinger.html

Rupert, M. (1997). *What is post modernism?* Accessed March 6, 2003 http://faculty.maxwell.syr.edu/merupert/teaching/postie.htm

Price, L. (2002). *Industry and sustainability*. Accessed March 6, 2003 http://www.kubatana.net/docs/env/indsust_lp020812.pdf

Sheyholislami, J. (2001). *Critical discourse analysis*. Accessed March 6, 2003 http://www.carleton.ca/~jsheyhol/articles/what%20is%20CDA.pdf

Thompson, M. (2002). *ICT, power, and development discourse: A critical analysis*. Accessed March 6, 2003 http://is.lse.ac.uk/discourse/ifip82discourse/thompson.pdf

van Dijk, T. A. (1988). *News as discourse*. Hillside, NJ: Erlbarum

van Dijk, T. A. (1999). Critical discourse analysis and conversation analysis. *Discourse and Society, 10*(4), 459-450.

van Dijk, T. A. (2000). *Critical discourse analysis*. Accessed March 6, 2003 http://www.discourse-in-society.org/teun.html and http://www.discourse-in-society.org/OldArticles/Ideological%20discourse%20analysis.pdf and al

Wodak, R., & Ludwig, C. (Eds). (1999). *Challenges in a changing world: Issues in critical discourse analysis*. Vienna: Passagenverlag.

Transformative Practice: New Pathways to Leadership

Transformative Practice: New Pathways to Leadership

Chapter 13: Authentic Educational Pedagogies

For educators in the profession, transformative practice must be preceded by queries such as "*How effective is my pedagogy?*" *Did the students and I really learn, and what was the quality of that learning experience?*" These questions need to be posed by all educators: primary, middle school, high school, community college, university, and non-formal. Personal and professional transformation includes reflection and consideration of paradigms, philosophies, and pedagogies—all related to practice.

The concept of *authentic productive pedagogie*s is not novel to the profession but has the potential to have great bearing on practice.[1] The productive pedagogy model provides a conceptual and pragmatic framework for ensuring that learning meets professional standards of intellectual rigor and connectedness in a supportive environment that recognizes and values diversity. The following section defines pedagogy before moving on to explore the model in detail.

Primer on the Meaning of Pedagogy

Pedagogy is an old word that refers to the art or science of teaching. It stems from the Greek root words *paideia* (as in encyclo*paedia*) and *paidagogos*, in which *paida* refers to children. Paideia (pedagogy) refers to the

---

[1] Dr. Janet Reynolds, of Australia, took the initiative to develop examples of this approach for home economics teachers (2002, 2003). Her work prompted the inclusion of this idea in this book on transformative practice. I thank her for this intellectual vision.

Transformative Practice: New Pathways to Leadership

process of imparting knowledge and skills, along with the activities and strategies for teaching. Paideia also refers to a process of education that considers each student's true and genuine human nature. Pedagogy combines the ethos of cultural ideals and habits and produces education that prepares individuals for liberty, freedom, nobility, and beauty. This approach leads to good citizenship (Wikipedia, 2005).

The Greeks distinguished this type of learning from the more mechanical style involved in teaching the techniques of a trade (*vanavsos*). They deemed the mechanical approach to be necessary, but not fit for preparing people to be citizens because it did not allow for self-education, reading, or conversing with others. They further believed that reason was the highest level to which humanity could aspire; therefore, most human activity should concern itself with reason (theory, reflection, contemplation, dialogue). A narrow focus on the technical, mechanical, and rote learning styles offered by one particular pedagogy is not enough to develop an engaged citizenry. Such a view leads individuals to prioritize monetary rewards instead of viewing work as an activity that serves truth, others, and justice. The Latin word for pedagogy is *education* and the two words are often used interchangeably (Wikipedia, 2005).

Technical, Mechanistic Pedagogy

Consideration of pedagogy's Greek origins serves to illustrate the long history of concern that educators have held with regard to the teaching mind-set. Even centuries ago, scholars wanted to ensure that educators focused not on the technical, mechanical, rote-learning approach but on an approach that

Transformative Practice: New Pathways to Leadership

engaged citizens through reflection, dialogue, and social critique. Students can experience very different learning results that are highly dependant upon which of these pedagogical styles is employed.

When a technical, mechanistic pedagogy is used, students learn to be passive observers and receivers of information and *expert* knowledge. The expert with that information is often the teacher, who may or may not possess real expertise. In this model, the teacher/expert is not questioned. Reality is fixed; there is no place for uncertainty or the mystery of learning. Reality exists independently of the observer; there is no place for exploration. The technically oriented teacher assumes that nature can be understood by breaking it down into smaller and smaller parts, and no concern is shown for the relationship among the parts. Once divided, it is assumed that natural objects can resume their original form. Linear cause and effect relationships gain prominence because they can be known, predicted, and controlled. This pedagogical approach encourages teachers to embrace technological progress as inherently good (Miller & Ramos, 2000). The technical, mechanistic pedagogy also supports a *separative consciousness* that gives rise to fragmented curricula and age graded classes. It assumes that conflict is inevitable, leading to pervasive competition in schools. Students are graded against one another based upon the amount of memorized data they can repeat. This pedagogy values efficiency at the cost of effectiveness and efficacy, and the environment is intended to facilitate the transfer of skills to enable students to compete for jobs that make the economy stronger. The social values

taught are those sanctioned by the elite for transmission to the next generation. This creates a wall around knowledge that excludes transformative change that might challenge sanctioned values. Finally, learning is limited to the *mechanics* of school life, and does not extend into life itself (Miller & Ramos, 2000).

Reflective, Dialectic, Critical Pedagogy

A non-technical, non-mechanical teaching approach encourages students to be independent, empowered thinkers. They can connect new learning to their own experiences and *make meaning* of their learning. Students can make decisions about their own learning needs, participate in the learning process, and reflect on the whole process. They consider their learning in relation to what the community needs (local context) rather than in abstract isolation. They engage in dialogue in a community of learners. The teacher moves the scope of the students' learning beyond the formal classroom and respects learning in a broader context. Finally, learners become agents of hope and social change because of new awareness, connections, and possibilities (Miller & Ramos, 2000). Entrenchment of this pedagogical approach is found in the Productive Pedagogy Model.

Overview of the Productive Pedagogy Model

The Productive Pedagogy approach to curriculum development and teaching is concerned with producing a particular kind of student: a critical, reflective, intellectually rigorous world citizen. The word *produce* can mean not only to make a profit but also to bring forth, to form by artistic effort, to bring into existence or foster development, and to help

Transformative Practice: New Pathways to Leadership

create. Those who embrace the Productive Pedagogy model want to produce *citizens*—students who employ higher order thinking and intellectual rigor and who feel connected to the wider community and to the world. This connection arises from a supportive classroom that respects diversity and inclusiveness.

This model for curriculum development and classroom strategies was developed in the mid 90s by Newmann, Secada, and Wehlage (1995) as a guide for authentic assessment via authentic pedagogy. The authors theorized that an *authentic* pedagogy includes three major components: (a) student construction of knowledge using higher order, complex, critical thinking skills, (b) disciplined inquiry so students can view connections and relationships via dialogue, leading to shared understandings of ideas and issues, and (c) instruction that involves real problems and that makes connections between what is learned in class and students' lives outside of school. This is a powerful pedagogical approach.

The work of Newmann, Secada, and Wehlage (1995) also included the creation of 20 teaching strategies that they collapsed into four pedagogies: (a) intellectual rigor, or quality, (b) connectedness, (c) recognition of differences, and (d) a supportive environment in the classroom. In 2001, Australia's Queensland Department of Education released an educational policy initiative using this model. They coined the term "Productive Pedagogy," affirming that the model is a balanced theoretical framework that enables teachers to reflect critically on their work. They use the term pedagogy interchangeably with teaching strategy, embracing the older Greek idea that pedagogy is

Transformative Practice: New Pathways to Leadership

synonymous with teaching activities and strategies.

Table 1 provides an overview of Productive Pedagogy. Of the 20 teaching strategies collapsed under the four main themes, six are related to intellectual inquiry, four to connectedness, and five each to a supportive classroom learning culture/environment and recognition of differences.

Table 1: Four Dimensions of Productive Pedagogy
(extrapolated from Chalmers, 2000; Dashwood, 2003)

Intellectual Rigor (Quality)	Relevance (Connectedness)
♦ *higher order thinking*—transform ideas, information, and meanings with critical analysis and reasoned judgment ♦ *deep knowledge*—establish complex connections to central concepts ♦ *deep understanding*—explore complex relationships and draw conclusions ♦ *substantive conversation*—use dialogue, sustained exchanges, synthesis, and critical reasoning ♦ *knowledge as problematic*—critically question, second-guess, and examine the discipline's textbooks and ideas ♦ *meta-language*—use discourse analysis to reveal power relationships in written text	♦ *connectedness to the world*—examine issues in the curriculum that resemble the real-life contexts of students and their families ♦ *problem-based curriculum*—solve real-life issues by sustained attention to them beyond the classroom ♦ *knowledge integration*—purposely connect two or more subject areas, paradigms, and fields of study ♦ *background knowledge*—link learning to students' backgrounds, lived experiences, and worldviews
Socially Supportive Learning Environment	**Recognition of Differences**
♦ *student directed*—use collaborative approaches via student-centered groups and teams; give students some say in the pace, direction, and outcomes ♦ *social support*—encourage mutual respect, a non-violent approach to conflict, and a positive, peaceful environment ♦ *academic engagement*—keep students engaged, involved, and on-task during class work so they do not disrupt others ♦ *self-regulation*—create a democratic classroom where students manage themselves and the learning environment ♦ *explicit criteria*—state expectations against which student performance is judged	♦ *cultural knowledge*—purposely value knowledge from all cultures and bring culture into the learning environment ♦ *inclusivity*—view class as a heterogeneous, diverse group, and plan learning experiences accordingly ♦ *narrative style of teaching*—use a narrative approach rather than an expository one that merely informs students ♦ *group identity and community*—build a sense of community and identity by challenging assumptions about "others" ♦ *active citizenship*—foster democratic behavior in the learning environment

Transformative Practice: New Pathways to Leadership

Intellectual Rigor

To facilitate intellectual rigor, teachers must create activities that enable students to work in an environment of risk and uncertainty. Students must have the opportunity to work on issues that are presented as problems in the real world, and teachers must strive to create complex connections between central concepts in the course or discipline. Instead of dealing with bits and pieces of disconnected information, students should delve deeply into an issue over a sustained period. It is especially important for teachers to give students the opportunity to apply the techniques of critical discourse analysis (metalanguage) to ascertain the power relationships that are shaping the issues under examination.

Students should be encouraged to critique and question textbooks, ideas, other written materials, and knowledge from many sources. Instead of accepting information from the teacher, students must create their own knowledge by discovering relationships, patterns, and meanings. This can be achieved though sustained classroom dialogue that extends beyond one class, and even beyond the formal classroom. In seminars, students should use critical reasoning skills to make distinctions, apply ideas, form generalizations, and pose new questions. Higher order thinking, such as analysis, synthesis, evaluation, and judgment, enables students to manipulate information and ideas in ways that transform the original material into something that is meaningful for them. This approach to learning helps students improve their ability to glean deep social, political, and economic implications from the curriculum content.

Transformative Practice: New Pathways to Leadership

Connectedness

To facilitate connections between what students learn in school and their lives outside of school, teachers must create activities that are based on real-life problems and issues. Students then interweave information gleaned from their lived experiences with the lessons learned in other courses and within the current learning experience. Knowledge integration depends upon respectful recognition of the knowledge that students bring to the classroom. Students begin to see the deep connections between what they are learning and what they are living in the larger societal contexts of home, neighborhood, sports, friends, family, or church. Educational experiences that incorporate real-world problems and issues have no "one correct" answer. Students often experience this learning process as a strong and significant force in their lives that moves them to influence others on social causes. They take social action outside the classroom in the understanding that all things are connected and that they can make a difference.

Supportive Classroom Environment

To facilitate intellectual rigor and connectedness, educators must foster a learning environment that respects students as legitimate partners. This dimension of Productive Pedagogy mainly deals with classroom management strategies that keep students on task, deeply involved with each other, and engaged with the topic or issue: Teachers facilitate collaborative and cooperative group learning so that students can assume responsibility for their own learning and that of their peers. A concerted effort must be made to provide support

Transformative Practice: New Pathways to Leadership

in this social environment so that students meet high expectations, find challenging work, and understand the learning outcomes, rules of class conduct, and parameters of acceptable behavior. Students learn that the teacher expects serious psychological investment in the class work, which includes attentiveness, respect for others, and enthusiasm. Teachers welcome, even solicit, contributions from all students who are expected to put forth their best effort at all times. When students receive this information in advance, there is no need for discipline because students regulate their own behavior to achieve their learning goals.

Recognition of Differences

Finally, teachers need to ensure that students know about and value a wide range of cultures. Students should also be encouraged to create positive human relationships, and to help create a sense of community in the learning environment. Implicit in all of this are the values of respect, appreciation, and esteem. Teachers create curricula, courses, units, lessons, and assignments that include more than one culture. Each of these cultures holds full status within the curriculum, including consideration of their beliefs, languages, practices, and ways of knowing in order to balance the dominant group(s) in the classroom. Ultimately, the concept of a dominant culture declines. Teachers work to help students appreciate that there are multiple cultural claims to knowledge and that every custom, practice, and view of the world is valid and legitimate. Teachers also ensure that non-dominant groups are fully represented in all classroom activities by facilitating their participation. Groups are

acknowledged to encourage their willingness and ability to contribute to the class.

Teachers that adopt a narrative approach to teaching can expedite this principle of inclusiveness and the valuing of other ways of knowing. Unlike the expository approach, a narrative style creates space for stories, biographies, cultural texts, and verbal historical accounts instead of relying upon written reports and technical proficiency demonstrations. It is of paramount importance that teachers challenge racism by moving beyond tolerance in a way that positively recognizes and develops various group identities. Finally, teachers must promote active citizenship in the classroom and must ensure that each student has the opportunity to create and participate in a democratic learning environment.

Summary

The enhancement of intellectual quality and rigor involves recognition that knowledge is not a fixed body of information. It requires higher-order thinking and a problem-solving approach to knowledge that communicates ideas and arguments instead of expecting students to memorize specific answers. Students do *learning work* rather than busy work. Most of all, this teaching style engages students in big ideas and complex understandings. Connectedness and relevance result when students connect different aspects of learning to experiences and to the world beyond the classroom. A socially supportive learning environment is a democratic one that enables students to influence activities and how they are implemented. It also involves a high degree of

Transformative Practice: New Pathways to Leadership

self-regulation by the students. More than making a warm, happy place, this approach is concerned with the creation of a learning culture that has high expectations of students and encourages risk taking. Finally, recognition of differences encompasses inclusivity of non-dominant groups and positive development of group identities.

Implications for the Profession

Authentic educational pedagogies are predicated on mindful practice. All educators have to make an informed, reflective decision about how they want to teach and "be" as professionals. They have to decide what kind of student they want to create, and they have to appreciate that the pedagogy they embrace in their practice really does dictate the shape of future citizens. Do they want to consciously practice from the technical, mechanistic (Greek *vanavsos*) paradigm or from the authentic, reflective, critical paradigm? Do they want to create individuals who do not question anything or do they want to create citizens who challenge the status quo, the power structures in society, and their sense of justice, peace, and diversity?

From a transformative perspective, the latter approach is advocated. To transform is to markedly change one's approach to life. Professionals exist to improve the well-being and the quality of day-to-day life of individuals and families. If they do not teach students and co-learners the merits of intellectual rigor and connectedness, in a supportive learning environment that recognizes and values diversity, how can they ever expect them to find their inner power as citizens? Those who do not have inner power are less able to see the inequities and injustices in society that keep them oppressed and marginalized. Quality of living cannot be optimized.

It is important to consider the virtues of an authentic educational pedagogy in working toward transformative practice. Rather than attempt to apply all four dimensions simultaneously, educators are advised to examine them separately before bringing them together as an integrated teaching approach. Professional learning groups or communities are helpful in exploring each of the 20 separate strategies in the four areas. Dialogue and study circles are essential to expedite changes in ways of thinking and practicing and to create safe, respectful learning environments. Every dimension of the Productive Pedagogy model has been around for decades. What is new is the synthesis and integration of these ideas into an authentic pedagogy for the 21st century. This is a good example of a model that focuses on the teacher and the student as co-learners in an ever-changing world. It helps educators prepare citizens instead of mere workers and consumers. It is a future-oriented approach to practice that can truly be transformative.

References

Chalmers, H. (2000). *Integration of productive pedagogies and principles of effective learning and teaching*. Retrieved June 8, 2005 from http://www.teachers.ash.org.au/bce/Pedagogies%202.doc

Dashwood, A. (2003). *Talk and productive pedagogies*. Retrieved June 8, 2005 from http://www.afmlta.asn.au/afmlta/conference/Ann%20Dashwood.pdf

Miller, V., & Ramos, A. M. (2000). *Transformative teacher education for a culture of peace*. Retrieved February 25, 2005 from http://www-

unix.oit.umass.edu/
~vmiller/transout.htm

Newmann, F. M., Secada, W. G., & Wehlage, G. G. (1995). *Guide to authentic instruction and assessment: Vision, standards and scoring*. Madison: Wisconsin Center for Education Research.

Queensland Department of Education. (2001). *New basics project: Productive pedagogies*. Brisbane: Author. Retrieved February 25, 2005 from http://education.qld.gov.au/corporate/newbasics/html/pedagogies/pedagog.html

Reynolds, J. (2002). Intellectual rigor in home economics classrooms. *Journal of the HEIA, 9*(4), 19-23,

Reynolds, J. (2003). Connectedness in home economics classrooms. *Journal of the HEIA, 10*(1), 29-32.

Wikipedia. (2005). *Paideia*. Retrieved February 25, 2005 from http://en.wikipedia.org/wiki/Paideia

Transformative Practice: *New Pathways to Leadership*

Transformative Practice: New Pathways to Leadership

Chapter 14: Intellectual Curiosity and Skeptical Thinking

Professionals can become bogged down by day-to-day routines at times, inhibiting the intellectual stimulation, curiosity, and skeptical thinking that are vital components of professional scholarship and practice. This phenomenon may work to the detriment of the profession's knowledge base by restraining growth and change. Brown and Paolucci (1978) identified six key characteristics of any profession. By applying the following ideas to home economics/family and consumer sciences, it becomes evident that intellectual curiosity and skeptical thinking are paramount to the integrity of the profession.

♦ A profession provides a a social end, or a set of services that are beneficial to society as a whole. Home economics/family and consumer sciences, for example, must contend with the challenging reality that layman think they can provide services for individuals and families because everyone lives day-to-day in some form of home environment. The profession recognizes this and builds its practice upon ethics and social issues, not just technical, how-to practice.

♦ The set of services provided for the benefit of society involves intellectual activity, especially moral judgments. Service requires professionals to focus scholarly activity on the critique of existing knowledge, and compels practitioners to determine if the common wisdom meets the evolving needs of individuals and families in the current environment.

279

Transformative Practice: New Pathways to Leadership

- Formal study and professional training are vigorously supervised to ensure that those practicing in the field are educated to engage in morally defensible work. Entrance into the *practice* of the profession is thoroughly screened through a process of licensing or certification to ensure that standards are met.
- A profession's scope and purpose are limited by the necessary level of competence and independent, intellectual thought required to practice. The complexity of knowledge and practice within the profession, however, remain unlimited. Most significantly, although a field may develop specializations to encompass the profession's full scope, all of them must adhere to the agreed upon social end (see first bullet).
- The knowledge appropriate to home economics/family and consumer sciences is not unique. What is unique is the focus on perennial problems that families encounter from one generation to another and an integrative perspective that draws information and insights from a number of disciplines. Professional knowledge has practical use for the social end of the profession, specifically individual and family well-being and quality of life.
- Professionals must engage in self-reflection and self-critique so they can present themselves to the public in such a way that society has a clear understanding of what the profession offers. Those who cannot accomplish this run the risk of asking inappropriate questions, posing the wrong problems, and missing the underlying causes of individual

Transformative Practice: New Pathways to Leadership

and family dysfunction. Pre-service and in-service initiatives must respect the "spirit of inquiry" and facilitate opportunities to improve and refine theory and practice. Members of a true profession must critique the human condition and investigate social issues and power structures. Praxis must be concerned with inequality in society and seek to link insights produced by ongoing critique to engage in social and political action.

These characteristics clearly demonstrate that professionals must possess intellectual curiousity and must be able to use skeptical thinking to confidently resist ideas presented by others without first examining them critically. Questioning dogma and unspoken assumptions by expressing skeptical doubt is humbling and constructive. It leads to rational thought, a full examination of the available options, and it opens unlimited vistas for professional rigor (Shenour, 1998). The following section examines the concepts of intellectual curiosity and skeptical thinking in more depth.

Essential Intellectual Traits

Elder and Paul (2004) identified eight essential intellectual traits. They noted that well cultivated thinkers possess a high degree of intellectual humility as opposed to arrogance and demonstrate integrity rather than hypocrisy. In addition, they display perseverance instead of lazy thinking, courage versus cowardice, empathy instead of closed-mindedness, autonomy rather than conformity, confidence and trust in people's ability to reason instead of distrusting reason and evidence, and, finally, fair-

mindedness rather than the intellectual unfairness that leads to advocating for one's own self interest.

Of interest to this discussion are several more detailed nuances of essential intellectual traits. Individuals have to be willing to struggle with confusion and unsettled questions over an extended period of time to achieve deeper understandings and insights. They must be willing to honestly admit to discrepancies and inconsistencies in their own thoughts and actions. Persons must not passively or uncritically accept what they have learned because it may have been false or misleading. They must have the courage to seek the truth and debunk the myths embedded in others' ideas and in ideas that come from their own group (Elder & Paul, 2004).

Professionals must resist the impulse to identify truth based solely upon the evidence of their own long-standing belief systems. Instead, they need to listen to and understand the perspectives of others to empathize with their truth. Empathy refers to one's ability to comprehend and relate to someone else's experiences and circumstances. Professionals must be able to identify with the emotions that an individual would experience in a given situation, then imagine themselves subjected to similar circumstances in order to experience an appropriate response. Afterward, the professional must behave in a way that takes those feelings into account. Exercising intellectual empathy in this way makes it easier to exercise intellectual fairness, because those who experience empathy are better able to treat all viewpoints alike instead of protecting their own

feelings or advancing their own vested interests (Elder & Paul, 2004).

Intellectual Curiosity

Where does intellectual curiosity fit into this process? Although Elder and Paul (2004) did not refer to this intellectual trait, it is paramount to being a well-cultivated thinker. Arnone (2003) described curiousity as an individual's search for relief from boredom, and explained that it could also be aroused by uncertainty and conceptual conflict. The discomfort inherent in this conflict can spur one to seek knowledge. Many of those inside the Zone of Curiosity are engaged in exploration, excitement, and sustained interest. They attempt to fill the *intellectual gap* between what they know and what they want to know. This heightened state of intellectual awareness, in the context of uncertainty and the unknown, is an important motivator for scholarship. There are, however, two other sides to the Zone of Curiosity. Some can experience a lack of motivation or interest, others enter a state of anxiety due to over-stimulation. This anxiety leads to defensiveness, disinterest, and avoidance. It is important to remember that what might stimulate curiosity in one person might result in anxiety in another. With this in mind, Maw and Maw (as cited in Arnone, 2003) define curiosity as a

- positive reaction to new, strange, incongruent, or mysterious elements in one's environment;
- need or desire to know more about oneself or one's environment;
- continual scanning of surroundings for new experiences; and
- persistent examination and exploration of stimuli in order to know more about them and oneself.

If being *curious* indicates a drive to seek information and interaction with one's environment and with other beings in one's vicinity (Wikipedia, 2005b), what is *intellectual* curiosity? Maki (2002) defined it as "the ability to question, challenge, look at an issue from multiple perspectives, seek more information before rushing to judgment, raise questions, deliberate, and craft well-reasoned judgments" (p. 1). Intellectually curious professionals have a strong desire to ask penetrating questions, to identity fallacies in underlying assumptions and challenges, and to question existing practice or the status quo. They are fascinated by issues and problems within their field and they are attracted to new avenues of exploration to address these perennial problems. Intellectually curious professionals are also driven to uncover new information and insights that may challenge existing theories or practices (Maki, 2000). Brown and Paolucci (1978) stated that members of a true profession respect the *spirit of inquiry* and facilitate constant attempts to improve and refine theory and practice. Members engage in scholarly activity that focuses on the critique of existing knowledge related to the evolving needs of individuals and families in the current environment. These insights cannot be achieved or incorporated into the field if practitioners are not intellectually curious.

Skeptical Thinking

Skeptical thinking is especially germane to intellectual curiosity because effective skepticism requires critical analysis combined with the desire and ability to obtain the best information (Lane, 2003). One must be a skeptic in order to exhibit intellectual curiousity through testing

Transformative Practice: New Pathways to Leadership

spoken assumptions, questioning unspoken beliefs that are taken for granted, identifying fallacies, and questioning dogma. All professions need more members who habitually doubt or question. Each field of study could benefit from having more members who are prepared to be cautious in drawing their own conclusions about the world and who are willing to change their minds if new information appears (Alberta Skeptics, 2005). Conversely, skeptics must not attempt to convince others that the skeptic alone holds the torch of truth to bring light to the darkness. A more modest, realistic, and achievable goal is for the skeptic to encourage others to consider the possibility that they may be mistaken in their assumptions and conclusions (Shenour, 1998).

It is important to note that skepticism differs from cynicism. Skeptics do not assume that the world is bad, evil, or corrupt. They are not contemptuous of nor do they mock the virtues of others. They do believe, however, that hidden power and agendas exist within the positions that individuals and organizations take on issues, and that these influence the messages they send. Skeptics do not automatically or unthinkingly disbelieve. Instead, they critically examine whether the knowledge and perceptions they encounter are true and whether they have good reasons to believe a given message or position.

Skepticism requires some training, patience, and practice. Skeptical thinking is difficult, not because it is unnatural but because more credulous attitudes require less *intellectual* work and are thus easier to adopt and maintain (Warburton, 2000). The un-skeptical mind is easy prey to misconceptions and irrational notions that

masquerade as logic. For example, many people do not question the notion that consumerism leads to the good life or that consumers exist to serve the market. For the sake of free trade and foreign relations, it must be acceptable to cut health, education, and welfare systems. If people cannot pay for something, they must not deserve it. Corporate-led globalization is the prevailing paradigm that shapes these assumptions and the State policies that follow from this line of reasoning (McGregor, 2001). Survival of the fittest, deregulation, privatization, decentralization, and individualism are the underlying assumptions that give form to the current penchant for war, resource exploitation, austerity measures, and the like. In turn, these measures have led to insecurity, injustice, lack of peace, and explicit violence. They have also given rise to inequitable and unjust economies, societies, and political systems. The current global situation leaves little room for delusions or for failure to correctly understand State, media, right-wing, and corporate messages (Alberta Skeptics, 2005).

Following are several concepts of value to professionals who wish to become more adept skeptical thinkers:

♦ In essence, skeptical thinking gives individuals the ability to recognize a fallacious, misleading, or fraudulent argument that someone else is using for self-interest. Sagan (1995) offers several suggestions for achieving this awareness. First, determine whether a statement or position is open to questioning and ascertain if it is based on good judgment, reasoning, or evidence (see third bullet). Second, ask if it is worthy of belief

Transformative Practice: New Pathways to Leadership

simply because it is precise, convincing, and seems to be true, then look for information and facts from different sources and points of view to find evidence that can be confirmed. Finally, consider many potential hypotheses and remain open to rejecting the favored interpretation.

- Skeptical or critical thinkers must feel confident posing a *particular* set of questions that will enable them to check the quality of reasoning behind a problem, issue, or situation (Paul & Elder, 2004). These questions must become second nature. Nine standards are used to frame these questions (see Table 1).
- Critical thinking falls within the framework of skepticism (Wikipedia, 2005a). In this context, critical does not mean to find fault with something. Rather, it refers to one's ability to unveil the unspoken assumptions and power structures that underlie a given issue. Critical thinkers develop thinking skills, have the ability and intellectual commitment to think critically, and use those skills to guide professional practice. Most importantly, a professional is willing to accept the results of this process and to act upon them. Thinking critically does not guarantee that a person will arrive at the "correct" conclusion, but it does increase the likelihood of that result by addressing personal biases. Individuals must accept that they have subconscious biases; they need to adopt a humble stance and leave the ego behind. Although professionals may discard entrenched beliefs, they are still vulnerable to blind spots within subjects about which they are ignorant or prejudiced (Wikipedia, 2005a).

Transformative Practice: New Pathways to Leadership

Table 1: Nine Universal Intellectual Standards and the Questions to Apply when Checking the Quality of Someone's Reasoning on an Issue (Paul & Elder, 2004)

Clarity	◆ Could you elaborate further or disclose your idea bit by bit? ◆ Can you say it in another way? ◆ Can you tell me how you understand this particular issue or problem? ◆ Could you give me an example? ◆ Can you show me what you mean?
Accuracy	◆ Is that really true or correct? ◆ How can we find out if it is true? ◆ How can we check that out?
Precision	◆ Can you be more specific, provide more details? ◆ Can you give a more exact, more clear description? ◆ Can you restate your answer and make it more concise? ◆ I would like to be certain I understood what you said. Can you clarify your answer so your reasoning is more evident?
Relevance	◆ How does that point bear on the issue we are discussing? ◆ What does that have to do with what we are discussing? ◆ How does that particular point help us with the issue?
Depth	◆ How does your answer address the many parts of this complex issue? ◆ Does that answer acknowledge the most significant aspects of this issue? ◆ What are some of the difficulties with which we have to deal? ◆ What are the opportunities with this issue?
Breadth	◆ Do we need to look at this from other perspectives? ◆ Do we need another point of view to move beyond this one stance? ◆ Do we need to approach this another way?
Logic	◆ Earlier, you implied this but now you say this. Can both be true? ◆ How does what you just said follow from other points you have made? ◆ Does this all make sense when taken together as a whole argument? ◆ Does what you say follow from the evidence you presented?
Significance	◆ Is this the most significant problem to consider? ◆ Is this the central idea in your argument on which to focus? ◆ Which of these facts and opinions are most important?
Fairness	◆ Do you have a vested interest in this issue? ◆ Are you accurately representing the views of others and their vested interest? ◆ Are you just and unbiased in your answers and positions?

Transformative Practice: New Pathways to Leadership

Challenging Another's Belief System

Skeptical, critical thinking and intellectual curiosity often reveal disconcerting evidence that challenges an individual's belief system. Indeed, most professionals have acquired their existing beliefs from many sources and lived experiences. They are confident that they have objectively analyzed the world around them. They trust their intuitive perceptions and the accuracy of their positions. They give no thought to the possibility that they use self-centered, rather than intellectual, standards to determine what to believe and what to reject, therefore they do not realize that their reasoning may be flawed due to an unexamined belief system (Paul & Elder, 2004).

Lester (2000) provided a compelling discussion of the difficulties a skeptic faces when trying to influence others to change their beliefs. Challenges also arise when sharing the results of activities that exercise one's intellectual curiosity. He made the valuable observation that beliefs do not die easily because they have an incredible staying power or shelf life that he called *survival value*. Evidence that proves a belief is misplaced is seldom enough to change minds. In the face of this reality, skeptics and those advancing insights gained through their intellectual curiosity must examine the implications of what it means to change beliefs. What effect will this change have on a person's fundamental worldview? One has to acknowledge that the human brain needs to maintain its belief system in order to maintain a sense of wholeness, consistency, and control. Skeptics have to be able to deal with the existential or philosophical anxiety that arises when personal and philosophical beliefs are challenged. Lester

Transformative Practice: New Pathways to Leadership

maintained that a person's brain literally fights for its life when beliefs are challenged as it struggles to preserve its sense of survival and equilibrium. The personal case study below illustrates this phenomenon.

When people succeed in changing their beliefs, they overcome the rudimentary biological urge to rely upon an internalized framework to make sense of the world around them. This idea may seem farfetched, but

Personal Case Study

My intellectual curiosity was tweaked when my students kept asking me, "What is the difference between the left and the right" in regard to ideologies? After acknowledging that I did not have a clue, that the students had hit one of my blind spots, I embarked upon a quest to find out. I was indeed humbled by what I did not know. After struggling with an amazing amount of new information, I discovered the neo-liberal ideology and learned about corporate-led globalization, capitalism, and Social Darwinism. But, more importantly, I learned that I had spent far too many years accepting the doctrine being imposed by the powerful business elite in Canada and the world. I realized that I had to change the way I taught and decided to shift my research agenda toward explaining the oppressive market mindset. My ideas were embraced by most students and other home economists who were ready to have their beliefs challenged. But, I also met resistance from business, economics, and public relations students who were deeply indoctrinated in the neo-liberal regime. I also, inadvertently, created anxiety in students and fellow home economists by being too passionate and not receptive enough to their angst at having their long held beliefs disputed. I often hear comments like, *"Why weren't we told this stuff before? I am so confused now. I don't want to change. I want to change but do not know how or am not ready."* I often have to rein myself in and remember that not everyone in the profession is as intellectually curious as I am. I feel frustrated that they are not and wonder why this is so? I now have to come to terms with the insights I have learned about myself as I have learned to be more skeptical (reflective practice). I had to learn that it is not the same thing as being cynical. I will always have the "spirit of inquiry" but am now more sensitive to other's propensity to bring this approach to their practice. For me, intellectual work is what life is about. For others, it is the last thing in which they want to engage. But, in order to remain relevant as a profession, we all have to "scratch the intellectual itch" and learn to be more skeptical, more likely to question the status quo to understand whose interest is being served, and who is being oppressed or exploited. The profession needs more of us to habitually question and doubt.

Transformative Practice: New Pathways to Leadership

it can serve as a useful metaphor for guiding skeptics or intellectually curious scholars. They must engage other skeptics with care and compassion and continue to examine the long view instead of merely trying to win the battle at hand. Appreciating that defensiveness makes people dig in their heals can help the skeptic to remember that it is the truth that matters in the long run. Skeptics must remain unfailingly dignified, tactful, and respectful and must always act with integrity. Eventually, those who resist challenges to their beliefs may listen if they have been treated with respect (Lester, 2000).

Conclusion

To remain relevant to the demands of a rapidly transforming world, a profession must nurture members' intellectual curiosity and skepticism of dogma. It must merge academic rigor and practice with the thrill of discovery and the desire to debunk societal messages of power and control. Professionals must continue to find ways to stimulate their minds and encourage discourse so they can actively create an intelligent community of scholars and practitioners who share the responsibility of advancing and securing the future of their profession. To instill and foster intellectual curiosity and skeptical thinking is to encourage a disposition to learn. To ignore the importance of being intellectually curious and skeptical is to risk diminishing, if not losing, the endowment of curiosity conferred upon all at birth (Arnone, 2003).

The world can be a source of excitement, inspiration, and profound mystery. Professionals who strive to be intellectually curious and skeptical of doctrine will make great strides in transforming practice as they look for new ideas, read widely, construct new theories or new ways of doing things, and challenge the status quo (personal communication, Dorothy Mitstifer, November 2, 2004). These professionals have the capacity to become the cultivated thinkers that Brown and Paolucci (1978) called for in their description of a true profession and its members. A profession must always critique its existing knowledge and doctrines, and it must continuously gauge how well these match evolving needs within the current environment. Intellectual curiosity and skepticism are necessary mind-sets for transformative practice and leadership.

References

Alberta Skeptics. (2005). About skepticism. Retrieved February 21, 2005 from http://abskeptic.htmlplanet.com/about_skepticism.htm

Arnone, M. P. (2003). Using instructional design strategies to foster curiosity. Retrieved February 21, 2005 from http://www.ericdigests.org/2004-3/foster.html

Brown, M., & Paolucci, B. (1978). Home economics: A definition (mimeograph). Washington, DC: AAFCS

Elder, L., & Paul, R. (2004). Foundations of critical thinking. Dillon Beach, CA: The Foundation for Critical Thinking.

Lane, L. (2003). Skeptical thinking. Retrieved February 21, 2005 from http://www.geocities.com/lclane2/skeptic.html

Lester, G. W. (2000, November). Why bad beliefs don't die. Skeptical Inquirer. Retrieved February 21, 2005 from http://www.csicop.org/si/2000-11/beliefs.html

Maki, P. (2002, May). Moving from paperwork to pedagogy: Channelling intellectual curiosity into a commitment to assessment. AAHE Bulletin.com. Retrieved February 21, 2005 from http://aahebulletin.com/public/archive/paperwork.asp?pf=1

McGregor, S. L. T. (2001). Neoliberalism and health care. International Journal of Consumer Studies, 25(2), 82-89.

Paul, R., & Elder, L. (2004). A miniature guide to critical thinking concepts and tools. Dillon Beach, CA:

The Foundation for Critical Thinking.

Sagan, C. (1995). Demon-haunted world. New York: Random House.

Shneour, E. A. (1998, July/August). Planting a seed of doubt. Skeptical Inquirer Magazine at http://www.csicop.org/si/9807/seed.html

Warburton, N. (2000). Thinking from A to Z. Scarborough, ON: Routledge

Wikipedia. (2005a). Critical thinking. Retrieved February 21, 2005 from http://www.wikipedia.org/critical-thinking

Wikipedia. (2005b). Curiosity. Retrieved February 21, 2005 at http://www.wikipedia.org/wiki/curiosity

Transformative Practice: New Pathways to Leadership

Transformative Practice: New Pathways to Leadership

Chapter 15: Philosophical Well-being*

This chapter addresses the specific needs of home economics/family and consumer sciences professionals with regard to *philosophical well-being*. The assumption is that professionals cannot transform their practice or the profession as a whole until they make a concrete decision to nurture the well-being of the field's professional philosophy. Because this has not happened, the modern profession of home economics/family and consumer sciences is currently not well. It is philosophically deficient and impoverished, and something must be done to rectify the situation.

Although a collection of scholars is chipping away at codifying the philosophy of the profession, it is the responsibility of each individual member to clarify and refine his or her own philosophical well-being. Consider that "for any set of philosophical ideas to make a difference in human well-being, it must *'aspire* to inspire'" (Pietersen, 2001, p. 8). Brilliant ideas may be put forward to serve as the philosophical underpinnings of the profession, but scholarly rhetoric will still fail to inspire individual practice unless each practitioner is prepared to receive and reflect upon these ideas.

When practitioners clarify and refine their philosophy of life concurrently with what it means to be a member of the profession, inspiration can become a regular part of their daily reflection and can lead to philosophical well-being. In turn, these professionals can more

---

* Earlier version published in *Human Sciences Working Papers Archive*, http://www.kon.org/hswp/index.html.

consciously strive to facilitate the philosophical well-being of individuals and families, leading to a more critical and reflective citizenry. Knowledge of this concept can bring each practitioner closer to the professional ideal of transformative practice. In order to transform, people have to change inside. Each individual's philosophy is an internal state of affairs that is expressed through professional practice. It must be made explicit so that it can be examined, refined, and transformed.

Developing the Concept of Philosophical Well-being

It is helpful to explore the familiar notion of *well-being* as the foundation for a discussion of philosophical well-being. Although it is a given that family well-being is the focus of the home economics/family and consumer sciences profession, Smith (2003) and others have suggested that the profession has not reached a consensus on what well-being means because there are many competing definitions that serve to make any understanding of the term imprecise. Tiberius (2003) agreed, noting that some believe there is no common notion of well-being while others contend that a universal notion of well-being does exist, despite cultural variations. Well-being is generally defined as *something in a good state*, where the 'something' is a human or a social system. What is meant by *good* remains unclear, however (Veenhoven, 2003).

The conventional approach is to define well-being along seven dimensions: emotional, social, economic, physical, spiritual, environmental, and political (McGregor, 2004, McGregor & Goldsmith, 1998). Veenhoven (2003) approached well-being from a different perspective by adding

Transformative Practice: New Pathways to Leadership

four "kinds of things that are well." The first involves living conditions, such as standard of living and social equality. The second is an internal fitness or ability to cope with life's problems. Personal enjoyment of one's daily life is a third type of thing that can be well, involving happiness and satisfaction in a way that is similar to the concept of quality of life. The fourth area has a moral focus and relates to the meaning of life such that the *good life* is good for something more than itself. In other words, life holds some higher value than self-interest, such as ecological preservation or social equity and justice.

Philosophical well-being, therefore, is the healthy state of one's ability to think, reason, acquire, critique, and apply knowledge and paradigms. The Wikipedia Encyclopedia (2004) defined philosophy as the act of constantly improving one's understanding by way of thinking and discussion. The Philosophy Dictionary (2002) defined philosophy as a love of wisdom. Philosophy is careful thought about the fundamental nature of the world, the grounds for human knowledge, and the evaluation of human conduct. These sources do not marry the concept of philosophy with well-being, but Plato defined it as the preservation of one's soul, claiming that it is better to be at odds with the whole world than to be at odds with oneself (Folks, 2002). To live in a state of harmony, each individual must regularly attempt to define what life is about. Professionals must also ask themselves, "Why am I doing what I do, and what is the impact of my actions? What are the underpinnings of my practice? Am I philosoph-ically sick or well?"

Henry (1995) is the scholar who comes closest to exploring the philosophical dimension of well-being by conceptualizing "political well-being" as *empowerment and autonomy* based upon moral and ethical freedom. Political well-being, or an internal sense of power and autonomy, is construed as (a) being in control of one's life, (b) possessing the ability and freedom to make decisions, (c) being aware of and able to anticipate the consequences of one's actions, and (d) having the skills to act on one's decisions. When this dimension of well-being is achieved, individuals no longer unquestioningly accept societal practices that are frequently taken for granted, practices that reinforce inequality and injustice.

Although Henry's (1995) notion of political well-being brought the profession closer to having a philosophy that is well, it does not go far enough. To be politically well, one must have a sense of personal and political freedom and control. This leads to the likelihood that one will engage in reasoned political and social actions that take into account the impact on others and strive for the greater good. At this point, the concept falls short of capturing the essence of a healthy philosophy. Henry (1995) and McGregor and Goldsmith (1998) also introduced the notion of spiritual well-being. The spiritual aspect of well-being encompasses the joy and sense of completeness associated with the holistic connectedness of the world, an appreciation of nature as a dynamic ecosystem, the pure joy of living, and peace and faith gained from insights and moments of growth and enlightenment. This definition moves the profession closer to a better understanding of the nebulous concept of philosophical well-being.

Transformative Practice: New Pathways to Leadership

Gulick (1998) does not use the term *philosophical well-being* but his ideas are useful in developing the concept because he posits that people contribute to their own well-being *using philosophy*. To accomplish this, one must first reflectively explore why one does what one does and the consequences of actions. Second, one has to engage in critical reflection. Third, one has to pay attention to and foster the existentially meaningful experiences that make life worth living. Fourth, a moral and ethical dimension demands that the existential experiences that make life worth living should involve benefits to the whole human community. Finally, one must be open to things in the world to determine their depth, weight, and complexity and to appreciate the mystery of life. Gulick's ideas contribute to a discussion of professional philosophical well-being when practitioners (a) reflect upon why they do what they do (and the subsequent consequences), (b) foster community-focused meaningful experiences that make life worth living for everyone, and (c) embrace the mystery of life.

It seems that philosophical well-being is achieved by examining the world and one's relationship with that world. The objective is to make morally responsible decisions that benefit all humanity and nature. This entails questioning the prevailing worldview and pondering the impact of practice by using the theories and models that stem from it. To be *philosophically well*, each professional must consider how practice might need to change to reflect the insights gained through a defined, deep, thorough, and mature understanding of life. In this way, one becomes a philosopher, seeking

reason and truth by thinking, meditating, deliberating about, and celebrating life.

Philosophical Isolation: Breaking out of the Intellectual Cage

Philosophers have a rich repertoire of theoretical and paradigm perspectives at their disposal. Therefore, they are especially adept at envisioning the implications and assumptions behind the thinking that guides their practice and the world within which they live and work (Wikipedia Encyclopedia, 2004). This is a standard of practice that transformative professionals can achieve by cultivating their philosophical well-being. To that end, professionals must question whether they are endowed with a rich repertoire of perspectives that moves beyond the prevailing world paradigm of capitalism, "free" markets, corporate-led globalization, consumerism, and Social Darwinism. They must also examine whether they are philosophers or mere practitioners locked in an intellectual cage constructed by formal education and unchanged by a life in practice. The philosophical professional recognizes that the world has changed and asks "Have I?" Only in this way can an individual find the freedom to pursue intellectual and philosophical growth.

Several questions arise from this discussion. How is practice affected if professionals are unsure of their life and professional philosophies, or if they are philosophically ill? How can professionals engage in critical practice if they have not clarified their own philosophical well-being? What happens to practice if professionals cannot reconcile themselves with the new philosophy being espoused for the

Transformative Practice: New Pathways to Leadership

profession as a whole? How does this lack of congruency affect actions taken to facilitate the understanding of individuals and families as they strive for well-being, including philosophical well-being? For example, can today's professionals facilitate critical reflection by consumers, enabling them to critique the world in which they live and make morally responsible decisions that minimize structural violence in the marketplace? Are professionals equipped to help individuals and families to see the merit of fostering community-focused and meaningful experiences that make life worth living for everyone instead of remaining self-centered? Do professionals possess the philosophical awareness necessary to help people to embrace the mystery of life instead of craving certainty and resisting change (McGregor, 2003a, b, c)? If the three philosophical cornerstones of professional identity are not in sync—personal philosophy, professional philosophy, and the philosophy of the profession as a whole—professionals are less able to practice in such a way that truly improves family well-being and society at large (Vaines, 1990).

Professionals do not have to define and refine their philosophical well-being on their own. Schuster (1999) clarified that philosophy means friendship (*philo*) and wisdom (*sophia*). What better way to develop one's understanding of wisdom and professional capital than in concert with friends, new and old? He notes that person-to-person exchanges that examine life have disappeared and have been replaced with academic papers and scholarly work. The challenge is to keep a meaningful inner and interpersonal conversation going. He points out that

Transformative Practice: New Pathways to Leadership

"healing through meetings" serves to break the isolation capsule that professionals tend to place around themselves, a process that can lead to transformation. Dialogue and other encounters that shape philosophical well-being are not bound to a particular routine or to a specific place. The effort to become philosophically well is worthwhile because cultivating philosophical well-being can change or recreate lives in a positive manner.

Getting Started

A *well-lived professional life* is contingent upon philosophical well-being. Although technological advances, scientific knowledge, and aesthetics can make life easier and more pleasant, the art of philosophizing or engaging in skeptical intellectual curiosity must come first to make life truly worthwhile (Russell, 1987). There are several ways for professionals to begin this process. The following section does not define *what* to talk about, but instead shares ideas that participants can use to begin the conversation:

- **Philosophical Cafés—** Professionals can take direction from other fields by establishing and participating in philosophical cafes, either online or in real time. The former started in 1997 in Paris with the Café-Philo. An American version can be seen at http://www.cafe-philo.org/.
- **Cyberspace Cafés—** Café Utne is another example of a cyberspace meeting place where people and ideas can interface, http://cafeutne.org/café/ Home economics/ family and consumer sciences professionals could easily design and establish such a venue to host dialogue rather than more traditional commercial interactions.

Transformative Practice: New Pathways to Leadership

- **Salons and Dialogues**—Salons can be organized and implemented to encourage dialogue. The word salon is French for *drawing room*. Salons, or small groups of people who gather for conversation, are making a comeback. *Utne Reader* has useful guides on how to conduct salons at its website (Sandra & Spayde, 2002; Utne, 1991). Dialogue involves a shared exploration toward greater understanding, connection, or possibility. Bohm, Factor, and Garrett (2000) discussed dialogue and how to conduct it in ways that encourage intellectual growth. Kappa Omicron Nu also provides discussion on dialogue in its newsletter, aptly named *Dialogue* (Mitstifer, 1996). Margaret Wheatley (2002) examines the importance of conversations in ways that are helpful in the exploration of philosophical well-being.
- **Virtual Salons or Chat Sites**—E-mail-based virtual salons or chat sites can be established to cover the topic of philosophical well-being. These venues require a *salon-keeper* to guide the conversation in ways that are stimulating and transformative. These tools can serve as an extension of static distribution lists by facilitating online discussion about philosophical well-being. Some good examples of the etiquette, logistics, and other procedures that are involved in establishing educational chat rooms are available at http://www.siec.k12.in.us/~west/edu/chat.htm
- **Study Circles**—Locally based study circles can be formed to explore philosophical well-

Transformative Practice: New Pathways to Leadership

being. A study circle is a group of 8-12 people from different backgrounds and viewpoints who meet several times to talk about an issue. This idea is particularly beneficial in light of the profession's existing structure. It provides a vehicle for connecting the many professionals who have specialized and moved away from a central philosophical core. In a study circle, everyone has an equal voice and participants try to understand each other's views. They do not have to agree with each other. The idea is to share concerns and look for ways to make things better. A facilitator helps the group to focus on different views and ensures that the discussion runs smoothly. The Study Circle Resource Center provides useful information regarding this format. It can be obtained from http://www.studycircles.org/ or by calling 860- 928- 2626.

♦ **Reading Circles**—The idea of reading circles is often credited to Paulo Freire. He developed "culture circles," or problem-solving study groups to guide discussion and learning experiences. Reading Circle members read the agreed upon material before gathering to discuss it. State or local area groups can establish Reading Circles with some coordination from a central source. Several ideas for structuring a reading circle are available from the Vancouver Community Network site at http://www.vcn.bc.ca/citizens-handbook/2_15_discussion_group.html. Brown and Hayes (2001) also provide a model of reading circles as a mode of professional learning.

Transformative Practice: New Pathways to Leadership

- **Web based networking**—Professionals can follow the lead of The New Civilization Network, http://www.newciv.org/, to set up a web-based forum capable of linking practitioners who are committed to becoming philosophically well.
- **On-Line Philosophical Well-being Journal**—Professionals can organize and contribute to an online journal for posting think pieces about the concept of philosophical well-being. The Human Sciences Working Papers Archive, found at http://www.kon.org/hswp/index.html, offers an existing framework that is well-suited to this purpose.

Summary

Members of the profession cannot transform their individual practice or the profession as a whole until they make a conscious choice and an ongoing, concerted effort to nurture the wellness of their professional philosophy. A well-lived professional life is contingent upon the philosophical well-being achieved when professionals are consciously aware of why they are doing what they do, along with the impact that their actions will have on the well-being and quality of life of individuals and families. Practicing from a state of unawareness is irresponsible because each action and inaction involves the risk of creating potential harm instead of providing the intended help. This harm can be avoided, or at least mitigated, when professionals nurture a meaningful inner and interpersonal conversation about practice. These mental and oral conversations create a rich repertoire of theoretical and paradigmatic perspectives that professionals can draw upon to address the myriad of pressing issues that families face each day in a complex, interconnected world.

References

Bohm, D., Factor, D., & Garrett, P. (2000). *Dialogue.* Retrieved January 25, 2004 from http://www.muc.de/~heuvel/dialogue/dialogue_proposal.html#2

Brown, M., & Hayes, H. (2001, November). Professional reading circles. *ultiBase Archives*, Retrieved January 25, 2004 from http://ultibase.rmit.edu.au/Articles/nov01/brown1.htm

Folks, J. J. (2002). Remembrance and healing in Poe's narrative of childhood grief. *Queen: A Journal of Rhetoric and Power, Special Issue.* Retrieved January 22, 2004 from http://www.ars-rhetorica.net/Queen/VolumeSpecialIssue/Articles/Folks.pdf

Gulick, W. B. (1998, August). Philosophy as a contributor of well-being. Paper presented at the 20th *World Congress of Philosophy Paideia*. Boston, MA. On line proceedings Retrieved January 22, 2004 from http://www.bu.edu/wcp/Papers/Educ/EducGuli.htm

Henry, M. I. (1995). Is well-being the focus of home economics? A report on an Australian study. *Proceedings of the Home Economics Institute of Australia conference* (pp. 79-84). Fremantle, Australia: HEIA.

McGregor, S. L. T. (2003a). Consumerism as a source of structural violence. *KON Human Science Working Paper Series.* Retrieved February 10, 2004 from http://www.kon.org/hswp/archive/consumerism.html

McGregor, S. L. T. (2003b). Critical science approach: A primer. *Kappa Omicron Nu FORUM, 15* (1). Retrieved February 10, 2004 from http://www.kon.org/cfp/critical_science_primer.pdf

McGregor, S. L. T. (2003c). Postmodernism, consumerism and a culture of peace. *Kappa Omicron Nu FORUM, 13*(2). Retrieved February 10, 2004 from http://www.kon.org/archives/forum/13-2/mcgregor.html

McGregor, S. L. T. (2004). Taking the home economics paradigm into the 21st century. In N. Aria (Ed.), *IFHE Post Congress Proceedings for A New Paradigm for Home Economics.* Japan Association of Home Economics Education. Available at http://www.consultmcgregor.com

McGregor, S. L. T., & Goldsmith, E. B. (1998).

Transformative Practice: New Pathways to Leadership

Expanding our understanding of quality of life, standard of living, and well-being. *Journal of Family and Consumer Sciences, 90* (2), 2-6, 22.

Mitstifer, D. I. (1996). Dialogue. *Kappa Omicron Nu Dialogue, 6*(1), 1-3.

Philosophy Dictionary. (2002). *Philosophy*. Retrieved January 22, 2004 from http://www.philosophypages.com/dy/p5.htm#phiy

Pietersen, H. (2001). Philosophy and well-being. *The Examined Life On-Line Philosophy Journal, 2*(5). Retrieved January 22, 2004 from http://examinedlifejournal.com/articles/template.php?shorttitle=wellbeing&authorid=17

Russell, B. (1987). Moral standards and social well-being. In A. Seckel (Ed.), *On ethics, sex and marriage* (pp. 129-149). New York: Prometheus Books.

Sandra, J., & Spayde, J. (2002). *Salons: The joy of conversation*. Gabriola Island, BC: New Society Publishers.

Schuster, S. S. (1999). Philosophy practices as alternative ways to well-being. *Radical Psychology, 1*(1). Retrieved February 10, 2004 from http://www.yorku.ca/danaa/vol1-1/Schuster.htm

Smith, F. (2003) Pie in the sky? Reaching consensus on a political/moral focus. *Kappa Omicron Nu FORUM, 15*(1). Retrieved February 10, 2004 from http://www.kon.org/archives/forum/15-1/smith.pdf

Tiberius, V. (2003). *Cultural differences and philosophical accounts of well-being*. Retrieved January 22, 2004 from http://www.tc.umn.edu/~tiberius/my_papers/wb%20and%20culture%203.pdf 28 pages

Utne, E. (1991). The salon keepers companion. *Utne Reader Web Special Archive Issues* Retrieved February 10, 2004 from http://www.utne.com/web_special/web_specials_archives/articles/2977-1.html

Vaines, E. (1990). Philosophical orientations and home economics: An introduction. *Canadian Home Economics Journal, 40*(1), 6-11.

Veenhoven, R. (2003). Subjective measures of well-being. In M. McGillivray (Ed.) *Measuring human well-being*. Retrieved February 10, 2004 from http://www.eur.nl/fsw/research/veenhoven/Pub2000s/SWB-WIDERchapterRV2.rtf

Wheatley, M. (2002). *Turning to one another*. San Francisco: Barrett-Koehler.

Wikipedia Encyclopedia. (2004). *Philosophical counseling*. Retrieved January 22, 2004 from http://en.wikipedia.org/wiki/Philosophical_counseling

Transformative Practice: New Pathways to Leadership

Transformative Practice: New Pathways to Leadership

Chapter 16: Communities of Practice

When professional practitioners do not push the limits of their field of study, the body of knowledge stagnates. A special kind of community is needed to perform for this transcending and transformative work. Wenger (1998a, b) offered the concept of communities of practice (CoP) as a venue for this boundary-pushing activity that can profoundly change practice in the field: "Communities of practice are social groups who share their expertise and passion about a topic and interact on an ongoing basis to further their learning in this domain" (Wenger & Snyder, 2001, p. 3). When working in a community of practice, the term *practice* takes on a meaning other than "to do something." Instead, it becomes "a way of *talking about* the shared historical and social resources, frameworks, and perspectives that can sustain mutual engagement in action" [italics added] (Wenger, 1998, p. 5).

The intent of these communities of practice is to steward a particular practice and to nurture, enrich, spread, and entrench a valued contribution to a profession. Members of a community of practice negotiate what has meaning for them. In this case, *negotiate* means "continuous interaction, gradual achievement, and a give-and-take approach" (Wenger, 1998b, p. 53). Three key processes thus unfold, specifically (a) an emerging identity of one's self while (b) actively participating in the group learning process to (c) steward a particular aspect of practice. Because individuals derive meaning in life by "doing with others," the

Transformative Practice: New Pathways to Leadership

group needs them and they need the group. This is a powerful synergy and a welcomed approach to practice within a profession. The rest of the chapter will focus on strategies for forming, managing, leading, and nurturing these communities.

CoPs are Different from Other Social Groups

CoPs differ from other social groups on four basic criteria: their purpose, who belongs, what holds them together, and how long they last (Nickols, 2000; Wenger & Snyder, 2000). Other social groups in a work context include formal team work groups, project teams and task forces, and informal networks. Work teams are formed by management to do ongoing daily work, have a defined membership, have deadlines and deliverables, and report to the boss. They last until the work is done. Project teams or task forces are formed by management for a specific task or assignment within a particular time frame, have a defined membership, have project goals and milestones, and last until the work is done and then disband. Informal networks, as a set of relationships, are not necessarily "about something." They collect and share information of common interest and do so because people perceive a value in belonging and they get value from participating in the network. The network will last as long as people have a reason to stay connected and to share information. The network does not have a topic, does not shape the person's identity, nor does it create a shared practice.

A community of practice, on the other hand, has self-selected members who are committed to the expertise that forms the basis of their practice. A CoP is organized around

Transformative Practice: New Pathways to Leadership

"what matters" to the members. The membership involves whoever participates and contributes to the practice. People can participate in different ways and to different degrees. Belonging to the community changes the person's identity. Within the CoP, members continue to develop their expertise and to define their role or place in the community. It endures as long as there is interest in improving the practice of the domain and an interest in maintaining the community. The community has a life cycle. It comes together because someone sees a need and people self-select or are recruited. It develops and evolves through sharing knowledge, problem solving, and improving practice. It can wind down because the value of being a member diminishes as the problems of practice are solved or as practice improves. Finally, it can shut down and disperse according to the timing, the logic of continuing, the rhythm, and the social energy of the shared learning (Nickols, 2000; Wenger, 1998b; Wenger & Snyder, 2000).

Wenger (1998b) enriched this discussion of the life cycle of a community of practice with a slightly different approach. He identified five stages of development with associated member activities. In the first stage, professionals face similar situations without the benefit of a shared practice. At this stage, people learn about each other and realize the potential of discovering commonalties.

In the second stage, individuals coalesce into a group, celebrate their potential as they explore connectedness, define the joint enterprise that they will work on together, and negotiate their way into and around the community by continuous interaction, gradual

Transformative Practice: New Pathways to Leadership

achievement, and a give-and-take approach.

Third, the members of the community of practice are very active in developing their practice by engaging in joint work, creating artifacts or documents, and adapting, renewing, and committing to mutual relationships. As they commit to stewarding the competencies of a profession, they discuss novel ideas and keep up with developments inside and outside the field. Instead of sharing best practices, they work together on problems. Collaborative inquiry makes people want to belong so they can be part of a dynamic, forward-looking professional community of practice. Members of the CoP are interacting, not just to accomplish work but to clarify and define that work. The higher purpose is to create new knowledge for the profession. This purpose can be realized because synergy is created between members who build upon the profession and the knowledge base.

In the fourth stage of the community's life cycle, members no longer engage as intensely but the community is still alive, is a force within the profession, and is a recognized center of knowledge. The community is established and goes through cycles of activities. Energy is sustained, some interest is renewed, and members continue to find a voice and influence.

In the final stage, the community of practice is no longer central to the profession or its members but it has a special place in everyone's identity. People start to disperse at this stage by staying in touch, holding reunions, and calling each other for advice. People share stories, preserve artifacts from their collective work, and collect memorabilia in memory of the community.

Transformative Practice: New Pathways to Leadership

Designing and Creating a Community of Practice

To create a community of practice, it is paramount for the design to allow learning to occur instead of merely instituting a new organizational structure. Wenger, McDermott and Snyder (2002) suggested seven principles to follow when designing and cultivating a community of practice. The main goal of these principles is to create a community of practice that is alive, growing, evolving, flexible, and responsive to its inner and outer environments. The objective is to find and to emphasize the inner character and energy of the collection of community members so that the community can be self-directed, spontaneous, and natural. Participants' dormant capabilities must be leveraged so they can contribute to the lively work of the community of practice. The following discussion details each of these principles and incorporates relevant ideas from McDermott's (2001) discussion of 10 critical factors to ensure success when building communities of practice.

Evolution

Instead of creating a community from scratch, someone *shepherds* the evolution of the community. Shepherds show people the way to the community, which often stems from existing networks or collections of people with similar interests and passions. The intent of this principle is to help the community to coalesce and develop, rather than impose a specific structure upon it. The latter negates the dynamic nature that a CoP must exhibit in order to thrive and energetically unfold. Once people are drawn to the group and relationships begin to form or solidify, community members reflect upon what they need to do their work and

313

Transformative Practice: New Pathways to Leadership

redesign the elements that make up the community, such as a website, list serve, working papers, weekly meetings, or conference calls. The structure of the community must take into account the geographic distribution, cultural orientations, and the size of the group as well as the cohesiveness of the group and the kind of knowledge that is being shared and stewarded. The structures that are put into place must catalyze the group to evolve and grow. The greatest danger of growing communities is for them to lose energy and drift into apathy. Steps have to be taken to maintain the energy level, to get others involved, and to remain on the cutting edge of the field. These steps include (a) getting respected leaders and thinkers involved as early as possible, (b) creating regular forums and events so participants have a sense of history and evolution, (c) holding live events to build commonality, enthusiasm, and trust, and (d) maintaining personal, one-on-one contact so that individuals feel connected when they first arrive at the regular forums.

Dialogue

A community of practice needs both an insider and outsider point of view. If the design of a CoP involves those outside the community and those inside it, the content of communications should facilitate a dialogue about what the community can achieve and the environment needed for that action. An insider has an appreciation for the needs of the community, the challenges of the field, and the knowledge that needs to be shared or stewarded. An outsider's involvement can sharpen the community's understanding of the strategic potential it has relative to other

Transformative Practice: New Pathways to Leadership

communities or those not involved in the field of study. Designing the CoP to ensure this dialogue can provide an invaluable head start in becoming established and gaining focus. When applying this principle, the designers arrange for events that focus on solving problems rather than presenting best practices. To create real dialogue about cutting edge issues, organizers must ask participants to explain the logic of their approach to solving problems. This dialogue helps the community to discuss both existing and alternative assumptions and encourages members to think together rather than engage in a battle of positions. One effective way to build connections is to work in three-person groups before interacting as a whole community. This approach builds incremental trust so that people feel comfortable talking openly. The development of CoP profiles fosters relationships and enhances the intellectual work of the community.

Participation

A CoP should be designed so that people can choose to participate on a level that reflects their current and potential interests and commitment. CoPs should have a range of roles that include both opportunities for newcomers and leadership for the old timers. These levels of participation include core (15%), active (20%), peripheral (65%), and intellectual neighbors (those surrounding the community with an interest in its work). The *core* group of high contributors builds the fire at the center to draw people into the community's current work. It also does most of the work of the community. Core group members are not always world leaders in the field, but they all demonstrate a passion for the topic and the community. Members of the core group are likely candidates for the coordinator role. *Active* members are regular attendees but only participate when the flame draws them to the core. Sometimes they are "lurkers" who only participate occasionally. Those on the boundary of the community, the *peripherals,* seem inactive at first glance. In reality, they are often quiet observers learning from a different perspective. Their level of involvement and current commitment may be lower because of lack of time, lack of what they see as a legitimate voice, or a sense of having no authority. Another related group includes the legitimate peripheral participants who hang out at the boundary between the center and the periphery. They are not responsible for the conversation and dialogue but they are free to join whenever they wish. As the topic being addressed by the community shifts, so does the identity of those in the core, active, and peripheral participation groups. Indeed, those designing a community of practice must adhere to this principle by incorporating benches for those on the sideline, spaces for semi-private conversations, and room for small initiatives that temporarily unite participants to the core.

Spaces

To continue from the previous discussion, the principle of shifting roles requires CoP designers to create private space for one-on-one or small-group conversations and public spaces for all community members to interact in conferences or meetings. When the relationships among the members are strong, the events are much richer. Conversely, when the events are richer, the personal connections become richer. The public events also provide rituals that foster the

Transformative Practice: New Pathways to Leadership

culture of the community and help those working in the private spaces to appreciate the level of sophistication and intellectual assets that the community stewards, how CoPs rally around key principles, and what influence they have on the profession as a whole. For this reason, the design of the community must provide for flexible, extendable gathering places and an infrastructure that includes both high tech and a soft touch.

Value

Communities of practice thrive because they provide value both to the members and to the parent profession. Because the impact of the CoP typically takes time to emerge, application of this principle requires an initial respect for the value of the community to its members. Members who experience value are more inclined to contribute to the systematic development of the body of knowledge that will be accessible to the profession at large. To gauge this value, members need to know that they are expected to share the logic and reasoning behind their work. The rationale is not always self-evident, so members must communicate in ways that help others to understand the value of participating in the community. Most importantly, codifying the value helps gauge the impact of the community of practice.

Familiarity and Excitement

This principle holds that a CoP must be designed in such a way that people feel at home but also know that they can expect to experience new ideas and new people on an ongoing basis. An interesting paradox drives the application of this principle. Although familiarity can invite candid discussions, it breeds resistance to the

Transformative Practice: New Pathways to Leadership

excitement of new ideas and contributions. The challenge is to provide a level of novelty and excitement that complements the familiarity of everyday activities. This can be done by inviting controversial speakers whose views are different but respected and who challenge normal ways of thinking. The objective is to encourage spontaneous contact among people while still respecting the need for comfort zones. The intended result is a *lively* community where people feel connected, excited, and engaged with new ideas and new people in a common adventure.

Rhythm

This principle requires the establishment of a suitable pace for member activities. A vibrant community of practice must have a rhythm—a regular pattern of activities, a cadence that sets the pace for interactions. When the beat is strong, the community has a sense of familiarity, movement, and liveliness. When the beat is too fast, overwhelmed members burn out. When it is too slow, members become sluggish and uninspired. Although the beat will change as the community evolves, it is very important to implement the right pace at the right time. This is achieved by including familiar and exciting events along with frequent private conversations, and by facilitating the inherent ebb and flow of people back and forth from the core to the sidelines. The rhythm of the community is the strongest indicator of its aliveness.

Stam (2003) devised an on-line questionnaire to help professionals develop a community of practice. Her instrument helped the respondent to determine common interests and scope (Wenger, McDermott, &

Transformative Practice: New Pathways to Leadership

Snyder, 2002). It also asked why a community of practice was needed, questioned what was missing in the current structure, and helped to pinpoint what should be the primary aim of the CoP. To answer the latter, respondents could select from among best practices, stimulating collaboration, developing new knowledge, creating synergy, and delivering solutions to problems. Stam also included a section on the perceived benefits of creating and joining a CoP, both for the individual members and for the organization. The instrument inquired about the time people were prepared to invest, the size of the group, potential members, and the quality of prospective members. Other questions dealt with the expectations and assurances members might have regarding the content, specifically pinpointing what information would be valued, solicited, and constantly received. Still other questions explored the roles that organizers wished to play within the community of practice (e.g., champion, general member, facilitator/coordinator/broker, thinker, and practice leader, or sponsor) and how they anticipated meeting, along with their ideas regarding the level of support that could be expected from existing management.

Nickols (2003) and LeMoult (2002) provided more detail on the different roles people play in the community. The Champion provides the energy and enthusiasm in the role as chief organizer of events and communications. The Facilitator is responsible for clarifying communications, drawing out the reticent, and making sure dissenting views are heard and honored—all subject to the will of the group. The Practice Leader is the acknowledged leader of

Transformative Practice: New Pathways to Leadership

the whole community because of competence in the particular domain and scope of the community of practice. The person in this role shifts in and out, depending on the issues and concerns of the CoP. The Practice Leader always emerges rather than being appointed. The Members share the primary responsibility for participating actively, learning, and sharing what they learn. The Integrator serves as the liaison between the CoP and the outside world and also ensures that there is little duplication of information shared within the CoP. This person is the internal communications/external liaison officer. If the community of practice is sponsored (instead of self-organizing), the Sponsor has the primary role of garnering support and visibility for the community of practice. In this case, the intent of the CoP is to steward a particular practice and to nurture, enrich, spread, and entrench a valued contribution to the profession. In this role, the Sponsor deals with resource issues such as time and funding, and plays a key role in ensuring that the community's mission and expected outcomes are agreed upon and respected.

Indicators that a Community Has Formed

The previous section focused on how to design or create a community of practice, but it is also important to explore the circumstances or events that might indicate that a community of practice has already formed or is evolving. Nickols (2000) detailed several of these factors. First, people have a strong sense of identity that is tied to the community. Continuing mutual relationships exist that may be either rough or smooth in nature. People are learning shared ways of doing things that did not exist before. They are sharing an evolving

Transformative Practice: New Pathways to Leadership

language, special jargon, terms, and shortcuts including acronyms. The perspectives that are shared reflect a common way of viewing the world. Community members are developing common stories, legends, lore, and inside jokes. There is a widespread and shared awareness of each other's competencies, contributions, strengths, and shortcomings.

A rapid flow of relevant information occurs in conjunction with conversations about the content. This flow comes swiftly to the point, rather than emerging after a long lead-in, which is not necessary due to the existence of an agreed upon domain. There is an effective grapevine that facilitates the flow of information, and there is a rapid diffusion of innovations—people quickly adopt what works. Members act in such a way that others know they are members in good standing. There is

a fairly broad consensus among members regarding who is in the community and who is not. These members are creating common tools, methods, and artifacts to facilitate the work of the community. CoP members are likely to be writing and producing publications on a regular basis, they often invite others to special briefings on their results and insights. Members also demonstrate an ability to assess the effectiveness of actions and the usefulness of the work they have accomplished (Nickols, 2000).

Three Dimensions of a Community of Practice

A community of practice is not like other communities. It is a group that is characterized along the three dimensions of (a) the joint enterprise that determines what the group is about, (b) the mutual engagement it diplays when working on shared tasks, and (c) the

shared repertoire or common methods and approaches it creates to do the work (Wenger, 1998a).

Joint Enterprise

Joint enterprise refers to members' agreement on the tasks that will be worked on within the community of practice. People in the community negotiate an understanding of their engagement in common tasks. As participants agree upon the joint enterprise or undertaking, they also negotiate a system of joint responsibility through which they are held accountable to one another. In this process, participants decide what matters to them and how they will exercise responsibility. They ensure that members sufficiently understand the enterprise so they can contribute to its success and share in the identity of a given community of practice, as each member may belong to multiple CoPs at the same time. As this shared identity evolves, participants negotiate their joint enterprise. They develop a respect for the complexity that is inherent in responding to changing conditions, and for the resources that shape their shared work.

Mutual Engagement

In mutual engagement, people work together on a regular and sustained basis. They participate in the joint enterprise, or the shared tasks, actions, and activities that have meaning for them. Community members perform some kind of work on an on-going basis—work that has a larger purpose beyond the community itself. This engagement encourages and depends upon diversity. Not only does being in the community involve doing something together, it also means clarifying what is being done and changing how it is done. Because people

Transformative Practice: New Pathways to Leadership

are paying attention to and have an interest in whatever the community has in common, they become bound together as a social entity. The social nature of their group identity necessitates that members respect (a) the differences in person- alities and competencies and (b) the unique identity and space that each person holds in the community while (c) developing strong interpersonal relationships. This mutual engagement forms the social foundation for the community's work because it enables and supports regular interaction among members, allowing for trust and sharing.

Shared Repertoire

Not only do people negotiate the nature of the work, they also develop a repertoire or inventory of communal practices, resources, and ways of doing things that they share as they do this work. This shared repertoire develops over time and ranges from concrete to abstract. It includes routines, methods, information, models and theories, sensibilities, vocabulary and shared language, and artifacts that include documents and forms. It also involves a common sense of appropriate actions, tools, lessons learned, stories, gestures, processes, concepts, genres, standards, competencies, and principles. This repertoire may include common dress or styles by which they express their identity and membership in the group. The result of this shared repertoire is a *cultural context* that constitutes the foundation of the community's work.

The Concept of Identity in Communities of Practice

Wenger and Snyder (2000) understood that communities of practice are *social learning systems* wherein participants keep company with and relate to others. Thus, the

interactions between people shape identity. This section examines how individuals come to see themselves as members of a specific community of practice—how they identify with a community and its focus. As people learn, grow, and work within the community, their identities change.

There are three levels of belonging to a community of practice that contribute to the formation of a participant's identity within the the group: engagement, imagination, and alignment. Members participate in and engage with other members of the community by creating ideas through imaginative exchanges—ideas that are operationalized through personal and contextual alignment.

Engagement

Engagement refers to participation in the community. When participants value work in the community, they come to belong to that community. Engagement is a process of simultaneously doing, discovering, and becoming. In a community of practice, one engages with people but also with ideas. Engagement demands involvement in culturally authentic practices with sufficient continuity to concurrently build upon learners' existing knowledge while encouraging them to explore new territory and ideas. As members engage with one another, the community forms and evolves. Through this participation, the community shapes a mechanism for creating documents, websites, videos, and other collateral to make their intellectual work concrete and accessible to others. Designed properly, the community of practice will have built-in time for reflexivity and for sharing perspectives with others in the community. Through this engagement, or participation and reification, members of the community continue to negotiate a shared understanding of their collective work. Engagement ensures that both individual members and the community as a whole continually rejuvenate themselves. As the character of engagement shifts so does the nature of the practice itself.

Imagination

Imagination gives members of the CoP a sense of the possible. It causes them to reflect upon who they are and who they can be within an expanded image of the broader world. Through imagination, members are encouraged to explore new possibilities, to open up new trajectories, and to conceive of new futures. The theory of CoP understands trajectory to mean a series of successive states of being through which a system or community proceeds over time. It can also represent the anticipated long-term behavior of the community. Imagination involves finding meaning over time and in different settings so that the community does not stagnate. A culture of creativity and exploration better enables members to envision their future roles, contributions, and work.

Imagination addresses the extent to which members create images of the world and envision connections through time and space. This happens because they learn to extrapolate from experiences and to imagine specific cases based upon more general ones. An ability to imagine the broader community that the CoP connects to through its work relates to this aspect of imagination. It allows participants to form a link between their experiences with the world outside the community and those

Transformative Practice: New Pathways to Leadership

inside the CoP. This connection leads people to recognize similarities and distinctions between these experiences, allowing them to position themselves relative to the wider, prevailing practices. This re-orientation and exploration also enables members to identify more closely with the chosen community of practice and to identify the boundaries of the community—boundaries that beckon members to cross and explore.

In order for imagination to take place, the community must suspend the production of objects and documents that give form to the community's work. In this state of suspension, a space is created for reinventing and imagining new enterprises, new practices, and new communities. Imagining provides a mechanism for discovery that leads the processes of the community toward greater innovation.

Creating rich representations of alternative perspectives gives the community a chance to reflect upon its own knowledge, bringing about new ways of doing things and viewing the world. Through imaginative leaps, members can see the world in new ways and can see themselves as different persons.

Alignment

Imagination does not necessarily result in action. Alignment becomes central during these circumstances because it is through alignment that members do what is necessary to take part in the community. There are several ways to understand the notion of alignment. First, it can denote the extent to which members coordinate their energy and activities to fit within broader social structures, along with the limits of their contributions to

Transformative Practice: New Pathways to Leadership

social enterprises. Alignment is concerned with the adjustment that members make in their understanding of the work of the community as it relates to a wider context. If alignment is achieved, the community is able to marshal, bind, and direct resources for the activities of the community. When each element is properly aligned, a community of practice has the ability to coordinate perspectives and actions in order to direct energies to a common purpose or mission.

Second, alignment is the process through which persons contribute to the community. This involves discipline, accountability, coordination, and meeting the expectations of others. New participants are expected to align their actions with those of the more experienced community members until such time as their thinking might influence the old-timers to view things differently. When this happens, the nature of everyone's participation or engagement changes. Moreover, when energies inside the community are aligned, the community can do better work in the wider community and connect with discourses in such a way that community members can participate in and critique discourse.

Third, tensions can arise as members straddle the boundaries of different communities of practice (Wenger, 1998a). In this instance, alignment refers to coordinating multiple identities and perhaps conflicting perspectives among multiple CoPs. In effect, members have to *disengage* in order to understand other points of view. Several CoPs can be viewed as a constellation of interconnected communities of practice that form a "learning architecture." The notion of reconciling identity in

Transformative Practice: New Pathways to Leadership

one community with that of others is central to the idea of participating concurrently in an assemblage of communities of practice. As noted earlier, the sense of self and identity emerges and changes as members engage in a community of practice. If they are engaging in several different communities, it makes sense that varying notions of self will emerge and need to be coordinated. The concept of boundaries is relevant at this point because learning about self, others, and shared work within a community of practice means dealing with boundaries. These boundaries are not simply lines that divide the inside of the community from the outside. They also form a complex social landscape of boundaries and edges or peripheries that open and close through various forms of participation.

Brokering by an intermediate agent in social transactions and relationships is vital to this participation and interaction. This go-between must engage in the complex process of translating, coordinating, and aligning many different perspectives and viewpoints as people enter into and work within the community. The broker must have enough legitimacy to influence the development of practice within the community by mobilizing attention to issues, addressing conflicting interests, and introducing new elements into the dialogue (Wenger, 1998a). This person may be accepted into the group, but risks being rejected as an intruder.

An Emergent Future for the Profession

A community of practice does not exist outside of its membership (Smethurst, 1997), but the aliveness, energy, flexibility, and responsiveness of these communities can be

Transformative Practice: New Pathways to Leadership

leveraged and diffused throughout the profession (Wenger, McDermott, & Snyder, 2002). The mere act of stewarding a particular practice within the profession can serve to motivate other practitioners to enter into existing groups or to create new communities of practice. If enough of these caretakers emerge to sustain the field's knowledge base, the profession can be more assured of future stability and evolution. Modeling Smethurst's metaphor (1997), practitioners must push the limits of the field of study. To continue to do only that which is already known brings destruction or stagnation to both the actors and the profession. Professionals must reach into the unknown, into the white space where new ideas are generated. A community of practice can be that white space, that social landscape where people can make things known and bring themselves into the unknown. In doing so, these communities pull the profession along with them. As the profession is exposed to this new knowing through the energy of the communities of practice, the new knowledge slowly becomes familiar, comfortable, and safe. Meanwhile, the communities of practice are forever foraging into the white space, pulling the profession along with them. This emergent approach offers a promising new future for any profession because communities of practice exist to problem solve and to innovate, and because they can be catalysts for keeping a field alive, vibrant, relevant, and transformative.

References

LeMoult, D. (2002). *How to make a CoP fly?* Accessed July 14, 2004 at http://www.knowledgeboard.com/cgi-bin/item.cgi?id=98480&d=pnd

McDermott, R. (2001). *Knowing in community.*

Accessed July 14, 2004 at http://www.co-i-l.com/coil/knowledge-garden/cop/knowing.shtml

Nickols, F. (2000). *Communities of practice: Definition, indicators & identifying characteristics.* Accessed July 14, 2004 at http://home.att.net/~discon/KM/CoPCharacteristics.htm

Nickols, F. (2003). *Communities of practice.* Accessed July 14, 2004 at http://home.att.net/~discon/KM/CoPOverview.pdf

Smethhurst, J. B. (1997, Summer). Communities of practice and language patterns. *Journal of Transition Management,* 2(3). Retrieved March 9, 2006 from http://www.mgtaylor.com/mgtaylor/jotm/summer97/community_of_practice.htm

Stam, C. (2003, April). Thema: Communities of practice. *Intellectual Capital Newsletter,* accessed July 14, 2004 at http://www.intellectualcapital.nl/e-zine/ICN3.html.

Wenger, E. C. (1998a). *Communities of practice.* Cambridge, NewYork: Cambridge University Press.

Wenger, E. C. (1998b). *Communities of practice: Learning as a social system.* Accessed July 14, 2004 at http://www.co-i-l.com/coil/knowledge-garden/cop/lss.shtml

Wenger, E. C., McDermott, R., & Snyder, W. (2002). *Seven principles for cultivating communities of practice.* Accessed July 14, 2004 at http://hbswk.hbs.edu/pubitem.jhtml?id=2855&t=organizations

Wenger, E. C., & Snyder, W. M. (2000). Communities of practice: The organizational frontier. *Harvard Business Review,* 78(1), 139-145.

Wenger, E. C., & Snyder, W. M. (2001). Communities of practice: The organizational frontier. *Harvard Business Review On Organizational Learning* (pp. 1-20). Boston: Harvard Business School Press.

Resources for further study

Gallagher, K., Mason, R. M., & Vandenbosch, F. (2004). *Managing the tension in IS projects: Balancing alignment, engagement, perspective and imagination.* http://csdl.computer.org/comp/proceedings/hicss/2004/2056/08/205680254a.pdf

Parkes, A., & Dilnet, R. (224). *Community of practice.* Accessed July 14, 2004 at http://www1.ecom.unimelb.edu.au/accwww/subjects_acc/320/lectures/KMS%20-%20Session%208%20COP%20Presentation.pps

Transformative Practice: New Pathways to Leadership

Chapter 17: Knowledge Management: Turning Personal Knowledge into Professional Knowledge

Professions can benefit from the consideration of knowledge management as a relevant aspect of practice (Mitstifer, 2000, 2001). To that end, this chapter explores cultivation of a profession-wide mindset, or a professional ethos for valuing tacit knowledge, comprising *personal* know-how rooted in individual experiences, personal beliefs, perspectives, and values. Consider that practitioners have accumulated *intellectual capital* since they left higher education. How do a profession's communities of practice go about obtaining and sharing this tacit knowledge? How does the profession respect and codify the knowledge that professionals create through practice and through participation in groups? How does the profession leverage assets that are buried in a human minds in order to make them available to a broader group upon whose practice the profession depends? In other words, how does the profession turn personal knowledge into professional knowledge? One answer is knowledge management. This is a relatively new idea from the business literature, conceptualized barely a decade ago in Sweden by Karl-Erik Sveiby (National Electronic Library for Health [NeLH], 2003; Polanyi, 1983; Sullivan, 2000).

Why Manage Intellectual Capital?

Knowledge management is based upon the principle that a profession's most valuable resource is the knowledge of its people—its *intellectual assets* or *intellectual capital*

(Synder & Wilson, 1998). Intellectual assets are the proprietary knowledge of individuals that can become critical to a profession's overall vision and strategic plan (Sullivan, 2000). Three basic questions need to be posed: "Do we *know* what we know? Do we *share* what we know? Do we *use* what we know to the best effect?" The tacit knowledge of individual members of the profession is the key to answering these questions, thus creating new value for the profession. This new value does not mean just having a competitive advantage (although that does have some relevance). Rather, it means knowledge as the *capacity for effective social action* while engaged in a wide range of relationships with policy makers, the private sector, the volunteer sector, the media, and the public (NeLH, 2003). By managing tacit knowledge, a profession is able to routinely **convert the ideas of its practitioners into ideas that sustain it**. A profession needs to appreciate that its collective knowledge is the profession's intellectual asset and that there must be strategies, policies, and tools to manage this asset (Barclay & Murray, 1997).

The profession of home economics/family and consumer sciences has a particular need to manage its intellectual capital for many reasons. It is a small profession that does not have market leverage, it is experiencing inertia, and it lacks sufficient fiscal and capital resources. The profession must be much more flexible and able to make better decisions because even small mistakes can be cumulatively fatal. Moreover, an aging cohort will lead to a great loss of knowledge for the profession, therefore the profession needs to focus

Transformative Practice: New Pathways to Leadership

on its intellectual capital in order to continue to exist. Focusing on a formal, explicit body of knowledge is simply not enough anymore. The profession needs to tap the minds of all professionals so that it can leverage their internal knowledge. Life and society are changing too fast for the profession to manage information. It needs to mine the *tacit data* or the brainpower of the members so knowledge is not lost, so that wisdom can be shared, and so that the personal experiences of practitioners can be scaffolded into the formal, explicit body of knowledge.

Mapping the field's tacit knowledge may also uncover new ground for the profession. Knowledge maps help organizations and professions to uncover areas of vulnerability, to ascertain the whereabouts of critical knowledge, and to understand the impact of knowledge within key professional processes. The knowledge mapping process, coupled with knowledge harvesting, can help to identify vital areas of expertise, prioritize relevant knowledge, understand where gaps exist, and develop plans to improve (American Productivity and Quality Center [APQC], n.d.). Managed knowledge enables professional or organizational members to deal with current situations and to effectively envision and create the future. If people can generate a collection of tacit knowledge for on-demand access, then each person can possess the sum total of every pertinent fact or concept that anyone in the profession or organization has ever learned (Bellinger, 2004).

If practitioners accept that research and development have a relatively short payback time in terms of a profession's productivity and performance, then a mental space can be established for valuing the experiences, personal beliefs, perspectives, and values of individuals—the profession's intellectual capital. The value of thoughts informed by a lifetime of experience is worth calculating because it is a way to identify ideas that the world needs, maybe before people know they need them. Knowledge needs to reach the audiences who can productively use it (McKinsey & Company, 2003). It is important to find out what is known along with the cost of not knowing. Professionals can benefit from having access to other professionals and their knowledge (Davenport, 1998; NeLH, 2003).

A Knowledge Economy

Although Sveiby (1996) used the term knowledge management, he argued that no one but the individual in question could manage it because the knowledge resides in that person's head alone. More appropriate terminology for this dynamic new thrust may center on "knowledge focused," where professions "see the world from a knowledge perspective." Although in agreement with Sveiby, this chapter uses the conventional term knowledge management to convey this perspective, an approach that differs from the prevailing information perspective. The need for knowledge management has been triggered by the relentless pace of change in society and organizations, making information outdated and knowledge more valued. It is also needed because we live in a knowledge economy.

A discussion about managing knowledge merits a brief note on the nuances of a knowledge economy. We live in an information society and a knowledge economy (NeLH, 2003). This means economies now put much more emphasis on what people know as a factor of producing goods and services than on their physical labor and raw resources, as was common in the industrial economy. In a knowledge economy, firms are more inclined to codify information by writing it down and storing it. With information technology (internet, intranet, e-mail, and other communication tools), this information is much more readily diffused and transported than are people, products, services, or raw materials. The result is an economy that depends upon businesses that engage in (a) continual learning, (b) bridging different areas of mental competencies, such as communication, interpersonal, initiative, creativity, problem solving, or a predisposition to change, and (c) networking. Two other results are that knowledge becomes a commodity that is not exhausted when consumed and that the tacit knowledge found in an individual's head is becoming difficult to capture because it is not written down. The new economy depends upon the creation, diffusion, and use of tacit knowledge (Houghton & Sheehan, 2000).

To be successful and innovative in this new economy, businesses and professions must foster and manage knowledge-intensive and learning-intensive relationships with employees, other businesses, and with actors such as governments, researchers, universities, and civil society organizations. A business will only be successful if it is able to maintain and distribute a stock of relevant knowledge. In addition, the economy in which all of this happens is organized differently

than it would be for ordinary commodities. At the core of the economy are the businesses that create, produce, and distribute goods and services, but all benefit from the input made by knowledge-based services. Knowledge is not destroyed when it is consumed; therefore spreading innovations, ideas, and information far and wide creates bigger markets where consumers can obtain the same commodity again and again (Houghton & Sheehan, 2000).

A knowledge-driven economy is the current reality, so knowledge management is a clear challenge. The business model of the information age is marked by fundamental rather than incremental change. Because change often alters the very *essence* of things, it is increasingly difficult to plan for the long term. Professions must shift to a more flexible "anticipation of surprise" model rather than adhere to the "predication of the future" model. To handle surprises, an organization requires an approach that can match the right person with the right information at the right time. Knowledge management may be the answer because it culls knowledge from the deep recesses of people's minds and collates this diverse data to make it available to others in a community of practice. The more complex the profession, the greater the chance that value and potential is being lost or misplaced. Marshalling bits and pieces of knowledge about processes, insights, and stories can add value that leads both to innovations and to increased effectiveness and efficacy (Abramson, 1998).

Information versus Knowledge

It is important to distinguish between information and

Transformative Practice: New Pathways to Leadership

knowledge. Gottschalk (2002) provided a useful discussion of these differences. He noted that although information can be stored on paper or in computers, knowledge can only be stored in the human brain. Information becomes knowledge when the human brain processes it. Knowledge is information combined with experience, context, interpretation, critical reflection, intuition, and creativity. He also described six characteristics that distinguish knowledge from information. Knowledge (a) is a human act, (b) is the residue of thinking, (c) is created in the present moment, (d) belongs to communities, (e) circulates through communities, and (f) is created at the boundaries of old knowledge.

Bellinger (2004) suggested that information relates to descriptions, definitions, or prescriptions while knowledge comprises strategy, practice, methods, and approaches. Wisdom embodies principles, insights, moral character, and archetypes. He further noted that with information, one can understand the relationships between bits of data; with knowledge one can understand patterns in the information; and with wisdom one can understand the principles responsible for the patterns. Information "is what it is" and its significance depends upon the context. Each person can interpret bits of information differently. There is a potential for knowledge when patterns exist among the pieces of data and information, but it only becomes knowledge when someone is able to see the patterns and understand their implications. These patterns have a completeness to them that simple information does not. Knowledge flows from sufficient data and information amassed to form a complete pattern that is understood. For example, if one has a great deal of enrollment data, one might be able to gain knowledge by finding patterns among the data to determine why enrollment is declining. Without the ability to see the connections among the bits of information, one cannot gain knowledge about the decline. Bellinger adds that wisdom arises when one understands the principles behind the patterns, principles that are completely independent of any context and stand the test of time and place.

Types of Knowledge

Knowledge is derived from information, but it is richer and more meaningful. Knowledge includes familiarity, awareness, and understanding gained through experience, reflection, and study, and it results from comparing results, identifying consequences, and making connections (NeLH, 2003). Nickols (as cited in Barclay & Murray, 1997) provided a distinction between knowledge *as a defined body of information* and knowledge *as a person's state of being with respect to the defined body of information*. Using home economics/family and consumer sciences as an example, the defined body of knowledge incorporates the field's facts, opinions, ideas, positions, theories, principles, values, and models or other conceptual frameworks. Individuals in the profession are in various states of awareness, ignorance, familiarity, understanding, and facility with the defined body of knowledge. In fact, many U.S. and Canadian efforts have been undertaken recently to identify the key components of this defined body of

Transformative Practice: New Pathways to Leadership

knowledge, but little has been done to grasp the individual practitioner's state of being with respect to it.

Those who write within the knowledge management literature often describe the different types of knowledge that need to be managed. Sveiby (1996) identified two levels of application and study as the research and practice of (a) individuals and (b) organizations, especially business enterprises. This chapter extends this level to the research and practice within a profession. Choo (2003) offered three types of organizational knowledge: tacit, explicit, and cultural. As noted earlier, tacit knowledge is that contained within a person's head, and if it is to be useful to others it must be encapsulated and converted to concrete form. Explicit knowledge is written down and is more easily communicated and shared (McKinsey & Company, 2003). Examples include written documents, databases, spreadsheets, CDs or DVDs, videos, audiotapes, images, and training course manuals (NeLH, 2003). Cultural knowledge refers to habits in the workplace that reflect the affective and cognitive structures. Cultural knowledge encompasses the assumptions, beliefs, conventions, and expectations used to assign value and significance to the new information that is brought into the workplace (Choo, 2003).

Gottschalk (2002) described another approach, noting that an organization can have core, advanced, or innovative knowledge. Core knowledge is what an organization or professional has to know just to be in business. Possessing this knowledge does not give the organization a competitive advantage the way advanced knowledge does. Innovative knowledge helps make a profession stand out in its specific market such that it can differentiate itself from others. If a profession wants to be even more influential and lead by changing rules and introducing entirely new ways of doing business, it will draw on its innovative knowledge.

All of these approaches are useful when applied to a profession. Like businesses and organizations, professions must utilize both tacit and explicit knowledge and must also capture the nuances of workplace culture that affect knowledge creation and dissemination. In addition, professions can designate associations and university programs as the stewards of core knowledge. They can also draw from specialization organizations to obtain the advanced knowledge necessary to give practitioners a professional edge. Honor societies and leadership associations can generate innovative knowledge for the profession, and university programs and professional associations can help professionals to lead by changing the rules and finding new ways to practice.

More on mapping tacit knowledge

Knowledge management involves directing the *process of knowing* in addition to organizing the collected body of knowledge (Godbout, 1996). Three components must be taken into consideration by professions or professional organizations that wish to map and manage tacit knowledge: people, processes, and technology (NeLH, 2003). The people component refers to the culture of the organization or profession. People must value ongoing learning and information sharing

Transformative Practice: New Pathways to Leadership

along with the qualities of respect, openness, and support. Professionals must have time for reflection instead of always operating under pressure. They must feel inspired to innovate and learn from their mistakes, so the organization must not foster a "blame and shame" culture.

The process component encourages the profession or organization to ask "How are things done around here?" The answer should involve people working together in ways that enable the mapping, management, and sharing of tacit knowledge. Although technology is necessary (often in the form of internet, intranets, e-mail, and data bases or e-libraries), it must fit into the culture and processes that practitioners actually use to accomplish professional goals. Technology that does not complement existing procedures will not be used. In addition, technology must facilitate convenient access to the information rather than simply creating a repository of static documents. It is essential that the collected tacit knowledge be made available to many people instead of remaining in the heads of a few collectors (NeLH, 2003).

Although it is unspoken and unwritten by definition, tacit knowledge consists of information and understanding that have a significant impact upon practice. However, not only is the information not known to others, it is often not known to the person "who knows it" (Grey, 2003). For example, it is one thing to know how to conduct an effective small group activity and debriefing session, but it is quite another to formulate coherent instructions that enable someone else to direct this dynamic, complex activity. Eliciting and sharing this tacit knowledge requires extensive personal contact and trust with the "knower." Professionals must have easier access to one another to create a knowledge environment and mind-set. Hence, the synergy between two other dimensions of knowledge management comes into play: collecting and connecting. *Collecting* involves linking people with information, and *connecting* involves linking people with other people. Connecting activities include skills directories, expert and annotated staff directories, collaborative working groups, and communities of practice. A wonderful synergy can be established if there is balance between collection and connection. Professionals who require specific information must be connected to those who know it. In collecting what is learned from this interface, more codified tacit information becomes accessible within a growing collection of codified knowledge. Another important element in the knowledge mind-set is an awareness that the quality of the knowledge collected does not depend on whether it is new or old. Instead, the knowledge is deemed valuable if it is relevant. Does it work in practice? Does someone need it? The right knowledge must be allowed to flow where it is needed, when it is needed (NeLH, 2003).

Stages of Knowledge Management Process Applied to the Profession

Professionals often assign an inordinate amount of weight to objective data collection, unbiased observations, and the value contained in measurements and numbers. Those who wish to discover tacit knowledge must adopt a different paradigm, engaging in *adventurous research* by leaving behind any idea of what they think they will find. Seeking tacit knowledge

Transformative Practice: New Pathways to Leadership

with a predetermined map can cause the explorer to miss the most significant tacit landmarks (Grey, 2000). With that in mind, the following section suggests a five-stage process to apply knowledge management (KM) to a profession, drawing from APQC (n.d.), Clark (2002), Davenport (1998), Lopez et al. (2001), and NeLH (2003).

Champion—Someone must champion the idea within the profession, much as Dorothy Mitstifer was an early champion for knowledge management in the field of home economics/family and consumer sciences. Energized by the vision of knowledge management's (KM) value, the champion searches for opportunities to share it with others. This work should inspire others to explore the idea and to share in journals, newsletters, conferences, and similar outlets.

Pioneers Explore and Investigate—Although the champion advocates the potential of the KM perspective, other professionals break new ground by exploring and experimenting with the idea. These pioneers work together to share a clear, tangible picture of the benefits and shortfalls of the KM perceptive. They relate their professional goals, principles, and mission to the benefits of KM in order to illustrate that there is a good fit. They seek out communities of practice that value the capture of their peers' tacit knowledge. Importantly, these pioneers act as agents of change whose explorations reveal the most important factors in motivating their profession to embrace KM. Pioneers use these factors to advocate for the cause, or to "sell the idea" to the wider community. These motivating factors often include improved efficiency and effectiveness. KM also assists in keeping up with competitors, streamlining access to information, capturing the voices of the elders, simplifying processes, and ensuring a profession's future. Because information technology is key to KM, pioneers examine how to

capitalize on technology to capture, codify, and share tacit knowledge. Finally, because many diverse people must "buy in," the pioneers must build the foundation for a knowledge-sharing culture. They must collect the profession's social norms, practices, and values to determine if members are ready to share knowledge instead of hoarding it for personal gain.

Create a KM Task Force—In order for the KM perspective to become a profession-wide initiative, the champion and the pioneers need to create a task force or steering committee to lead members into a KM future. The task force must explore the management and measurement of five dimensions of KM initiatives: culture, people, informational content, process, and technology. They must also appreciate that KM initiatives require investments in kind that involve both financing and technology. Finally, the task force conducts pilot studies of KM to illustrate that it is a valuable enterprise for the profession. These studies involve four stages, during which the task force (a) acquires tacit information from selected people, (b) codifies and organizes the written or recorded data, (c) uses information technology to distribute it and make it accessible, and (d) determines if people use it. As an example of a KM pilot study, the International Federation of Home Economics (IFHE) Canada interviewed three retired home economists about their role within the organization by capturing their tacit knowledge on videotape. Once the information was recorded, IFHE Canada arranged for it to be shared across the country and encouraged people to use it in their work. Although the video and distribution methods utilized low tech resources, this project used knowledge management to capture the tacit knowledge of elders in the profession.

Beyond Pilots to Profession: Wide Use—In order to move to the broader adoption of the

Transformative Practice: New Pathways to Leadership

KM perspective, it is important to tap into the values of members and relevant associations to see if a culture shift is occurring. Have people begun to embrace the notion of sharing tacit knowledge? Expanding KM will require experts who are good at mapping tacit knowledge and forming communities of practice in order to create and solicit this information. KM needs to be seen as a strategic and necessary component of professional growth and security. The importance of KM expands when professionals with high visibility and respected authority have blessed the process. The backing of respected leaders results in an increasing number of professionals who embrace the value of tacit knowledge and its role in sustaining the profession or organization. Evidence of this wider acceptance can be seen in the launch of intranets, the adoption of Wiki technology (software that facilitates collaborative on-line document editing), and in mapping strategies that capture tacit knowledge. The resulting product can take the form of a living thesaurus of codified, tacit knowledge.

Sustainable Profession-wide Adoption — The creation of formal infrastructures and processes is critical to the adoption of a KM perspective throughout the profession, and a funding source will be required to implement many of these new initiatives. First, knowledge providers must be connected to the knowledge users in a seamless community of practitioners using face-to-face interaction and Wiki technology or community driven websites. Other suggestions for implementing a broad KM adoption include the following:

- An oversight group can be created to capture lessons learned from various attempts to manage knowledge, regardless of their level of success.
- It is better to develop an expansion strategy that centers upon distinct organizations or institutions rather than taking a blanket approach.
- Organizations can create a Chief Knowledge Officer (CKO) position to ensure a sustainable KM effort.

345

- A core group of KM facilitators can be trained and made available to conduct new initiatives and ongoing support.

Further, sufficient resources must be allocated to allay slippage and reversal to old practices, and both pre-professionals and existing professionals must be trained in KM competencies (Newman, 2002). A comprehensive public strategy is also required, and some confusion is to be expected during early stages of adoption as people learn to manage tacit knowledge. Ideally, however, KM will become linked to a profession's business and socialization model. Capturing, codifying, and sharing tacit knowledge will become the norm, and the profession gains the reputation of a knowledge-sharing enterprise because everyone from senior leadership to novices will value the knowledge management perspective.

Discussion and Conclusion

By most estimates, the largest part of organizational knowledge escapes awareness, notice, and conversation; it slips beneath the collective radar, avoids codification and validation, and remains undiscovered by traditional knowledge-mapping activities (Grey, 2000, p. 1).

Failure to harvest and disseminate tacit knowledge as a valuable resource is a great loss to any profession. Members cannot avail themselves of the thought processes, insights, experiences, or lessons learned if these lessons have not been written down or captured and shared using technology. Because individuals create their own meanings when exposed to knowledge, work experiences, consultancies, and other information, much is lost when these meanings and

Transformative Practice: New Pathways to Leadership

interpretations are not made explicit. The learning curve for new professionals may be unnecessarily extended, as well. This information is also necessary to sustain and intellectually enrich the profession as a whole, so a profession must acknowledge that too much is lost if it does not capture what people know. Knowledge assets—ideas, concepts, processes, know-how—are valuable and legitimate forms of knowledge that might include e-mails, memos, letters, and un-circulated reports that have not been articulated to a wide audience (Freese, 2001). A profession must extract these ideas from practitioner's brains, file cabinets, and computers if its members are to obtain and understand tacit knowledge, interpret it within a context that is broader than that in which it was created, combine it with other types of information, and synthesize these unstructured forms of knowledge into new knowledge (Davenport, 1998).

One practitioner's knowledge should not remain solely in that person's possession, separate from the profession. It is emergent and requires dialogue, community, and time to evolve; hence, it needs to be shared. In this way, internal knowledge can be preserved and expanded upon within the professional community. The social capital that enables professional networks is not readily generated, making it even more important to share and use such knowledge. Even though some essence is often lost when one tries to capture tacit knowledge, it is worth the effort. Elements of knowledge can be lost when people are not aware of their heuristics (inner decision-making rules), thereby making it difficult to explain their experiences to others. It is also difficult to record all

Transformative Practice: New Pathways to Leadership

of the connections that make emergent knowledge so rich. Such knowledge is often generated through personal relationships, dialogue, personal reflections, and mental integration of insights and information. Information can be lost if it is taken out of context during harvesting, but this process can open the original information to new interpretations that differ from those held by the original knower. In any case, knowledge that exists inside a person's head is ephemeral, emergent, relational, and context dependent, and professionals have an obligation to capture it before it is lost (Grey, 2003).

Knowledge management has evolved to encompass innovation and creation, sharpened awareness, improved relationships and connections, and collaborative and continuous learning. It also involves personal identity, dialogue, trust, sharing, and fundamental change. Grey (2004) suggested that people define knowledge as a journey without end. A profession's members must set a goal to remain in the conversation and to learn from colleagues' internal distinctions and mental models, as well as from the profession's cultural knowledge. Transformation of practice through KM is almost certainly ensured.

References

Abramson, G. (1998, May 15). Intellectual capitalism: Turning knowledge into profit. *CIO Enterprise Online Magazine,* http://www.cio.com/archive/enterprise/051598_intellectual.html

American Productivity and Quality Center. (n.d.). *APQC's road map to knowledge management results: Stages of implementation.* Accessed June 11, 2004 at http://www.apqc.org/portal/apqc/site/generic?path=/site/km/apqc_roadmap.jhtml

Barclay, R., & Murray, P. (1997). *What is knowledge management?* Accessed November 14, 2003 at http:/

/www.media-access.com/whatis.html

Bellinger, G. (2004). *Knowledge management - emerging perspectives*. Accessed June 11, 2004 at http://www.systems-thinking.org/kmgmt/kmgmt.htm

Choo, C. W. (2003). *Making tacit knowledge explicit: Knowledge harvesting*. Accessed June 11, 2004 at http://choo.fis.utoronto.ca/UvA/learnerfirst/harvesting.html

Clark, D. (2002). *KM framework*. Accessed June 11, 2004 at http://www.nwlink.com/~donclark/km/framework.html

Davenport, T. H. (1998). *Some principles of knowledge management*. Accessed June 11, 2004 at http://www.mccombs.utexas.edu/kman/kmprin.htm

Freese, E. (2001). *Harveting knowledge from the organization's information assets*. Accessed June 11, 2004 at http://www.gca.org/papers/xmleurope2001/papers/html/s31-1.html

Godbout, A. J. (1996). *Information vs. knowledge*. Accessed June 11, 2004 at http://www.km-forum.org/ajg-002.htm

Gottschalk, P. (2002). A stages of growth model for knowledge management technology in law firms. *Online Journal of Information, Law & Technology, 2*, http://elj.warwick.ac.uk/jilt/02-2/gottschalk.html

Grey, D. (2000). *Mapping tacit*. Accessed June 11, 2004 at http://www.voght.com/cgi-bin/pywiki?MappingTacit

Grey, D. (2003). *Harvesting knowledge - can we really do it?* Accessed June 11, 2004 at http://denham.typepad.com/km/2003/10/harvesting_know.html

Grey, D. (2004, April). *Defining knowledge*. Accessed June 11, 2004 at http://denham.typepad.com/km/2004/04/defining_knowle.html

Houghton, J., & Sheehan, P. (2000). *A primer on the knowledge economy*. Accessed June 11, 2004 at http://www.cfses.com/documents/knowledgeeconprimer.pdf

Lopez, C., Sammis, S., Hofer-Alfeis, J., Lopez, K., Raybourne, C., & Neumann Wilson, J. (2001). *Measurement of knowledge management*. Accessed June 11, 2004 at http://www.kmadvantage.com/docs/km_articles/Measurement_for_KM.pdf

McKinsey & Company. (2003, February). *Rising to a knowledge management challenge on a national scale*. Accessed June 11, 2004 at http://www.knowledgewave.org.nz/forum_2003/background_reading/

Rising%20to%20a%20 knowledge%20management %20challenge.pdf

Mitstifer, D. (2000). Knowledge management (KM). *KON FORUM, 10*(2), 1-2.

Mitstifer, D. (2001). Knowledge management. *KON FORUM, 10*(3), 1-2.

National Electronic Library for Health. (2003). *Specialist library: Knowledge management.* Accessed November 14, 2003 at http://www.nelh.nhs.uk/knowledge_management/

Newman, B. (2002). *The education of the knowledge professions.* Accessed November 14, 2003 at http://www.3-cities.com/~bonewman/View%20-%20Education%20the%20Knowledge%20Professions.pdf

Polanyi, M. (1983). *The tacit dimension.* London: Routledge & Kegan Paul.

Sullivan, P. H. (2000). *Value driven intellectual capital.* Indianapolis, IN: Wiley.

Sveiby, K. E. (1996). *What is knowledge management?* Accessed November 14, 2003 at http://www.sveiby.com/articles/KnowledgeManagement.html

Synder, C., & Wilson, L. (1998). *The process of knowledge harvesting.* Accessed June 11, 2004 at http://www.users.cs.york.ac.uk/~kimble/teaching/mis/BIT98_harvest.doc

Transformative Practice: New Pathways to Leadership

Chapter 18: Globalization–Top-Down and Bottom-Up

Transformative professionals must understand the current phenomena of globalization because individuals and families are part of a world economy that has a deep and lasting impact on their well-being and quality of life. Indeed, the current face of globalization and the legacy of past phases of globalization are major factors in transforming the work of professionals in the new millennium.

This chapter explores the phenomena of corporate led, top-down globalization and juxtaposes this philosophy against that of a bottom-up, civil society movement that resists the negative impact of the top-down model. Professionals must embrace a holistic view of globalization if they want to bring issues of globalization into their practice. An assumption that globalization is entirely negative precludes professionals from appreciating the positive, far-reaching power that is played out in civil society as it tries to mitigate and redirect the impact of corporate-led globalization on people's rights, security, freedom, and futures.

Globalization Defined

Ask ten different people to define globalization, and you are likely to receive ten different answers (Marber, 2005). Globalization refers to the compression of the world and the intensification of the consciousness of the world as a whole. It also encompasses cross-border interactions, whether economic, political, or cultural (Marber, 2005; Robertson, 1991) and refers to the increased speed of time, space, and relations due to advances in telecommunications

Transformative Practice: New Pathways to Leadership

and technology, among other things. Globalization is viewed as a process of dynamic patterns of interaction and change that involves a growing *economic* interdependence between countries worldwide. Importantly, the term globalization is often heard in connection with economic phenomena, but it has implications far beyond the realm of economies as it encroaches on social, political, cultural, religious, linguistic, environmental, and familial realms. The broader conceptualization of globalization informs this chapter, which will now examine the different faces of top-down globalization over the centuries, followed by a similar exploration of globalization from the bottom-up.

Top-Down Globalization Over the Centuries

Verzola (1998) provided a powerful overview of three waves of globalization and makes a strong case that globalization has been occurring for centuries; today's version simply looks different. Table 1 summarizes his discussion of compelling world events. He notes that although humanity continues to live in the second wave of globalization, the third wave is upon us and we must give serious thought to dealing with this manifestation.

Robertson (2003) clarified that the third wave of globalization is different from the first two due to a mix of economic transformations, a conscious effort to put global policies in place, and social transformations set in motion by increased human interconnectedness. The third wave was shaped by currents of worldwide democratization that opened opportunities for structures and processes conducive to global cooperation as well as the attendant exploitation and oppression. The present

Transformative Practice: New Pathways to Leadership

Table 1: Summary of Three Waves of Globalization
(excerpted from Verzola, 1998)

Colonial experience **First** Wave 1870-1914	Anti-colonial experience **Second** wave 1950-1980	Neo-liberal experience **Third** wave 1980-present
"We will save you from yourself, we will bring you to the one true God for your own good, our culture is better than yours"	*"We bring jobs and technology, we will lend you development money, we will protect you from Communism"*	*"We will place iformation at your fingertips in a world without borders. Our global village allows a free flow of information and instant access to the world's libraries and a million TV channels"*
1. Military aggression and conquest by mercantilists and early industrial powers, especially in Britain—direct control.	1. Indirect economic control and *cultural* aggression led by Transnational Corporations (TNCs), that draw wealth from lands and communities using money as a commodity.	1. Information cyberlords, industrial cyberlords, and finance capitalists need mental labor, information, and markets for this information. Information and networked economies sell telecommunications, data exchange, media, entertainment, knowledge, computers, financial systems, biotechnology, and genetic engineering.
2. Brought in new religion and cultures to quell resistance and set up new colonial governments using local elites at lower levels of government (patronizing).	2. Global corporations shore up elite, military, and police with money and arms to win their loyalty and service, enabling corporations to do business outside the rules. Little market power for micro, small, and medium sized businesses.	2. Commodify everything and privatize services so all things, including relationships and cultures, are sold in the marketplace. Install capitalism as a market form to propagate commodification. Focus on individualism and survival of the fittest. The power of the state is seriously eroded so borders remain open for free trade. Social welfare declines.
3. Made citizens slaves and used them to extract precious metals from the land. Used the land to raise export crops and plundered the land for wealth.	3. Take wealth (raw materials and labor) away using: unequal trade, high interest rates on loans, low wages, profit repatriation.	3. Maintain a consumer society so the capitalist system continues to exist. People become slaves to the market and the workplace in order to earn money.
4. Replaced sustainable indigenous practices with unsustainable technology and practices.	4. Exploit land and natural resources (chemical agriculture and energy projects)—unsustainable production.	4. Continued engagement in unsustainable production with the added feature of unsustainable consumption.
5. Led to a lost people living in a lost and destroyed ecosystem/land.	5. Mass media controls minds. The media creates and expands markets to strengthen colonial hold.	5. Consumers are a lost people as third-world countries and ecosystems are exploited to satisfy first-world demands and transnational corporate greed. Continued use of the media to perpetuate the system.

stage of globalization, the third wave in a networked economy, is characterized by a specific set of features related to technology, markets and trade, relations and culture, state sovereignty, and social welfare (Broad, 2002; Cavanagh & Mander, 2004; Ellwood, 2001; McGregor, 2005; Robertson, 2003; Schaeffer, 2003).

Technology
- Massive technological change, particularly advances and cost reductions in telecommunications and transportation, are at the core of this wave of globalization. Technologies marking this era include computerization, miniaturization, digitization, satellite communications, fiber optics, nano-technology, and the Internet. The World Wide Web is a metaphor for the integration that is possible with technology; everyone with a computer can be continuously connected.
- Complex, real-time interactions now exist among people and among people and machines via information technology.

Markets and Trade
- Capitalism is the current form of market structure. Some define capitalism as *creative deconstruction* of inefficient means of production in the search for innovation to increase efficiency. It is a powerful economic system. The means of production and distribution are privately or corporately owned, and development is proportionate to the accumulation and reinvestment of profits gained in a free market.
- The world has a single market without a single state to regulate it. This state of affairs is further enhanced by new international trade

Transformative Practice: New Pathways to Leadership

institutions and regulations that are controlled by corporations striving for one giant global market.
- There is rapid growth of international financial transactions (buying and selling money) relative to the selling of goods and services, which used to be the mode of trade.
- There is faster growth in trade among transnational corporations (TNCs) than between local, national, or regional firms.
- Global markets for goods and services have emerged. This trend is augmented by the practice of making goods and services abroad instead of in home countries; hence, money does not stay in the community.
- There are many international alliances and competitions coupled with the use of international standards and benchmarks, as opposed to the previous system of national standards.

Relations and Culture

- A paradox exists with worldwide population growth accompanied by high death rates in some places.
- Trade agreements are prompting many countries to open their boundaries to one another. Unfortunately, the current wave of globalization undermines the strength, sustainability, and resilience of cultures and communities, just as in previous waves. Injustice, inequality, insecurity, and unrest abound as never before.
- There are sharpened regional disparities and inequalities in the form of a growing gap between haves and have-nots. This leads to warfare, terrorism, and conflict over scarce resources and cheap labor.

Transformative Practice: New Pathways to Leadership

State Sovereignty

- Governmental policy decisions often lead to decreased nationalism, more internationalism, and increased corporate control.
- Corporations can move to escape state regulations because there is no mechanism for states to act collectively. This increases corporate power over states and citizens.
- There are massive problems related to a loss of social cohesion, democracy, government sovereignty, and democratic citizenship.

Social Welfare

- Neoliberal trade principles have led to massive and debilitating cutbacks and privatization of health, education, and social welfare services.

In summary, paradoxes exist within the third wave of globalization from the top-down. Not only are relationships intensified, they also deteriorate. Local happenings are no longer isolated; they affect and are affected by global events. Distance and borders are undergoing reconceptualization. The globe is becoming a single space while localities simultaneously exist within the global sphere. Nation states are pressured by the presence of international systems. Efforts to ensure national security and peace threaten human security and inner peace. An expanding global consciousness threatens both individual and family connectedness and belonging. A globalized world is integrated but not harmonious, a single space but also diverse, and a construct of shared consciousness that is prone to fragmentation (Lechner, 2001; Mittelman, 2000).

Globalization from the Bottom-Up

It is because of the above paradoxes that

Transformative Practice: New Pathways to Leadership

globalization from the bottom-up has gained momentum. The top down model of the global economy is hugely subsidized and dependent upon a civil society framework comprising moral institutions and individuals who strive for economic, social and gender equity, as well as the basic civic staples of health, education, employment, and law and order. The bottom-up movement comprises the interests of labor, fair trade, gender, children, environment, indigenous peoples, animals, justice, peace, anti-war, anti-terrorism, anti-consumerism, and human rights.

A review of literature in the globalization from the bottom-up movement (also referred to as alter globalization or anti-corporate-led globalization) reveals a collection of strategies that professionals could easily embrace (sourced from ATTAC, DGB and VENRO, 2003; IBON Foundation Inc., 2001; Levinson, 2002; New Economics Foundation, 2003; Third World Network, 2003). Using the same headings as above, technology, markets and trade, relations and culture, government sovereignty and social welfare, the following text profiles globalization from the bottom-up.

Technology
- Mainstream Western media must be used responsibly and must be critically analyzed.
- There must be a place for the legitimate alternative voice of the globalization from the bottom-up movement. This vehicle is currently the Internet, but there are indications that this medium may come under much more control in the future.

Markets and Trade
- The world needs to reform international financial institutions to

limit financial speculation and to control the illegal movement of funds by the International Monetary Fund (IMF), World Bank (WB), banks, tax havens, and offshore financial centers.
- The world must allow for international bankruptcy and insolvency to replace IMF rescue missions using Structural Adjustment Programs (SAPs), which should be eliminated. Debtor cartels could be formed.
- All third world debt should be forgiven and replaced with a framework of justice and discipline for relations between sovereign debtors and international creditors.
- Worker, child labor, human rights, animal welfare, and ecological standards must be entrenched in the workplace and in product and service development processes.
- Corporations, along with small and medium-sized businesses, must be held socially accountable for their market actions.
- Public and social services should be kept out of trade agreements. Government social policy should not be used as a trade barrier.
- Strive for fairer trade.
- Strive for localization and mindful markets in conjunction with responsible consumer behavior and global citizenship.
- Stop corporate patent protectionism by limiting intellectual property rights and ending patents on traditional knowledge about biological resources such as seeds and medicine.

Relations and Cultures
- Increase equality between women and men. Gender and women's rights need to be expanded.

Transformative Practice: New Pathways to Leadership

- Stop the marginalization of women and the feminization of poverty.
- Make children's rights paramount.
- Stop trafficking and slavery.
- Mitigate the lasting, negative impact of colonialism, imperialism, and neoliberalism.
- Value families as society's basic democratic unit.

State Sovereignty

- Protect national and state sovereignty from TNC and WTO multilateral trade agreements. Both TNCs and the WTO actually have more authority than national governments in many instances.
- Dismantle the WTO and replace it with a more representative body.
- Ensure a voice at the table for civil society by democratizing the globalization process because *democracy needs proximity*.
- Augment national security with human security, peace, and non-violence.
- Place the needs and aspirations of ordinary people at the center of rules and policies.
- Revamp the United Nations.

Social and Environmental Welfare

- Stop cash cropping (reverse export-oriented industrial farming and import liberalization) and help small farmers regain livelihood, dignity, and food sovereignty and security as they practice sustainable agriculture and respect cultural and productive diversity.
- Use the money released by forgiveness of Third World debt (now called the Majority World) to eradicate poverty and build infrastructure and communities.
- Ensure that trade agreements do not undermine genuine

international human, social, labor, and environmental agreements.
♦ Eliminate extreme poverty, injustice, and inequality, especially through food security and human security.
♦ Ensure sustainable development and environmental protection.
♦ Encourage wealthy countries to repay Third World ecological and human rights debts.
♦ Regulate financial services, transport, tourism, electronics, and telecommunications for the benefit of nations, not TNCs.
♦ Strive for genetic biodiversity and social diversity. Question biotechnology.

In summary, globalization refers to greater movement of people, money, products, and ideas due to increased integration propelled by extended trade and investment. There has always been movement of goods, but improved technologies and reductions in trade and exchange barriers mean that the speed and size of these movements are much faster, broader, and larger. Globalization is an extremely complex web made up of many elements (Global Education, 2004; Robertson, 2003), as evidenced by the scope of the legitimate issues fielded by the globalization from the bottom-up movement: poverty, cultural integrity, security, local economies, resilient communities, debt reduction, democracy, corporate power, state effectiveness, sustainability, worker rights, gender equity, children's rights, social justice, and the role of the media. Each of these issues is a reflection of the paradoxes inherent in the current wave of globalization. The recent report of the World Commission on the Social Dimensions of Globalization tendered even more ideas about how to mitigate the

Transformative Practice: New Pathways to Leadership

impact of the third wave of globalization (International Labor Organization, 2004).

Implications

This final section discusses six ideas about what globalization means for professionals and how practice can become transformative. Transformative practice is centered around empowerment, diversity, and the assumption of respective responsibilities. It focuses on globalization of conscience and respect for universal values that transcend cultures, religions, and socio-economic circumstances. Transformative practice appreciates that clarity eventually *does* emerge from the confusion, distress, and uncertainty that people experience due to the impact of globalization. When dealing with this stress, professionals should not view an initial lack of consensus on issues as a failure, but as a progression toward empowerment and recognition. Small steps forward count (Bush & Folger, 1996). Professionals need to find a balance between focusing on historical antecedents, current moments, and future trends in regard to the pros and cons of globalization. The following section examines these ideas in more detail.

Holistic Understanding of Globalization

Professionals face the challenge of critiquing two concurrent movements, globalization from the top-down (led by corporations and complicit governments) and globalization from the bottom-up (led by members of civil society). Where the former strives for a global market economy dependant on capitalism and consumerism, the latter strives to mitigate or alleviate the negative impacts on citizens, the environment, and other species by forming mindful, local markets. The goal is to put a human face on globalization to offset the profound damage spawned by the top-down juggernaut. Accountability, transparency, and citizens' rights are the key principles that guide this work. Socially responsible action from all of the world's citizens is paramount, regardless of their positions in industry, government, or civil society.

The Third Wave of globalization is replete with threats to national sovereignty, citizenship, human rights, privacy, a sustainable future, freedom, peace, and human security. That is professionals must expand their understanding of globalization. The powerful and growing resistance and alternative movement is also a form of globalization, this time from the bottom-up. Lessons must be learned from both types of globalization. Professionals need to expand their appreciation of the types of globalization beyond economic expansion and integration. They also need to consider the globalization of language, learning, religion, ideas, technology, social, culture, and politics (Cheng, 2002). Only through this expanded awareness can practitioners foster individual, professional, and institutional change within the evolving phenomena of globalization.

Ongoing Critique of Globalization

Although globalization is not going to go away, its appearance will change as it evolves. More than being responsive to the trends and challenges of globalization, professionals have to be able to critique the phenomena sufficiently to forecast possible impacts and guide processes in a positive direction by

Transformative Practice: New Pathways to Leadership

taking a transformative leadership role. To that end, professionals can embrace another definition of globalization, that being the transfer, adaptation, and development of values, knowledge, technology, and behavioral norms across countries and societies in different parts of the world (globalization) and in local contexts (localization) with the goal of meeting individual needs and characteristics (individualization) (Cheng, 2002).

Respect Differing Perceptions of Globalization

Professionals need to note that there is a lack of consensus about how to view globalization. Some view globalization as the victory of American culture and neoliberal ideology. Others see it as a kind of imperialism rooted in economic domination, producing new kinds of colonial relations. Still others see globalization as a process that triggers basic questions about the meaning of democracy and community (Coleman, 1999). Many understand globalization to be about creating a world order without respect for race, nationality, geography, or religion. This would require a unification of culture, language, and politics. National economies would be subsumed and reshaped into a system of international processes and transactions. This "one-world" economy would evolve at the expense of national sovereignty and would reflect the development of a universal, homogenous state where all human needs are met by the global market (Pendleton, 1999).

Some view globalization as a positive process that is beneficial for everyone—the key to future world development. They also

Transformative Practice: New Pathways to Leadership

see it as inevitable and irreversible and this perspective is often referred to as the TINA, or There Is No Alternative, syndrome. Others, however, regard it with skepticism, fear, and hostility, believing that it profoundly increases inequality, threatens employment and living standards, and thwarts social progress. Thus it is viewed as a process that *is* reversible. From this perspective, many intriguing alternatives are available to alter the current trajectory of globalization, so this is referred to as the TAMARA, or There Are Many And Realistic Alternatives, syndrome. The home economics/family and consumer sciences profession should be part of the latter cadre, paving the way for alternatives to corporate-led globalization such that family, societal or community well-being, and the entire human condition are more secure, peaceful, and sustainable.

Become Future Oriented

Professionals must shift focus from the minutiae of the present to the trends that forecast the future. This shift entails (a) embracing a critical, reflective approach to practice so that individuals can unveil the power relationships that allow corporate-led globalization to dominate the scene, and (b) heralding the powerful alternatives promoted by the bottom-up movement. Professionals need to appreciate that cultural change within civil society is an indispensable condition for changing the economy and the markets as well as corporate power and state culpability. This change occurs by identifying, acting upon, and mobilizing around social issues. The magnitude of these issues can make it difficult to step back far enough to perceive the overall pattern, scope, and impact of globalization. However, some pressing issues

Transformative Practice:  New Pathways to Leadership

involve the extent and character of globalization's impact upon identity, social cohesion, national resiliency, democracy, authority, citizenship, and relationships with the non-human world.

Globalization of Conscience

Future research agendas, policy initiatives, and curricula development must investigate globalization as a multifaceted phenomenon and examine the impact of this powerful force on the human condition. This work needs to be done in concert with the growing, dynamic web of grassroots globalization while critiquing the corporate-led globalization movement. Paramount to this work is globalization of conscience so that the human condition is foremost in everyone's mind. The globalization of capital has created the globalization of conscience. People sense an intrusion in their lives and are crying out for political leaders to respond. Worldwide peace demonstrations represent this conscience. The idea is that community can act as an antidote and replacement for commodification and market ideals. The pressure from organizations in the bottom-up globalization movement is growing at an accelerated pace. As this global conscience gains strength, government and business actions will come under growing public scrutiny (Danaher & Mark, 2003; Hayden, 2003; McLellan, 1998). Professionals must be key stewards of this global conscience.

Universal Values and Diversity

In light of the global turmoil among cultures and religions that has stemmed from globalization, professionals must give attention to the overarching human values

that hold people together, making it easier to understand diverse populations. Kofi Annan (2003) speculated that "globalization has brought us closer together in the sense that we are affected by each others' actions—but not in the sense that we all share the benefits and the burdens" (p. 2). Universal values act as principles for societal progress that can be life-restoring and life-giving. They transcend cultural, religious, and socio-economic differences (Federman, 2001). Universal human values are cognitive representations of human motives, defined as the basis for human actions and decisions (Pogaènik, 2001).

Table 2 shares a collection of universal values culled from an array of sources. This collection reflects the worldwide search for a common global identity within the context of diversity. If one accepts that universal values apply to every individual and every society, then it is possible to suggest that these values are stable and that the changes in society that are caused by globalization bring new priorities, not new universal values (Pogaènik, 2001). In light of this idea, professionals must be flexible enough to help people realize universal values in ways they can actually apply in their specific circumstances. For example, Federman (2002) shared a compelling discussion of how different cultures and religions understand the universal value of compassion. This example demonstrated why professionals should not take universal values for granted, but should think about them carefully and rigorously, defend them, assert them, strengthen them, and live by them while helping others to do the same (Annan, 2003). In all their differences, cultures reflect common humanness and humanity (Christians & Traber, 1997).

Transformative Practice: New Pathways to Leadership

Table 2: Collection of Universal Values
(Baba, 2001; Dufour, 2000; The Center for Learning, 1999)

- power
- enjoyment and happiness
- unity
- benevolence
- self-direction, knowledge, actualization, and autonomy
- love and friendship
- non-violence
- justice and fairness
- compassion
- civility
- respect
- responsibility and accountability
- sense of community and belonging
- pluralism
- democracy
- tradition
- security
- empowerment
- achievement
- peace
- truth
- trustworthiness
- forgiveness
- equality and equity
- diversity and tolerance
- sustainability
- empathy and open-mindedness
- cooperation
- health and wellness
- freedom
- life

Conclusion

A transformative profession has a role to play in this current era of globalization because a space has opened up for its unique focus on individuals and families. Professionals must assume that they live in a globaliz*ing* condition, rather than a completely globalized condition. This optimistic view implies a space for transformative leadership, vision, and practice such that globalization unfolds in a way that supports well-being and quality of life for all. Support for bottom-up globalization reinforces a shift to equity, sustainability, and social welfare. Ongoing critique of top-down globalization reveals the challenges that compromise individual and familial progress and potential. This holistic approach to understanding globalization is necessary because globalization has intensified the complexity of the world situation. Professionals are reminded that transformative practice involves a marked increase in empowerment or self-determination, and in the capacity for recognition and responsiveness to others (Bush & Folger, 1996).

Professionals who practice from this stance are poised to ensure that a better world is possible. Acting in concert with others, professionals can have a voice in determining what the next wave of globalization looks like. Ideally, it will be a form that supports humanity: the opposite of the corporate vision of globalization that now prevails. Robertson (2003) and others openly discussed the possible collapse or implosion of the Third Wave of globalization from the top-down. He says that human connectedness, globalization of conscience, multicultural diversity, continued democratization, far-reaching cries for sustainability of the earth, and relentless striving for empowerment and autonomy pave the way for a future that manages the human condition more positively and affects global solutions based on inclusiveness. Professionals can strive to make the shockwaves of unprecedented empowerment and transformation the counterpoint to the shock waves of corporate-led globalization.

References

Annan, K. (2003, December 24). Do we still have universal values? *The Globalist*. Retrieved June 17, 2005 from http://www.theglobalist.com/DBWeb/praintStoryId.aspx?StoryID=3361

ATTAC, DGB and VENRO. (2003, March). *Making globalization equitable. ATTAC News Sand in the Wheels Newsletter*, pp. 6-11. Accessed February 9, 2005 at http://www.union-network.org/UNIsite/In_Depth/Interna_Relations/GATS/2003PDF/DGB-ATTAC-VENRO.pdf

Baba, S. S. (2001). *What are the universal values*? Retrieved June 17, 2005 from http://www.sathyasai.org.nz/sse_what_are.htm

Broad, R. (Ed.). (2002). *Global backlash*. New York: Rowman & Littlefield.

Bush, B., & Folger, J. (1996). *The promise of mediation.* San Francisco: Jossey-Bass.

Cavanagh, J., & Mander, J. (Eds.). (2004). *Alternatives to economic globalization.* San Francisco: Berrett-Koehler.

Cheng, Y. C. (2002). *Fostering local knowledge and wisdom in globalized education.* Retrieved February 9, 2005 at http://www.ied.edu.hk/cric/new/doc/speeches/18-21nov02.pdf

Christians, C. G., & Traber, M. (1997). *Communication ethics and universal values.* San Francisco: Sage.

Coleman, W. (1999). *The Institute on Globalization and the Human Condition: A research agenda.* Retrieved October 18, 1999 at http://www.humanities.mcmaster.ca/~global/institute/resrch~1.htm

Danaher, K., & Mark, J. (2003). *Grassroots globalization gets real.* Retrieved June 16, 2005 from http://www.alternet.org/story/15327

Dufour, G. (2000). *Universal values developed at Global Community 2000 World Congress on managing and measuring sustainable development.* Retrieved June 17, 2005 from http://www.telusplanet.net/public/global06/Universal.htm

Ellwood, W. (2001). *The no-nonsense guide to globalization.* Oxford, UK: New Internationalist.

Federman, J. (2001). *The need for diversity education.* Retrieved June 17, 2005 from http://www.topia.org/diversityeducation.html

Federman, J. (2002). *The search from common values.* Retrieved June 17, 2005 from http://www.topia.org/common_understanding.html

Global Education. (2004). *Globalization.* Retrieved June 16, 2005 from http://www.globaleducation.edna.edu.au/globaled/go/cache/offonce/pid/178;jsessionid=47FA3334C894BD73CEE4275A0FA5BB37

Hayden, T. (2003). *The status of progressive politics and the need for progressive state networks (speech).* Retrieved June 16, 2005 from http://www.hppn.org/pdf/HaydenSpeech.pdf

IBON Foundation Inc. (2001). *WTO: Shrink or sink.* Retrieved June 17, 2005 from http://www.twnside.org.sg/title/shrink.htm

International Labor Organization. (2004). *The report of the World Commission on the Social Dimensions of Globalization.* Geneva: Author. Available at http://www.ilo.org/public/english/fairglobalization/report/.

Lechner, F. J. (2001). *Globalization theories.* Retrieved January 18, 2006 from http://www.

Transformative Practice: New Pathways to Leadership

emory.edu/SOC/globalizaiton/theories03.html.

Levinson, M. (2002). Trading places: Globalization from the bottom up. *New Labor Forum Journal*, 11 accessed February 9, 2005 at http://qcpages.qc.edu/newlaborforum/html/11_article20.html

Marber, P. (2005). Globalization and its contents. *World Policy Journal*, 20(4), extract. http://www.worldpolicy.org/journal/sum05-1.htm

McGregor, S. L. T. (2005). Structural adjustment programs and human well-being. *International Journal of Consumer Studies*, 29(3), 170-180.

McLellan, Hon. A. (1998). *Notes for address: Vision and reality*. Retrieved June 16, 2005 from http://canada.justice.gc.ca/en/news/sp/1998/decla50.html

Mittelman, J.H. (2000). *The globalization syndrome*. Princeton, NJ: Princeton Press.

New Economics Foundation. (2003). *About us*. Accessed February 9, 2005 at http://www.jubilee2000uk.org/about/about.htm

Pendleton, M. (1999). Our allegiance: Australians or global citizens. *Murdoch University Electronic Journal of Law*, 6(3). Retrieved February 9, 2005 at http://www.murdoch.edu.au/elaw/issues/v6n3/pendleton63_text.html#Globalisation%20Defined_T

Pogaènik, V. (2001). *The theory of human values*. Retrieved June 17, 2005 from http://www.geocities.com/vidpogacnik/theory_values.htm

Robertson, R. (1991). The globalization paradigm: Thinking globally. In D. Bromley (Ed.), *Religion and Social Order* (pp. 1-10). Greenwich: JAI Press.

Robertson, R. (2003). *The three waves of globalization*. London: Zed Books.

Schaeffer, R. K. (2003). *Understanding globalization*. New York: Rowman and Littlefield.

The Center for Learning. (1999). *Universal values*. Retrieved June 17, 2005 from http://www.centerforlearning.org/universal_values.asp

Third World Network. (2003). *Proposals to reform the financial system*. Accessed February 9, 2005 at http://www.twnside.org.sg/crisis_10.htm

Verzola, R. (1998). Globalization, the third wave. *CorpWatch*, Accessed February 9, 2005 at http://www.corpwatch.org/article.php?id=1569

Transformative Practice: New Pathways to Leadership

Chapter 19: Re-conceptualizing Human and Social Development

The home economics/family and consumer sciences profession has always been concerned with human development and, more recently, social development through strong and resilient communities. In order to be seen as transformative, the profession must expand its traditional understanding of human development to incorporate the definitions used by the United Nations and by development and lending agencies. The profession understands human and social development to comprise the development process *of individuals* and their interaction with group members as they evolve through the course of their lives. It is concerned with the dynamics of individual human beings developing within the context of their families and communities. It focuses on parent/child relations, families as systems, family processes, and early childhood development processes (McGregor, 2005a). The UN and others view development as a series of actions that are taken by one country to strengthen the infrastructure of another. Growth refers to the actions taken by the nation itself, from within the country. The conventional perception of development is that of *economic* development with the intent of developing the economic system of a given nation. Newer dimensions of development being explored at the UN are those of human potential and the social context within which individuals live as *affected* by economic development.

Professionals who appreciate both the differences and the powerful synergy between these two approaches to

development (family dynamics and life cycle versus sustainable humans and societies) can envision a place for the profession in *sustainable* human and social development. It seems a natural fit. In order for the infrastructure of a country to be sustainable, the family as a democratic unit needs to be sustained. Professionals should not limit practice to the family within the home, they should instead extend their reach to include individuals and families as the focus of countrywide, infrastructure, development work that sustains people, societies, and nature.

The profession should be in the vanguard of human and social sustainable development (McGregor, 2005a). As such, members of the profession could be the ambassadors of human and social development. In order to take on this work, professionals must have a working understanding of the distinctions between economic, human, and social development, along with an appreciation of how this approach differs from the traditional life cycle and family dynamics approach. Hence, the following section briefly describes the notion of economic development as compared to newer conceptualizations of human and social development, followed by a discussion of nine implications for transforming practice in such a way that professionals can appreciate the synergy between the human development from the family life cycle and family dynamics approach and the sustainable human and societal perspective. The entire chapter is based on the assumption that all sustainable forms of development must integrate economic development with the well-being and potential of a nation's people, as well as the social system that supports them (UNESCO, 2002).

Economic Development

Economic development can mean different things. It can refer to (a) efforts to increase employment opportunities by getting new businesses to relocate to a community or by encouraging existing businesses to expand, (b) improvements in society's economic subsystem that are concerned with the production, consumption, and distribution of goods and services to meet human needs, or (c) the process of raising the level of prosperity and material living within a society through increases in its economic productivity and efficiency. In less industrialized regions, this process is achieved through an increase in industrial production and a relative decline in the importance of agricultural production. Economic development can also refer to the process of improving the quality of human life by increasing per capita income, reducing poverty, and enhancing individual economic opportunities (Iannone, 2005).

There is a profound link between economic and social justice. Economic justice refers to the moral principles that guide people as they design economies. Despite the best intentions, or sometimes due to deliberate misdirection, economic development causes less than optimal human and social development. This is especially true when that development is guided by Structural Adjustment Programs (SAPs) (McGregor, 1997, 2005b). Although under a new name now, (Poverty Reduction Strategy Papers, PRSP, World Bank, 2004), SAP programs have

failed to form a base for sustainable, balanced economic development. Instead, SAPs have created political, social, and individual harm. Policy tools of SAP-driven economic development include: exchange rates, deregulation, privatization, interest rates, and removal of trade barriers to facilitate exports. They also involve austerity programs, wage control and de-unionization, improved productivity and human capital, and the removal of restrictions on transnational corporations (Chossudovsky, 1991; O'Neill, 1992).

To benefit both national and family economies, externally imposed economic development initiatives should strive to achieve sustainability, institutional capacity and capability, poverty reduction, and empowerment. They should also focus upon gender relations, environmental protection, feasibility, good governance, dialogue, and participation (Mikkelsen, 1995). When economic development is undertaken under the rubric of SAPs, such actions impact negatively on earning power in the form of wages and salaries, and upon income distribution defined as the gap between rich and poor. Harmful effects can also be seen in standards of living, health, mortality, employment, education, and within social conditions and the resultant unrest. Most ironically, there is a negative impact upon the nation's ability to repay foreign debt and rebuild the economy, which the SAPs was originally intended to improve (Chossudovsky, 1991, 2004; O'Neill, 1992; McGregor, 1997).

Human Development

The profession can renew its concept of development beyond economic development

Transformative Practice: New Pathways to Leadership

and life cycle development to include human and social development. The two latter approaches are concerned with "poverty reducing growth." Although social development promotes social progress relative to economic progress, human development is concerned with the empowerment of the individuals and family units that make up society and are the backbone of the economy. Introduced by the United Nations as a development concept in 1990, sustainable human development not only generates economic growth, it is also (a) pro-jobs and income equity by distributing the benefits from economic growth equitably, (b) pro-nature by regenerating the environment rather than destroying it, and (c) pro-people by refusing to marginalize a nation's citizens. Additionally, sustainable human development gives priority to the poor through poverty reduction, enlarges peoples' choices and opportunities, and provides for women's participation in political decisions that affect their lives. The concept of human development has also evolved to include generational sustainability (United Nations, 1994).

The term human development is shorthand for the whole complex of issues, sectors, priorities, needs, and goals implied by the struggle or journey to make life better (Thornley & Perera, 2000). *Sustainable* human development refers to economic growth that empowers the individual. This growth occurs both through the formation of human capabilities (the abilities, knowledge, and skills that *persons* acquire and develop throughout their lives) and through the use of those capabilities to lead a long and healthy life, to be educated, to enjoy a decent standard of living,

375

to gain political freedom, and to secure human rights and self-respect. The 2004 *United Nations Human Development Report* identifies many factors that indicate that humans are developing in such a way that allows them to reach their full potential in a secure, equitable, and participatory context. These factors are listed in Table 1.

Social Development

Sustainable social development is the *context* within which human development occurs. Its chief characteristics are that it (a) is equitable and socially inclusive; (b) promotes local, national, and global institutions that are responsive, accountable, and inclusive; and (c) empowers poor and vulnerable people to participate effectively in development processes. These elements of social capital make *communities* more productive and provide more opportunities through trust, communication, teamwork, and reciprocity. Social development implies not only that individuals gain improved skills, increased knowledge, and higher levels of physical well-being or human development, but also that they enjoy equal opportunity to employ their skills productively and have a sufficient degree of economic security to experience stability and satisfaction in their lives (UNRISD, 1993).

Similarly, social development is related to political freedom and stability but it involves much more than formal constitutional democracy. Social development implies not only that people have a voice in government but also that they enjoy certain basic human rights, live in equitable and just societies, are free to make choices in their personal lives, and are able to carry out their daily

Transformative Practice: New Pathways to Leadership

Table 1: Indicators of Human Development
(UNDP, 2004)

Enlarging people's choices and providing opportunities
- poverty and income in developing countries (life expectancy past 40, literacy, no access to water, children underweight for age, below poverty line or making less than $1-2.00 per day)
- poverty and income in developed countries (life expectancy past 60, literacy, long term unemployment, below poverty line, or making $4-11.00 per day)

Leading a long and healthy life
- demographics (urban/rural, fertility, and age)
- public spending on health (contraceptives, immunization, number of doctors, birth attended by health personnel, public money spent on health, drugs)
- water, sanitation, and nutritional status
- global health crisis and risks (HIV/AIDS, malaria, TB, smoking)
- basic survival (mortality rates)

Acquiring knowledge
- public spending on education at all levels
- literacy and school enrollment (number of students in math, science, engineering)
- diffusion and creation of technology (phone, cell phones, Internet, patents, R&D)

Obtaining resources for a decent standard of living
- economic performance (GDP, CPI)
- inequality in income or consumption
- structure of trade (imports, exports)
- foreign aid (rich country contributions to development)
- debt relief and trade barrier rules
- flow of aid, private capital (FDI), debt service
- priorities in public spending (education, health, military and debt service)
- unemployment in OECD countries (not in Majority world) (average, youth, long term)

Preserving things for future generations
- energy and environment (energy consumption, ratification of energy/eco agreements)

Protecting personal security
- refugees and armaments (size of military, arms transfers)
- victims of crime (five types of crime)

Maintaining equality for all women and men
- gender related development index (life expectancy, literacy rate, school attendance, income)
- gender empowerment (seats in parliament, legislature, professions, income)
- gender inequality in education
- gender inequality in economic activity (working and in what sector: industry, services, agriculture)
- gender work burden and time allocation between market and non-market activities
- women's political participation (vote, positions in government)

activities free from fear of persecution or crime (UNRISD, 1993).

Increasing evidence shows that (a) social cohesion is critical for societies to prosper economically and for development to be sustainable, and (b) social progress alleviates human suffering. It also shows that social capital is not just the sum of the institutions that underpin a society; it is the **glue** that holds these institutions together. Table 2 lists the familiar dimensions of social development, the context for human and economic development. Societies that progress socially make headway against a collective vision of a *just society*. Economic justice refers to the moral

Table 2: Dimensions of Social Development 1969 UN Declaration on Social Progress and Development, the 1995 Copenhagen Declaration on Social Development, and the Geneva 2000 Social Development Summit (see Eurostep, 2000; United Nations, 1969

- access to basic education, completion of primary, and closure of the gender gap
- a life expectancy of no less than 60
- reduced mortality rates of infants and children under five
- reduced maternal mortality
- food security (access, safety, quantity, and cultural relevance)
- reduction of malnutrition
- primary health care so that people are healthy enough to lead socially and economically productive lives
- productive employment in equitable and favorable conditions of work
- income and wealth distribution
- access to family planning and child care facilities
- reduction of malaria mortality and morbidity (occurrence and death)
- elimination and control of major diseases
- increased adult literacy with emphasis on gender
- access to safe drinking water and proper sanitation
- affordable and adequate shelter for all
- provision of community services
- comprehensive rural and urban development to ensure healthier living conditions
- transportation and communication systems
- reduced discrimination against women
- reduced poverty

Transformative Practice: New Pathways to Leadership

principles that guide people as they design the economy. Justice in the economy is represented by mindful markets or the moral economics of care that place people and society first. The economy exists to serve the people rather than the reverse. In other words, people should not be pushed aside to facilitate economic development and growth.

Implications for Practice

Economic development that is not conducted with a human face leads to human suffering and lack of progress, non-resilient communities, and an inactive civil society. All of these factors are crucial to human and social development. The titles of the UNDP's human development reports over the years give a sense of the scope of the aspects that relate to human potential: cultural diversity, international development cooperation, democracy, technology, human rights, globalization, poverty, consumption, economic growth, gender, participation, global dimensions, and finances for the development process. These topics evidence the more invisible aspects of development—those that have a human and social face. Mahbub ul Haq (who led the global movement for recognition of the complex concept of human development) said that

> The basic purpose of development is to enlarge people's choices. In principle, these choices can be infinite and can change over time. People often value achievements that do not show up at all, or not immediately, in income or growth figures: greater access to knowledge, better nutrition and health services, more secure livelihoods, security against crime and physical violence, satisfying leisure hours, political and cultural

Transformative Practice: New Pathways to Leadership

freedoms and sense of participation in community activities. The objective of development is to create an enabling environment for people to enjoy long, healthy, and creative lives. (UNDP, 2005, p. 1)

This description of the commonplace, mundane nature of development resonates with the focus of the profession—the daily life of people in their communities. There is a good fit between the profession and human and social development because the latter focuses on the resiliency of communities and a rigorous civil society. Following are nine suggestions for transformative practice at the vanguard of sustainable human and social development. From this integrative perspective, professionals must:

Read Human Development Reports: Professionals need to read all of the UNDP Human Development reports and the wide array of material prepared prior to and following the World Summit on Social Development. The Human Development Reports compress the multiplicity and diversity of situations and experiences into three or four categories (see Table 1). This kind of macroscopic view of the world does not do justice to the local situation, or to the lived experience of diverse cultures and contexts (Sachs, 1998). Professionals must also bring their global, contextual, holistic perspective to this area of practice, noting the relationships and the fact that nothing happens in isolation. Instead of reporting the facts about human development progress using numerical indicators and scores, professionals should provide a normative critique of the human condition and should explore the power relationships that allow injustice, inequality, and insecurity to prevail.

Be Wary of SAPS and Hidden Agendas: In reading and critiquing the World Bank human and International Monetary Fund (IMF)

Transformative Practice: New Pathways to Leadership

social development reports, professionals must examine whose interest is being served. These reports focus on making it easier to implement economic development policies using the Poverty Reduction Strategy Papers (PRSP). These papers replace the old SAP tripartite Policy Framework Paper (PFP) drawn up for the IMF, World Bank (WB), and a local government for concessional loans. Governments receiving the money through a participatory process involving civil society and development partners, including the WB and the IMF, prepare the papers. The offensive assumption is that if they come up with their own poverty reduction program they cannot blame the WB for any fallout from trying to meet the terms of the loan (McGregor, 2005b). Brazier (2004) claimed that these programs were renamed because the term SAP was so tainted. Even the WB and IMF admitted that there has been little evidence of success using these policy instruments.

Become Familiar with Human Rights and Responsibilities: Because human and social development and human rights are mutually reinforcing, professionals must become familiar with the concept and reality of human rights (McGregor, 2001). Development and rights serve the well-being and dignity of all people and build self-respect and the respect of others. Hand-in-hand with this suggestion to become familiar with human rights is the recommendation that professionals examine and follow the global movement towards a UN declaration of human responsibilities (Martinez, 2003). Those advocating for human responsibilities argue that inherent dignity (and the equal and inalienable rights of all members of the human family) is the foundation of freedom, justice, and peace in the world and implies obligations or responsibilities.

Heed World Summit on Social Development Program of Action: The 2000 World Summit for Social Development in Geneva yielded nine

381

commitments in the Platform of Action that fosters social development. These factors include (a) creation of an enabling environment so that people can achieve social development, (b) poverty eradication, (c) employment, (d) gender equality, (e) education and health, and (f) social integration (International Institute for Sustainable Development, 2000). Although most of these factors are self explanatory, it is necessary to expand on social integration as a commitment. Notably, the 4,791 government delegates and 2,045 Non-governmental organizations (NGO) delegates agreed that they "recognize the key role of the family in social development, cohesion, and integration and call for appropriate actions to meet family needs" (p. 10). Professionals can use this clause as leverage when lobbying for human and social development issues. Furthermore, the entire Program of Action provides a platform from which the new social development initiatives can be launched. The final outcome document, as adopted by the Plenary of the UN 24th Special Session, is available from the United Nations (2000).

Challenge and Work to Replace the Prevailing Development Paradigm: Professionals have to shift paradigms and rethink who is at fault when human and social development is thwarted by or in spite of economic development. Sachs (1998) put forward some challenging notions. Although inequality is commonly viewed as a shortcoming of the powerless, it can instead be seen as a fault of the powerful. The point is not to change the poor but to change the rich. There should not be an attack on poverty but rather an attack on wealth. The classical idea of equity was bound to just measures rather than mere growth. This paradigm shift rejects the top-down, corporate-led, capitalistic development model and replaces it with alternatives to globalization: localization, mindful markets, and strong civil society. Human and social development become the ends with

Transformative Practice: New Pathways to Leadership

economic development the means, not the other way around.

Respect the Concept of Civil Society: Professionals must familiarize themselves with the concept of civil society, a notion that has only recently entered the professional lexicon. Civil society comprises all non-state organizations in which people come together to satisfy certain needs, pursue goals, and take an active part in state affairs. It is an essential element of social and human development and it is inherently linked with participatory democracy. Professionals who become more involved in strengthening civil society are better able to convey the concerns of citizens and help to ensure that government policies become more reflective of the circumstances in which people live. Collectively, civil society can bring pressure to bear on the bureaucracy so that the interests of citizens are served. Participants and champions of civil society help to preserve cultural values upon which a functioning society is founded: peace, literacy, security, non-violence, respect, and solidarity. Civil society sets the stage for ethnic, religious, and cultural actors to get to know and understand one another so that they are better able to live in harmony (Schmitt, 2004).

Pursue Roles in the Political Arena and Governance: The success of all types of development (economic, human, and social) depends upon the quality of governance in a nation, thus there is a role here for transformative practice and leadership. Professionals must be involved in the political arena to contribute to transparency, accountability, citizen participation, and the application of the principles of justice and human rights. This is particularly important in the arenas of politics, finance, law, and public service. Part of the political role is the mobilization of strategies and principles to implement effectiveness, efficiency, cooperation, prioritization of health and educational goals over military ambitions; and collaboration among state, local communities, the private sector, and development organizations (Schmitt, 2004).

Promote Family as a Democratic Unit: Professionals can pursue several actions that facilitate quality governance in order to foster human and social development. The Vienna NGO Committee on the Family (1994) prepared these ideas for the first ever UN World Summit on Social Development, which took place in Copenhagen in 1995. The committee suggested that development work recognize the family as the basic social institution, an undisputable social network vital for contributions to humans and society. It directed the UN to pay attention to the tenets of the 1994 International Year of the Family, one of which is that families deserve special attention in social development initiatives. It maintained that social progress implies constant and dynamic interaction between family structures and the larger environment. Therefore, families must be considered in all development policies. Families should be able to define their own needs and then act upon them. To ensure this level of empowerment, families need to be recognized as a valid social development agent. The committee argued that any long-term poverty reduction initiatives depend heavily on the maturity of individuals, and it was agreed that the family is the main environment where people mature as citizens.

Employ a Critical Science Approach: Professionals need to bring a critical science approach to their practice with the intent of helping people to find their inner power and inner voice so that they can feel empowered to take action in their local communities and at the global level. In this way, professionals can foster a climate conducive to human and social development. As long as people feel oppressed and exploited, their reactions may be violent and vindictive in nature.

Transformative Practice: New Pathways to Leadership

People need to feel good about themselves and must feel freed from inner and outer constraints on their daily decisions. They need to be able to imagine a decent society for all people and be able to work in a consistent fashion to attain that future.

This is where professionals play a most vital role: in creating safe environments and situations where people can examine their unspoken assumptions and the hidden power agendas that keep them marginalized. Human and social development depends upon an empowered citizenry. Once the goal of greater physical, social, cultural, and economic security extends to larger sections of society, there will be an inexorable pressure to further the progress toward this goal. To that laudable end, the human community needs professionals to engage in transformative practice.

References

Martinez, M. A. (2003) *Declaration of on Human Social Responsibilities.* Retrieved February 16, 2005 from http://www.unhchr.ch/Huridocda/Huridoca.nsf/(Symbol)/E.CN.4.2003.105.En?Opendocument

Brazier, C. (2004, March). The power and the folly. *New Internationalist, 365,* pp. 9-11.

Chossudovsky, M. (1991, March). *The third-world structural adjustment programme.* Unpublished document at Halifax, NS: Saint Mary's University IDS Programme.

Chossudovsky, M. (2004, February 4). *The destabilization of Haiti.* Accessed April 27, 2004 from http://globalresearch.ca/articles/CHO402D.html

Copenhagen Declaration on Social Development. (1995). Accessed April 27, 2004 at http://www.un.org/esa/socdev/wssd/agreements/decparti.htm

Eurostep. (2000, April). *Eurostep position paper on Geneva 2000* Accessed April 27, 2004 at http://www.earthsummit2002.org/wssd/wssd5/wssd5r8i.htm

Iannone, D. (2005, March 16). Defining economic development. *Economic Development Futures Journal,*

385

3. Retrieved January 19, 2006 from http://www.doniannone.com/edfutures/2005/03/defining-economic-development.html.

International Institute for Sustainable Development. (2000). *Summary of the 24th special session of the General Assembly:26 June - 1 July 2000*. Retrieved February 16, 2005 from http://www.iisd.ca/vol10/enb1063e.html

McGregor, S. L. T. (1997). The impact of economic reform on Ghanian families. *Canadian Home Economics Journal, 47*(3), 110-115.

McGregor, S. L. T. (2001). *Leadership for the human family: Reflective human action for a culture of peace*. Retrieved February 16, 2005 from http://www.kon.org/leadership/peace.html

McGregor, S. L. T. (2005a). Positioning home economics on the vanguard of human and social development. *Keynote at the Home Economics Institute of Home Economics Conference (CD Rom)*. Tasmania. Paper available at http://www.consultmcgregor.com

McGregor, S. L. T. (2005b). Structural adjustment programs and human well-being. *International Journal of Consumer Studies, 29*(3), 170-180.

Mikkelsen, B. (1995). *Methods for development work and research*. Thousand Oakes, CA: Sage.

O'Neill, B. (1992). *Structural adjustment*. Ottawa, ON: Oxfam Canada

Sachs, W. (1998). On earth as it is in the west? *SEF News, 1*. Retrieved May 27, 1999 from http://bicc.uni-bonn.de/sef/publications/news/no1/sachs.html

Schmitt, K. (2004). *Social development*. Retrieved February 16, 2005 from http://www.novartis foundation.com/en/articles/development/social_development.htm

Thornley, A., & Perera, R. (2000). Education and human development. *CIDA Development Express, 3*, Retrieved February 15, 2005 from http://www.acdi-cida.gc.ca/cida_ind.nsf/0/08ea99383db05a9085256964006a5c27?OpenDocument

UNESCO. (2002, March). *Position paper: Enhancing global sustainability*. Retrieved January 19, 2006 from http://unesdoc.unesco.org/images/0012/001253/125351e.pdf.

United Nations. (1969). *Declaration on Social Progress and Development* Accessed April 27, 2004 at http://www.unhchr.ch/html/menu3/b/m_progre.htm

United Nations. (1994). *United Nations Human Development Report* (1994). New York: Oxford, Oxford University Press. And at http://hdr.undp.org/reports/global/1994/en/ (Free).

United Nations. (2000, December 15). *General Assembly A/RES/S-24/2. Further initiatives for social development*. Retrieved June 16, 2005 from http://daccessdds.un.org/doc/UNDOC/GEN/N00/665/16/PDF/N0066516.pdf?OpenElement

United Nations Development Program. (2004). *Human development report*. Retrieved February 15, 2005 from http://hdr.undp.org/reports/global/2004/ and http://hdr.undp.org/reports/global/2004/pdf/hdr04_HDI.pdf

United Nations Development Program. (2005). *What is HD?* Retrieved February 15, 2005 from http://hdr.undp.org/hd/

UNRISD. (1993). *The crisis of social development in the 1990's*. http://www.unrisd.org/ . See full copy of report at http://meltingpot.fortunecity.com/lebanon/254/ghai.htm

Vienna NGO Committee on the Family. (1994). *Family and social development*. Retrieved February 16, 2005 from http://www.bic-un.bahai.org/pdf/94-0705.pdf

World Bank. (2004). *Overview of poverty reduction strategies*. Accessed April 27, 2004 from http://www.worldbank.org/poverty/strategies/overview.htm

Transformative Practice: New Pathways to Leadership

Transformative Practice: New Pathways to Leadership

Chapter 20: Transforming Consumption*

Inasmuch as professionals are tasked with transforming themselves and the people with whom they work, this chapter calls for radical change to transform the actions of individuals as consumers. Because 70% of all money is spent on goods and services in developed countries, professionals must work toward ethical consumption to ensure that this powerful force is held accountable.

Consumer Ethics

There is an important distinction to make before continuing. Unethical consumer behavior encompasses much more than stealing or shoplifting (Babakus, Cornwell, Mitchell, & Schelgelmilch, 2004). Dishonest or unethical consumption inflates the prices of products and services because retailers must recoup the losses incurred by these bad behaviors. Such dishonesty inflicts financial damage upon the industrial sector, the retailer or service provider, other consumers, and the economy. Consumption can also be perceived as unethical from a social, political, and environmental perspective because it can endanger the future, waste and deplete raw materials and precious resources, deprive people in other countries, dispossess future generations, and because it is oppressive. Unethical consumer behavior places many people at the margins of society as it makes consumers slaves to work and consumption

---

* Co-authored with Deirdra Shaw, Senior Lecturer in the Caledonian Business School, Division of Marketing, Glasgow Caledonian University, Scotland. Deirdra is developing an international reputation for her work in ethics and ethical decision making, and is co-editor of *The Ethical Consumer* (2005, Sage).

(McGregor, 2005). For these reasons, transformative practice requires a professional understanding of the act of consuming and hinges upon honesty and a strong ethical imperative.

Although intentionally dishonest consumption has always been a concern in the marketplace, socially responsible consumption that is similarly purposive has only become an issue within the past 30 years. Ethical purchasing is now a deliberate act that is shaped by political, social, religious, spiritual, environmental, and other motives as well as the traditional choice criteria of price and quality. Ethical consumers are concerned with the effects that a purchase will have on themselves, their neighbors, other species, and the environment. Increasingly, consumption has become politicized as individuals react to the stresses of the consumer society. People use consumption as a tool to maximize political effectiveness as governments lose sovereignty and corporations solidify their position of dominance over society from the neo-liberal market posture (Harrison, 1997; Harrison, Newholm, & Shaw, 2005).

Consumers can pose three simple questions to determine if their actions in the marketplace are ethical and principled or immoral and reprehensible. First, does this purchase harm humans, including the self and others? Second, does it harm other sentient creatures? Finally, does it harm the earth or the ecosystem? If the answer to any of these questions is yes, the behavior must be judged unethical (Collis et al., 1995). Unethical behavior demonstrates a lack of scruples. It enables one to seek a personal advantage at the expense of others, and it is a reflection of one's character and personal philosophy. The ramifications of unethical

Transformative Practice: New Pathways to Leadership

consumption are both far-reaching and long lasting. Professionals who are eager to pursue transformative practice may find this approach to consumption liberating because it provides a conceptual and philosophical framework to help people hold themselves accountable to themselves, others, and nature.

Conceptual Underpinnings of Ethical Consumption

Many approaches have been put forward to advance an ethical model of consumption. A typology of sorts includes green consumerism, ethical consumerism, voluntary simplicity, and anti-consumerism (Connolly & Shaw, forthcoming; Collis et al.,

Table 1: Four Types of Concerned Consumers
(from Harrison, 1997; Harrison, Newholm, & Shaw, 2005)

Ethical Consumption (Means to an end)			Ethics of Consumption (A different end)
Green Consumerism	**Ethical Consumerism**	**Voluntary Simplicity**	**Anti-consumerism**
Concerned with environmental and health issues, along with impact on ecosystem. Promotes the philosophy of 3Rs, or reduce, reuse, and recycle— *environmental movement*	Jointly concerned with environmental issues and social justice issues such as human rights, animal rights, and fair trade— *social movement*	Engages in voluntary reduction of consumption and/or consumption with a con-science. Alternate, non-mainstream lifestyle encourages people to "live simply on the earth" for self and community well-being and for the health of the earth— *resistance movement*	Promotes a major paradigm shift that challenges capitalism. Advocates for mindful non-consumer society with localized markets and development with a human and social face. Works toward a thinking society that challenges the status quo— *reform movement*

1995; Horowitz, 2002; Maniates, 2002; Strong, 1997; Shaw & Clarke, 1999). Table 1 illustrates the main differences between these four types of ethically concerned consumers.

Green Consumer

Green consumers purchase goods and services that replace existing, environmentally damaging products with friendlier goods that are less harmful to the earth. During the late 1980s and early 1990s, there was a dramatic increase in environmental awareness that resulted in the emergence of green consumerism (Brown, 1992; Peattie, 1992). Numerous green consumer guides were published and membership in environmental groups grew, providing consumers with more information. Although a great deal of research was conducted to identify and understand the green consumer (e.g., Antil, 1984; Henion, 1972; Kinnear, Taylor & Ahmed, 1974; Krause, 1993; Webster, 1975), much of this research focused on single issues such as recycling (Boldero, 1995) or energy resources (Rowlands, Parker, & Scott, 2002) rather than examining the complex array of related dimensions. The reality is that environmental concerns are complex and interactive. To make good decisions, consumers are faced with a multi-faceted and often non-resolvable set of concerns that sometimes extends beyond the initial environmental concern. Social justice, human rights, trade, worker, and human security issues may arise, values may conflict, and the consumer may feel trapped.

There is yet no universally accepted definition of the green consumer. A few examples illustrate this stage of conceptual development. Elkington and Hailes

(1989) described green consumers as individuals who avoid products that are likely to (a) endanger their health; (b) cause significant damage to the environment during manufacture, use, or disposal; (c) consume a disproportionate amount of energy; (d) cause unnecessary waste; (e) use materials derived from threatened species or environments; (f) involve unnecessary use of or cruelty to animals; and (g) adversely affect other countries. On the other hand, Strong (1996) addressed the issue of ethical consumption by noting a connection between environmental concerns and ethical issues. Strong believed that the green consumer has become ethically aware and has been joined by many consumers who believe in the principles of fair trade.

Confounding the dialogue, Shaw and Clarke (1999) stated that ethical consumers are distinguishable from green consumers by their concern for "deep-seated problems, such as those of the Third World" (p. 109) in addition to environmental problems. Shaw and Newholm (2002) further illustrated this lack of conceptual clarity when they stated, "the inextricable link between consumption and ethical problems, such as environmental degeneration and fairness in world trade, has resulted in the emergence of a group of consumers commonly referred to as ethical consumers" (p. 168). It is obvious that interconnectivity has developed around green and ethical consumption, illustrating the ambiguity in the distinction between these terms. This can be further illustrated by examining the literature on ethical consumers.

Ethical Consumers

Ethical consumerism is an expansion of green consumerism. It considers

a variety of issues that go beyond a product's green credentials, including whether or not the manufacturer invests in the arms trade or has supported oppressive regimes. By comprehensively monitoring the behavior of modern business, ethical consumers encourage trade that is as responsible as is possible, *within* the current economic system. Collis et al., (1995) and Shaw & Clarke (1999) argued that the distinction between green and ethical consumerism is important, since more wide-ranging ethical issues can add significantly to the complexity of consumer decisions.

The above position is reinforced by the internal complexity of individual issues that concern the ethical consumer. For example, global issues such as environmental degradation, worker's rights, and armaments are highly emotional topics for some because many of these "big issues [are] played out in a domestic setting" (Lunt & Livingstone, 1992, p. 166). This point is illustrated in an example provided by Newholm (1999) wherein environmental and fair-trade concerns are coupled together. He noted that, "In some way, these concerns are applicable to *every* product or service; yet, *conflicts* can arise between a concern to trade fairly with majority world countries, to promote their economies, and environmental problems of excessive transportation" (p. 167). This overlap demonstrates how one's understanding of one ethical situation, such as fair trade, can be transferred to another focus of consumer concern that is otherwise unconnected. Environmental degradation and the crossover of seemingly unrelated concerns can also significantly add to the complexity of decision-making. Indeed, this complexity serves to

highlight the interconnections that exist between green and ethical consumer concerns.

Although green and ethical consumerism have been the focus of much consumer research, marketers and consumer researchers are increasingly interested in the rejection or limiting of consumerism through movements that include voluntary simplicity and anti-consumerism (Craig-Lees & Hill, 2002; Etzioni, 1998; Shaw & Newholm, 2002). Thus, sustainability is being extended to other consumer lifestyles. Most notable in this search for consumptive resistance is the voluntary simplicity movement, which has been termed "countercultural, potentially subversive" and "mainstream" (Maniates, 2002, p. 199).

Voluntary Simplicity

Voluntary simplicity is a conscious decision to live more simply in a consumer society, or to live as far outside of the mainstream society as logistically possible (Maniates, 2002). These consumers make the daily decision to adhere to a sustainable, ecologically sensitive alternative to the Western consumer lifestyle. Beyond simply buying green or ethically produced goods, adherents to this movement believe that there are different ways of living, trading, and working that enable one to "live more lightly" on the Earth. Those who practice voluntary simplicity choose not to depend upon buying things to feel good about themselves. Instead, they reduce the stress, anxiety, and pressure that are produced by life in the mainstream consumer society. Terms such as downshifting and simple living have been used to describe this lifestyle.

Shama (1985) defined voluntary simplicity as a

lifestyle of low consumption, ecological responsibility, and self-sufficiency. Etzioni (1998) stated that if voluntary simplicity were constituted on a large scale it would significantly enhance society's ability to protect the environment. He contended that *voluntary simplifiers* are more likely to recycle, build compost heaps, and engage in other civic activities that indicate stewardship of the environment; simplifiers draw more satisfaction from nature than from conspicuous consumption. There is also, he believed, a converse correlation. As people become more environmentally conscious and committed, they are likely to find voluntary simplicity a lifestyle and ideology compatible with their environmental concerns.

A similar position is taken by Shaw and Newholm (2002) who contended that voluntary simplicity may be demonstrated among consumers whose behavior includes some ethical consideration of the environment and some social impact of their consumption choices. These consumers are termed *ethical simplifiers*. They also claim that, although ethical simplifiers may be concerned about consumption levels *per se*, radical anti-consumerism may not be an option for them in a society that requires or demands some level of consuming. For these consumers, the important decision is between whether to consume with sensitivity through the selection of more ethical or green alternatives or whether to reduce levels of consumption to a more sustainable level through voluntary simplicity. In this way, overall consumption levels may be reduced through car sharing for example, while other areas of consumption are refined to reflect ethical concerns,

Transformative Practice: New Pathways to Leadership

such as the purchase of fair trade products. Thus, voluntary simplicity may contain elements of both green and ethical consumerism.

Anti-Consumerism

Anti-consumerism challenges what it means to live in a consumer society. At what cost do we consume? To oppose hyper-consumerism involves challenging the values, ideologies, and assumptions of "the consumer society." Taking the view that the rich nations of the world are fundamentally damaging themselves, the planet, and others in the pursuit of material acquisition raises the question, "How much is enough?" Challenging the status quo requires a shift in paradigms. Through this shift, an individual's daily actions can contribute to saving the planet, increasing overall happiness and fulfillment (thereby reducing war, insecurity, injustice, and suffering), and preserving the world's spiritual and cultural traditions. Those who adopt this new worldview seek to transition from a thing-oriented society to a person-oriented society (Collis, et al, 1995; Horowitz, 2002). The last section of the chapter resumes this discussion of paradigm shifts.

Complex Intersections Between Four Consumer Concerns

The preceding section demonstrates that these four concepts are frequently combined into two general approaches to ethics and consumption. Green, ethical, and voluntary simplicity reflect an "ethical consumption" stance, wherein consumption is a medium for moral and political action. Anti-consumerism is concerned with the "ethics of consumption," which questions the morality of the entire capitalistic enterprise

from production and distribution to consumption and disposal (Harrison, Newholm, & Shaw, 2005). Viewing ethical consumption as political involves making the ethical dispositions that are already implicit in day-to-day consumption decisions visible. This process produces a change in consumers' sense of the scope and in the quality of their responsibilities to each other and nature. Focusing on the morality of the entire capitalistic system (the ethics of consumption) paves the way to envision a new market system that is people centered rather than money centered. This new system values localization, mindful markets, new conceptualizations of economics, a focus on human and social development, and a concern for the links between peace and consumerism.

The remainder of this chapter illustrates the complex links between green and ethical consumerism, voluntary simplicity, and anti-consumerism. On the surface, these appear to be four different concepts. In practice, however, their intersections create very complex consumer decisions. For example, many of the practices and experiences described by Connolly and Prothero (2003) in their study of *green* consumers in Ireland can be applied to studies of *ethical* consumers in the United Kingdom (Shaw & Clarke, 1999). It is not easy to separate green from ethical or to differentiate voluntary simplicity from anti-consumerism because they are all interconnected. Understanding this connectivity is central to transforming consumption. Particularly challenging issues include complex choice criteria, compromised rational

Transformative Practice: New Pathways to Leadership

decisions, economic votes for a political voice, and the paucity of marketplace alternatives. Following are detailed descriptions of each of these challenges.

Complex Choice Criteria

For ethically concerned consumers, a purchase may not be governed solely by self-interest but rather by an obligation to consume ethically. Thus, although many rational self-motivated consumers select coffee on the basis of factors such as price and taste, those concerned with ethical issues may be guided by a sense of obligation to others and by identification with ethical issues. Concerns such as a fair price for producers can take priority in the evaluation of product alternatives (Shaw, Shiu, & Clarke, 2000; Shaw & Shiu, 2003).

This evaluation process can become remarkably complex. As an example, consider a low involvement product like a banana. From an ethical stance, the choice criteria might include an evaluation of the purchase's impact upon other people. In this case, the consumer questions whether the banana is fairly traded, seeks information related to the health and/or environmental issue of organic production, and expresses an environmental concern regarding excess packaging. The consumer may consider the country of origin and the impact of transporting the banana across long distances, which may encourage the purchase of a locally produced alternative. These choices must be coupled with traditional choice criteria that include price, quality, convenience, and availability, and it must also take the preferences of others into consideration. The consumer may then find that no local alternatives exist for non-packaged organic produce, and this conflict with environmental concerns could force the consumer to seek alternative outlets or to compromise on choice criteria. Thus, even a traditionally low involvement product can require substantial decision-making effort on the part of the consumer.

Compromised Rational Choice

In the context of ethical consumption, it is difficult to support the concepts of perfect or rational choice. In reality, ethical consumers are likely to be uncertain about the information they receive and the consequences of their actions. This uncertainty results (a) from the complex interaction among the multiple ethical concerns that consumers wish to satisfy and (b) from changeable circumstances that arise when new information demands a re-evaluation of the decision-making criteria. Information is vital to the ethical consumer, and there is evidence that individuals are demanding more information (Burgess, Harrison, & Filius, 1995; Shaw & Duff, 2001) from labels, pressure groups, or selected media. This demand is not surprising, but the ability of individuals to digest and act upon the data is limited due to information overload (Shaw & Clarke, 1999). Jacoby (1984) and Keller and Staellin (1987) provided further discussion on the issue of information overload.

Although consumers may voice concerns about a number of issues over time, their attention is often confined to the limited number that they are able to consider when making consumption choices (Shaw & Clarke, 1999). This coping mechanism is evident in the overlapping nature of green, ethical, and voluntary simplicity concerns. Indeed, it is apparent from the complex process illustrated above that a single individual is unlikely to fully subscribe to one discrete typology of concerned consumers.

Economic Votes, Political Voice

Although concerned consumers take an anti-consumerist view of marketing and capitalism as societal problems, many use that very market system to find a solution. Such individuals use purchases like economic votes to demand more ethically responsible alternatives and practices. These ethical consumer actions may embrace both individualized and collective practices. Examples include boycotts (e.g., Smith, 1990) and buycotts (Friedman, 1996) of specific products, retailers, or producers. To clarify, boycotts discourage the purchase of unfriendly products or objectionable services while increasing public awareness of a company's unethical methods. Buycotts, on the other hand, encourage purchases in order to support ethical companies, increase the visibility of responsible products, or to otherwise support social justice.

Another recent development is the girlcott, which encourages socially responsible purchases that support small, often women or minority-owned businesses worldwide. Such actions are inevitably motivated by ethical concerns, but they also demonstrate marketplace consequences. For this reason, they can be regarded as a marketplace vote.

The ethical dilemmas addressed by marketplace actions are not always straightforward. They can be complicated by the imposition of Western values on citizens who work in developing countries. Child labor is taboo in most Western nations, but in other parts of the world it may be acceptable or at least necessary. There is, therefore, a complex array of economic implications that arise when Majority World consumers boycott third world products that are made under conditions deemed unethical by Northern standards.

Paucity of Alternatives in Marketplace

Niche markets have been created to satisfy consumer desires for ethically responsible products and services. Independent organic food retailers and the organic grocery sections found inside traditional retail chains could be viewed as an adaptation made in response to consumer votes (Dickinson & Carsky, 2005). Similar advances have been made in other areas, as evidenced by the increased availability of meat substitutes. Voting for these options has become easier due to clear labeling and improved availability. Ethical product sectors are now well established, with their own certification marks that aid in consumer decision-making. Examples include the fair trade movement, managed forest products, freedom foods produced through ethical farming, environmental reporting on consumer appliances, and the organics movement.

Other sectors of the economy remain more challenging for the ethical consumer, notably the fashion and clothing industry. Child labor and worker's rights issues exert significant pressure for similar action in this sector, but labeling and other consumer decision-making clues are not readily available. Although consumer

concerns surrounding sweatshop labor in clothing production have been well documented (Dickson, 1999; Tomolillo & Shaw, 2003), effective labeling and the availability of marketplace alternatives are lacking. Most apparel items found in the Canadian marketplace, for example, are made by sweatshop labor either overseas or within Canada, primarily involving girls under the age of 15. One or two major retailers control the national market and consciously use overseas sources. Consumers are forced to make choices based on imperfect information, and they lack an ideal alternative that adheres to their values. Choice, in these circumstances, becomes inherently more complex.

A Systemic Moral Conundrum

Ironically, goods produced using purely ethical means simply do not exist. Because production depends upon consuming, the dangers of consumption are an inherent part of the production process. There is general agreement among ethical consumers that consumption needs to be reduced through the imperative of careful, conscious consumption (Gabriel & Lang, 1995). Although consumers often demand more ethical product alternatives and business practices, such options remain in short supply. This lack of choice can often mean that the consumer is confronted by an ethical paradox. For example, consumers purchase fair trade produce in order to provide workers with a fair wage and improved conditions. In doing so, however, they sometimes encourage the shipment of produce halfway around the world, thus causing negative environmental consequences. This complexity highlights the

Transformative Practice: New Pathways to Leadership

on-going nature of concerns that are hard to reconcile with one another and with ethical consumption principles (Newholm, 2000).

Implications

The typology of concerned consumers (green, ethical, voluntary simplicity, and anti-consumerism) opens the door for some amazing opportunities. Many things must happen to encourage people to consume ethically. Even those who already try to consume ethically are faced with decision-making challenges in the marketplace. In order to facilitate an ethical stance in the market, professionals can obtain insight from the growing peace and social justice movement and from the trend toward global consumer citizenship. Professionals need to build consumer moral consciousness and encourage paradigm shift regarding consumption.

Peace and Social Justice

The discussion of issues faced by concerned consumers demonstrated ethical consumer decisions involving peace, security, human rights, gender equity, and justice. These were exemplified in the examples of sweatshop and child labor in production. Unethical consumerism is a source of structural violence. When there is unequal and unfair distribution of resources or there is a lack of human constraint caused by economic and political structures, structural violence occurs through a lack of peace and justice. Unequal accesses to resources, to political power, to education, to health care, or to legal standing are all forms of structural violence as noted by McGregor (2003). This complementary work can help professionals to educate citizens about the human implications of their consumer decisions.

Transformative Practice: New Pathways to Leadership

It is not enough to say, "Our consumption hurts other people." Consumers must know how and why such harm occurs. In order to communicate this knowledge, professionals must become familiar with peace and social justice issues and with conflict studies as they integrate new knowledge into their existing understanding of consumption.

Professionals who embark upon this learning journey can expect to encounter three stages of learning: incremental exposure (accretion), fine-tuning, and restructuring (Rumelhart & Norman, 1978). In the first stage, professionals begin to acquire knowledge, meanings, and beliefs about making consumption decisions from a peace and citizenship perspective. Then, their knowledge base begins to change as they are repeatedly exposed to experience, information, and reflection upon justice, rights, and consumption decisions. In this way, professionals add new meanings, understandings, and beliefs to their existing marketplace knowledge. In the second stage, a subtle change occurs with the development of "chunks of new knowledge." This change results in adjustment and fine-tuning of the professional's evolving understanding of ethical consumption from a peace perspective. Ultimately, professionals restructure their entire internal knowledge base as it relates to consumer decision-making. This restructuring involves the creation of new meaning structures, the reorganization of the old knowledge base to accommodate a new set of principles and values, or both (Peter & Olson, 1987).

Global Consumer Citizenship

Professionals need to embrace the emerging

notion of global consumer citizenship. Valuing people as citizens first and consumers second provides a powerful platform from which to understand the dynamics of ethical consumption. Individuals become more reluctant to harm others through their consuming habits when they view one another as fellow citizens instead of dismissing them as "the invisible other."

Global citizens (a) are aware of the wider world and have a sense of their own role in it, (b) respect and value diversity, (c) are willing to make the world a more equitable and sustainable place, and (d) take responsibility for their actions (Oxfam, 2000). Bryer (2000) noted that global citizens (a) know where and how to fit into the wider world and believe that they can develop the understanding and skills to make an impact for the better, (b) are self-aware, open, and sensitive to the needs of others, (c) understand the whole and appreciates their own connection to the world, and (d) know how to make a difference. Bryer added that being a global citizen is not just about understanding, attitudes, and values (e.g., human capital in the context of social capital). It is also about standing up, standing out, and taking action, and it requires one to participate in the world as a consumer citizen.

Global citizenship requires that individuals understand their responsibilities to others, to society, and to the environment by (a) examining the meaning of democracy and citizenship from differing points of view, including non-dominant, non-western perspectives, (b) exploring the various rights and obligations that citizens may have in their communities, nations, and the world, (c) understanding and reflecting upon their own lives, careers, and interests in relation to participatory democracy and the general welfare of the global society, and (d) exploring the relationship between global citizenship and responsibility to the environment. Transformative practice involves embracing the concept of consumer-citizenship (McGregor, 2005).

Building Consumer Moral Consciousness

Once a sufficient number of people gain the same ethical consciousness, the market will change quickly and automatically. In the end, it is the collective consciousness of the market that dictates ethical standards for the market. Awareness must be created where it does not already exist (Gustavsson, 1996). This sentiment implies that professionals have to facilitate the development of moral conscience in the marketplace. In defining moral consciousness, Tucker (1994) explained that, "when we can see into the complexity of a situation, look with penetrating insight into all of the possibilities, understand the true impact of each possible action, then we are using moral consciousness" (p. 1). He described a heightened awareness that allows individuals to choose consciously rather than instinctively or habitually.

A sense of connectedness is an integral part of moral consciousness. This awareness of the link that exists between everyone and everything demands that each person rise above a sense of personal self. The power of choice is also central to moral consciousness. Individuals can choose to respond to a situation automatically, or they can elect to consider the mix of right and wrong or good and bad among the possible actions and reactions. Being conscious of the moral quality of one's

choices is an important part of life that, once gained, can never be lost (McGregor, 2005, May).

Consumption decisions clearly exhibit a moral nature. Consumers who enter into each transaction conscious of the impact of their choices are less likely to make unethical and immoral decisions. If everything is valued as connected, one can no longer dismiss the potential negative impact of buying or not buying a given product or service. Those who approach each buying situation knowing both our side and the alternative find it harder to ignore insights gained by examining consumer choice from an ethical and moral imperative. In other words, individuals become incapable of dispensing with the truth when conscience is brought to bear in the marketplace. To engage the moral and ethical imperative entails a major paradigm shift.

Facilitating Paradigm Shifts

If any group of people anywhere in the world were asked, *"How many of you woke up this morning with the intention of destroying the world?"* nobody would raise a hand. Individuals engage in destructive behavior unintentionally, indicating that the action is embedded rather than the result of a conscious choice. Fortunately, embedded behaviors can be reversed. Life-changing lessons arise when individuals recognize a paradigm within themselves, understand how the paradigm affects them personally, and discover that actions can bring them closer to others or can separate them from both their fellow humans and other species (Hawken, 1993).

Paradigm shift begins with identification of anomalies—problems, realities, and facts that do not fit into the old

paradigm. Each person must define a new paradigm and build faith in it in order to let go of an old paradigm. Time in a neutral zone—the space for ending one way and becoming comfortable with another—provides breathing room for the hard work of change. Individuals also require touchstones in the form of guidelines and reference points for moving toward a new paradigm, and they need a safety net in the event of relapse or slippage because shifting paradigms is not easy work. Osborne and Plastrik (1996) offered guidelines for facilitating a paradigm shift from consumer to global citizen.

Conclusion

The delineation of four types of concerned consumers has revealed that it is relatively easy to apply the labels of green consumerism, ethical consumerism, voluntary simplicity, and anti-consumerism. However, the conceptual overlap and ambiguity that exists among the four types indicates that future theorists need to refine the theory of ethical consumption. Harrison, Newholm, and Shaw's (2005) distinction between ethical consumption and the ethics of consumption contributed to theory, as did the distinction between honest and unethical consumption. When examined alongside the interactions among the four types of concerns, these theories provided professionals with a useful, albeit incomplete, foundation for explaining the nuances and complexities of ethical consumption.

Individuals transform if they experience a disorienting dilemma regarding a consumer decision. They become frustrated and lost because familiar choice criteria are not effective in judging ethical principles.

Transformative Practice: New Pathways to Leadership

This chapter makes the case that professionals can transform consumption by expanding their understanding of it in light of ethical and moral imperatives. Ultimately, professionals need to develop the innate ability to know when it is necessary to shift paradigms in order to share this view of consumption through an ethical lens. This change in professional practice would impact the world dramatically, resulting in truly transformative practice.

References

Antil, J. H. (1984). Socially responsible consumers: Profile and implications for public policy. *Journal of Macromarketing*, Autumn, 18-39.

Babakus, E., Cornwell, T.B., Mitchell, V., & Schelgelmilch, B. (2004). Reactions to unethical consumer behaviour across six countries. *Journal of Consumer Marketing, 21*(4), 254-263.

Boldero, J. (1995). The prediction of household recycling of newspapers: The role of attitudes, intentions, and situational factors. *Journal of Applied Social Psychology, 25*(5), 440-462.

Brown, A. (1992). *The UK environment*. London: The Stationery Office Books.

Bryer, D. (2000). *Oxfam's global citizenship conference keynote*. Retrieved March 2002 from http://www.oxfam.org.uk/coolplanet/teachers/globciti/conf/gcconf2.htm

Burgess, J., Harrison, C., & Filius, P. (1995). *Making the Abstract Real: A Cross-cultural Study of Public Understanding of Global Environmental Change.* Unpublished Study. London: University College London.

Collis, C., Cooper, S., Fitzgerald, P., Lawson,, J., Purkiss, J., Ryan, J., & Thomas, A. (1995). *Never enough? Anti-consumerism campaign*. Retrieved February 23, 2005 from http://www.enough.org.uk

Connolly, J., & Prothero, A. (2003). Marketing to low-impact consumers in a high growth developing economy – An Irish story. In the Proceedings of the 8th Bangkok International Conference on Marketing and Development: Globalization, Transformation, and Quality of Life. Madison, WI: Omnipress (CD ROM).

Transformative Practice: New Pathways to Leadership

Connolly, J., & Shaw, D. (forthcoming). Identifying fair trade in consumption choice. *Journal of Strategic Marketing*.

Craig-Lees, M., & Hill, C. (2002). Understanding voluntary simplifiers. *Psychology and Marketing*, 19 (2), 187-210.

Dickson, M. A. (1999). US consumers' knowledge and concern with apparel sweatshops. *Journal of Fashion Marketing and Management*, 3(1), 44-45.

Dickinson, R., & Carsky, M. (2005). The consumer as voter: An economic perspective on ethical consumer behavior. In R. Harrison, T. Newholm & D. Shaw (Eds.), *The ethical consumer* (pp. 25-36). London: Sage.

Elkington, J., & Hailes, J. (1989). *The green consumer guide*. London: Gollancz Publishing.

Etzioni, A. (1998). Voluntary simplicity characterization, select psychological implications and societal consequences. *Journal of Economic Psychology*, 19, 619-643.

Friedman, M. (1996). A positive approach to organized consumer action: The "buycott" as an alternative to the boycott. *Journal of Consumer Research*, 19, 439-451.

Gabriel, Y., & Lang T. (1995). *The unmanageable consumer*. London: Sage.

Gustavsson, B. (1996). The ethical consciousness of the market. *Paper presented at Conference on Technology and Ethics*. Retrieved June 9, 2005 from http://www.fek.su.se/Home/gus/PAPERS/Ethconpa.htm

Harrison, R. (1997).*The rise and rise of ethical consumerism*. Accessed April 12, 2004 at http://www.ethicalconsumer.org/philosophy/riserise.htm

Harrison, R., Newholm, T., & Shaw, D. (Eds.) (2005). *The ethical consumer*. London: Sage.

Hawken, P.(1993). *The ecology of commerce*. New York: Harper Collins.

Henion, K. E. (1972). The effect of ecological relevant information on detergent sales. *Journal of Marketing Research*, February, 10-14.

Horowitz, B. (2002). *The new anti-consumerism*. Retrieved 9 June 2005 from http://www.sustainableenterprises.com/Planet/anticonsumer.htm

Jacoby, J. (1984). Perspectives on information overload. *Journal of Consumer Research*, 10, March, 432-435.

Keller, K.L., & Staellin, R. (1987). Effects of quality and quantity of information on decision effectiveness. *Journal of Consumer Research*, 14(2), 200-213.

Kinnear, T. C., Taylor, J. R, & Ahmed, S. A. (1974).

Ecologically concerned consumers: Who are they? *Journal of Marketing, 38*(April), 20-24.

Krause, D. (1993). Environmental consciousness - An empirical study. *Environment and Behavior, 25*(1), 126-142.

Lunt, P., & Livingstone, S. (1992). *Mass consumption and personal identity.* Berkshire, UK: Open University Press.

Maniates, M. (2002). In Search of Consumptive Resistance: The Voluntary Simplicity Movement. In T. Princen, M., Maniate, & K. Conca (Eds.), *Confronting consumption* (pp. 199-236). London: The MIT Press.

McGregor, S.L.T. (2003). Consumerism as a source of structural violence. *Kappa Omicron Nu Human Sciences Woking Paper Series.* Retrieved February 24, 2005 from http://www.kon.org/hswp/archive/consumerism.pdf

McGregor, S.L.T. (2005, May). The dynamics of shared responsibility: Strategies and initiatives for participatory consumerism. *Keynote at the 2nd Consumer Citizenship Network Conference*, Bratislava, Slovakia. Available at http://www.consultmcgregor.com

McGregor, S.L.T. (2005). Understanding consumer moral consciousness. *International Journal of Consumer Studies, 29*(5), pp. 437-447.

Newholm, T. (1999). Relocating the ethical consumer. In R. Norman (Ed.), Ethics and the Market (pp. 162-184). Aldershot, UK: Ashgate Publishing.

Newholm, T. (2000). Consumer exit, voice and loyalty: indicative, legitimation and regulatory role in agricultural and food ethics. *Journal of Agricultural and Environmental Ethics, 12*(2), 153-164.

Osborne, D., & Plastrik, P. (1996). *From banishing bureaucracy: The five strategies for reinventing government.* New York: Addison Wesley.

Oxfam. (2000). *Curriculum for global citizenship.* Retrieved February 23, 2005 from http://www.oxfam.org.uk/coolplanet/teachers/globciti/curric/index.htm

Peattie, K. (1992). *Green marketing,* London: Longman.

Peter, P., & Olson, J.C. (1987). *Consumer behaviour.* Homewood, IL: Irwin.

Rowlands, I. H., Parker, P., & Scott, D. (2002). Consumer perceptions of 'green power.' *Journal of Consumer Marketing, 19*(2), 112-129.

Rumelhart, D., & Norman, D. (1978). Accretion, tuning and restructuring: Three modes of learning. In J.

Cotton & R. Klatsky (Eds.), *Semantic factors of cognition* (pp. 37-53). Hillsdale, NJ: Lawrence Erlbaum.

Shama, A. (1985). The voluntary simplicity consumer, *Journal of Consumer Marketing* 2, 57-64.

Shaw, D., & Clarke, I. (1999). Belief formation in ethical consumer groups: an exploratory study. *Marketing Intelligence & Planning*, 17(2,3), 109-119.

Shaw, D. S., & Duff, R. (2001). Ethics and social responsibility in fashion and clothing choice, *European Marketing Academy Conference*. Bergen, Norway.

Shaw, D., & Newholm, T. (2002). Voluntary simplicity and the ethics of consumption, *Psychology and Marketing*, 19(2), 167-190.

Shaw, D. S., & Shiu, E. (2003). Ethics in consumer choice: A multivariate modelling approach. *European Journal of Marketing*, 37(10), 1485-1498.

Shaw, D. S., Shiu, E., & Clarke, I. (2000). The contribution of ethical obligation and self-identity to the theory of planned behaviour: An exploration of ethical consumers. *Journal of Marketing Management*, 16(8), 879-894.

Smith, N. C. 1990. *Morality and the Market: Consumer Pressure for Corporate Accountability*. London: Routledge.

Strong, C. (1996). Features contributing to the growth of ethical consumerism – a preliminary investigation. *Marketing Intelligence & Planning* ,14(5), 5-13.

Strong, C. (1997). The problems of translating fair trade principles into consumer purchase behaviour. *Marketing Intelligence and Planning*, 15(1), 32-37.

Tomolillo, D. A. C., & Shaw, D. (2003). Undressing the ethical issues in clothing choice. *Journal of New Product Design and Innovation Management*, 15(2).

Tucker, E. (1994). *The moral consciousness, above rules.* Retrieved 24 February 2005 from http://www.theos-l.com/archives/199401/tl00046.html

Webster, F. E. 1975. Determining the characteristics of the socially conscious consumer, *Journal of Consumer Research* (December), 188-196.

Transformative Practice: New Pathways to Leadership

Transformative Practice: New Pathways to Leadership

Postscript from the Editor, Dorothy I. Mitstifer

Recently I heard Lani Guinier liken children to canaries in the mines. Back in the 19th century canaries were used to determine whether there were lethal gases in the mines. Children, according to Guinier, should not be treated as victims but as evidence of what's wrong in the school environment. Perhaps Sue McGregor is the canary reacting to stresses and serving as a similar early warning system for home economics/family and consumer sciences. This book raises some critical questions and proposes some alternatives for change. Certainly these aren't the only ideas, and Sue would be first to say, "Bring 'em on."

Moving forward to find common ground will require respect for differences. Several controversies could thwart cooperation:

♦ Long-term vs. short-term opportunism – Pursuing short-term fixes may not be consistent with long-term vision.
♦ Inclusion vs. exclusion – Exclusion may risk support of the broader community, but inclusion may dilute the vision and action will drift aimlessly.
♦ Exploration vs. goal-orientation – Deliberation about vision and methods takes considerable time but adoption of clear goals and aggressive action may overlook some unintended consequences.
♦ Collaboration vs. competition – Perhaps both collaboration and competition have value, but will competition undermine cooperation?
♦ Attainment vs. compassion – In the rush to choose direction and advance

Transformative Practice: New Pathways to Leadership

the profession, care must be taken that the interests of society are uppermost.
- Self-interest vs. wider interests – Although self-interest is a motivator, the wider interests of society should not be harmed. Regarding home economics/family and consumer sciences, what are the wider interests for the specialty islands?

Moving forward will need shared values and commitment to change, personal responsibility for outcomes, and a bias for action.

Leadership guru, Rosabeth Moss Kanter, noted that all change efforts have roadblocks (1999). Because plans are based upon experience, assumptions, and predictions, leaders must be prepared to accept departures from plans. A path is unlikely to run straight and true, and plans are no different. Change teams must be prepared to respond, to troubleshoot, and to make adjustments and the case for them. After the excitement of launching change, reality sets in and enthusiasm drops. By revisiting the mission, progress can be recognized, remaining tasks can be identified, and enthusiasm can be renewed. The emergence of critics will be strongest after change is underway. Leaders will need to be prepared to respond to the criticism, remove obstacles, and push forward. Believers will emerge with tangible progress.

Change is usually seen as a threat, not an opportunity. But we need to question our way of doing business and open our mind to new possibilities. May this book inspire new possibilities.

Reference

Kanter, R. M. (1999). The enduring skills of change leaders. *Leader to Leader,13*, pp. 15-22.

Transformative Practice: New Pathways to Leadership

Index

A

Action

8-9, 13, 15, 65, 69, 89, 92, 94, 98-99, 104, 109, 110-120, 127-130, 134-137, 139, 141-145, 147-152, 154, 156, 174-175, 178, 180, 189, 191, 194, 196, 198-199, 211-215, 217, 222-223, 233, 239, 249, 256, 260, 272, 281-282, 297-299, 301, 305, 309, 314, 321-323, 326-327, 332, 358, 362, 365-366, 371, 374, 381, 384, 389-390, 397, 400-402, 406-408, 415-416

C

Change

1, 3-5, 10, 12, 14-15, 17-18, 23, 26, 30, 35, 38, 41, 49, 61, 69, 80-82, 94, 98, 100-101, 103, 105-106, 121-125, 129-130, 137, 142, 144-145, 150, 152-153, 155, 163-167, 169-179, 191-192, 196-197, 200-202, 205, 208-215, 222, 224, 229-235, 242, 260, 268, 275-276, 279, 285, 289-290, 296, 299-302, 309, 311, 318, 324, 327-328, 3 34-336, 343, 348, 352, 354, 362, 364, 366, 379, 382, 389, 398, 400, 405, 407, 409-410, 415-416

Consumer/Consumption

10, 11, 17, 31, 33-36, 37, 40-41, 44, 48-49, 58, 65, 83, 91, 95, 97, 116, 165, 167-169, 177, 183, 190, 221, 241, 276, 286, 300-301, 336, 353, 357-358, 373, 377, 379, 389-406, 408-410

Critical Science

16, 171, 205-210, 213-214, 216-218, 221-225, 245, 249, 259, 384

Critical Thinking

118, 175, 213, 215, 230-231, 236, 269, 287, 289

D

Development

8, 16-18, 26-27, 32-33, 36-37, 58, 61, 70, 98, 101, 106, 117, 126, 133-135, 137, 143, 148, 150, 154, 157, 163, 173, 193, 208, 215, 236, 268-269, 275, 311-312, 315, 317, 328, 333, 353-354, 358, 360, 363, 365, 371-385, 391-392, 398, 401, 405, 407

Transformative Practice: New Pathways to Leadership

E

Empowerment
9, 13, 16, 51, 61, 89, 106, 168, 209-211, 213, 234, 298, 361, 367-368, 374-375, 377, 384

Ethics
15, 17, 47, 49-50, 100, 103-104, 109, 112, 114, 118-120, 129-130, 149, 215, 217, 231, 236, 239-242, 261, 279, 298-299, 389-391, 393-409

G

Globalization
5, 16, 38, 40, 50, 59, 75, 168, 177, 219, 286, 290, 300, 351-357, 359-368, 379, 382

H

Home Economics
7, 9-10, 15, 58, 65, 83, 85, 91, 95, 97, 165, 177-178, 183, 190-193, 197-198, 250, 260, 265, 279-280, 295-296, 302, 332, 338, 343-344, 364, 371, 415-416

I

Inquiry
46, 55, 62, 68, 136, 168, 229, 235, 237, 240-241, 269-270, 281, 284, 290, 312

Intellectual
2, 16-17, 26, 39, 49, 56, 60, 62, 67, 69, 71-72, 74, 80, 102, 112, 171, 184, 193, 195, 199, 224, 265, 269-275, 279, 281, 282-285, 287-291, 300, 302-303, 315, 317, 324, 331-332, 334, 347, 358

Interdisciplinary
11, 16, 47, 55, 57-59, 63, 70

K

Knowledge
6, 9, 17, 25-26, 29, 32, 36, 43, 46-47, 50, 55, 58-67, 69, 71-74, 79-80, 97, 114, 121, 126, 128, 130, 137, 139, 164, 170, 179, 209, 211, 217,

Transformative Practice: New Pathways to Leadership

K

Knowledge *(continued)*
219, 221, 229-230, 233, 238, 240-241, 248, 250, 252, 257, 261, 266-274, 279-280, 283-285, 292, 296-297, 302, 309, 312, 314, 317, 319, 324, 326, 329, 331-348, 353, 358, 363, 367, 375-377, 379, 405

L

Leadership
14-15, 36, 51, 65, 97-102, 104, 106, 109, 111-112, 115-130, 133-135, 137, 139, 143, 148, 150-151, 154, 157, 173, 184, 188, 190-192, 210, 235-236, 239-240, 292, 315, 340, 346, 363, 367, 383, 416

N

Neoliberal
167-169, 356, 359, 363

P

Paradigm
1-5, 7-9, 12, 14-15, 17-18, 24, 33, 40, 43, 56, 77, 84, 87, 109, 164, 166, 170-172, 177, 205, 207, 230-232, 245, 265, 270, 275, 286, 297, 300, 305, 342, 382, 391, 397, 404, 408, 410

Pedagogy
17, 214-215, 219-220, 245, 265-266, 268-270, 272, 275-276

Perspective
2, 7, 11, 14-15, 45, 47, 51, 57-58, 61-67, 71, 85, 89, 95, 98, 102, 121-122, 128, 134-137, 153, 157-158, 166, 171-172, 190, 199, 203, 205, 212-213, 220, 229, 232, 234, 237, 241-242, 246, 253-256, 259, 275, 280, 282, 284, 288, 296, 300, 306, 309, 316, 321, 324, 326-328, 331, 334, 343-346, 364, 372, 380, 389, 405-406

Philosophy
2, 10, 47, 84-85, 87, 135, 148, 157, 167, 202, 207, 234, 260, 295, 297-301, 305, 351, 390-391

Postmodern
17, 21, 35-41, 43-51, 178

419

P

Power

16, 26, 32-33, 49, 51, 75, 81, 98-100, 103-105, 109-112, 117, 123-127, 129-130, 141-143, 151-152, 163, 166, 168-171, 174, 179, 201, 205-212, 214-215, 221-225, 230, 237-238, 245, 247-249, 251-254, 256-257, 259, 261, 270-271, 275, 281, 285, 287, 289, 291, 298, 351, 353, 356, 360, 364, 367, 374, 380, 382, 384-385, 404, 407

Practice

2, 6, 8-9, 12, 14-17, 21, 23, 41, 48-49, 51, 55-57, 59, 61, 64-65, 70, 72, 79-82, 88-91, 93-94, 97, 105-106, 114, 120, 129-130, 134, 145, 149, 165, 173-174, 184-186, 190, 196, 201-206, 208-214, 223-225, 232, 234, 238-242, 245, 249-251, 253, 260-261, 265, 273, 275-276, 279-281, 284-285, 287, 290-292, 295-300, 305, 309-328, 331, 336-337, 339-341, 343, 345-346, 348, 351, 353, 355, 359, 361, 364, 367-368, 372, 379-380, 383-385, 390-391, 395, 398, 401, 403, 407, 410

R

Reflective

15, 65, 109, 112-115, 118, 120, 124, 128, 134-135, 148-150, 154, 158, 167, 193-195, 198, 200, 206, 209, 216-217, 229, 232, 235, 237-242, 268, 275, 290, 296, 299, 364, 383

Relationships

4, 12-13, 16, 32-33, 51, 66, 76, 80, 83, 99, 104-105, 109, 112, 115, 118, 123-125, 129-130, 137, 140-142, 148-149, 156, 166, 175, 185-187, 203, 207, 210-212, 214, 219, 230, 233-234, 237-239, 245, 247-251, 267, 269-271, 273, 310, 312-313, 315-316, 320, 323, 328, 332, 335, 337, 348, 353, 356, 364, 380

S

Skeptical Thinking

16, 171, 279, 281, 284-286, 291

Strategic Thinking

145, 147

Transformative Practice: New Pathways to Leadership

T

Thinking
3, 5, 9, 14-15, 21, 29, 31, 37, 39-40, 45, 59-60, 82, 84, 89-90, 102, 109, 112, 129, 136, 151, 154, 156, 165, 167, 169, 187, 193, 195-199, 201-202, 211-212, 218, 224, 234, 271, 274, 276, 297, 300, 318, 327, 337, 391

Transdisciplinary
16, 55, 58-65, 67-70, 72-73, 77, 79, 81-82

Transformative
14, 16, 51, 65, 73, 90, 97, 100-101, 105-106, 129-130, 163, 170-172, 174, 176-177, 179, 183, 190, 203, 205, 208-210, 224, 229-231, 233-236, 240, 242, 245, 265, 275-276, 292, 296, 300, 303, 309, 329, 351, 361, 363, 367, 371, 383, 385, 390, 410

V

Vision/Visionary
15, 47, 59-60, 73, 76, 100-103, 106, 109, 123, 125-126, 128, 139, 144-147, 149, 156, 174, 178-179, 189, 193-195, 197-198, 239-240, 261, 265, 332, 343, 367-368, 378, 415

Transformative Practice: *New Pathways to Leadership*